Toward Great Dhaka

DIRECTIONS IN DEVELOPMENT
Countries and Regions

Toward Great Dhaka

A New Urban Development Paradigm Eastward

Julia Bird, Yue Li, Hossain Zillur Rahman,
Martin Rama, and Anthony J. Venables

WORLD BANK GROUP

Contents

Maps

Photos

Tables

Foreword

Dhaka is exceedingly important for Bangladesh. This historic, vibrant, and endearing city is home to one-tenth of the country's population. It generates at least one-fifth of its total economic output and provides more than 40 percent of its formal sector jobs. Dhaka has also been instrumental in reducing Bangladesh's poverty rate. The economic opportunities it offers attract migrants from around the country, improving their own living standards and those of the families they support through the money they send home. Tax revenue generated in Dhaka is used to finance investments and service delivery throughout the country.

At present, however, Dhaka faces seemingly impossible challenges. Despite unrelenting efforts to upgrade the city's infrastructure, congestion is increasing and travel speeds are declining. Dhaka also remains vulnerable to flooding and becoming waterlogged, often coming to a standstill during the heavy rains of the monsoon season. And service delivery is uneven. More than a fourth of its inhabitants live in slums, pollution is increasing, and the city sits at the bottom of global livability rankings. If these challenges are not addressed, it will be difficult for Dhaka to become a prosperous global city, and therefore difficult for Bangladesh to join the ranks of upper-middle-income countries.

The World Bank Group is committed to supporting Dhaka's urban development. The strong partnership with the City Corporations and specialized government agencies has so far focused on urban upgrading, urban resilience, water and sanitation, and clean air. A number of new projects are under preparation, including for a new Bus Rapid Transport line, water supply and sanitation, and urban upgrading. Over time, these initiatives will strengthen Dhaka's economic performance and make for a more livable city.

This report proposes an even more radical approach to put the city on a better urban development trajectory, one that could transform it into a truly great global city in just a few decades.

Dhaka currently has a unique opportunity, not readily available to other megacities in the world. Toward the east of its urban core, almost within walking distance from the most valuable parts of town, there is a vast expanse of mostly agricultural land. East Dhaka, an area with a surface similar to that of a major European city, could be developed with the right urban infrastructure from the start, decongesting the current city and becoming a modern economic pole for the country as a whole. The time to act is now. East Dhaka is already being developed in an unplanned way and this opportunity may soon pass.

Using state-of-the art modeling and detailed data from each neighborhood in Dhaka, the report shows that embracing a different urban development paradigm eastward would have high economic returns, while managing environment and social risks. Recognizing local institutional complexities, the report focuses on a few self-standing projects for the transformation of East Dhaka, each firmly anchored on Dhaka's existing master plans and technical studies. The annual investments these projects would require are within the range of long-term finance provided by the World Bank and other multilateral and bilateral organizations.

As a long-term development partner of Bangladesh, the World Bank Group stands ready to assist should the country decide to take on the transformational vision proposed in this report.

Qimiao Fan
Country Director for Bangladesh, Bhutan, and Nepal
The World Bank

Acknowledgments

The preparation of this report was led by Yue Li (World Bank). The core team also comprised Julia Bird (University of Oxford), Hossain Zillur Rahman (Power and Participation Research Center), Martin Rama (World Bank) and Anthony J. Venables (University of Oxford).

The work was conducted in close collaboration with the Social, Urban, Rural and Resilience Global Practice, and the Transport and Digital Development Global Practice at the World Bank. Hyoung Gun Wang and Shigeyuki Sakaki were the respective focal points. The report also benefited from substantive contributions by Ritika D'Souza, Virgilio Galdo and Yan (Sarah) Xu.

Valuable inputs were contributed by Susmita Dasgupta, Peter D. Ellis, Ruth Hill, Zahid Hussain, Swarna Kazi, Zahed Hossain Khan, Jon Kher Kaw, Keith Patrick Garrett, Poonam Pillai, Iffath Anwar Sharif, Nadia Sharmin, Lia Carol Sieghart and Sanjay Srivastava, all with the World Bank. The report also reflects insights provided by Ahasanul Hoque (consultant), M. Shafiqul Islam (consultant), Nihad Kabir (Metropolitan Chamber of Commerce and Industry, Bangladesh), Md. Akter Mahmud (Jahangirnagar University, Bangladesh), Maj. Gen. Abu Syeed Md. Masud (Special Works Organization, Bangladesh Army), S. M. Mahbubur Rahman (Institute of Water Modelling, Bangladesh) and Hongwei Yang (Urban Innovation Think-tank, China).

The preparation of the report greatly benefited from the presentation and discussion of the preliminary results at the International Conference on Development Options for Dhaka towards 2035, which was held in Dhaka on July 19, 2017. Special thanks are extended to the following for their participation and constructive engagement at this conference: Kazi Shafiqul Azam, secretary, Economic Relations Division of Ministry of Finance; M. Bazlul Karim Chaudhury, chairman, Rajdhani Unnayan Kartripakkha (RAJUK, Capital Development Authority); Kamal Abdul Naser Chowdhury, former principal secretary, Prime Minister's Office; Sheila Dikshit, former chief minister, Delhi; Khandaker Mosharraf Hossain, honorable minister of local government, Rural Development and Cooperatives; Annisul Huq, late mayor, Dhaka North City Corporation; Abul Kashem Khan, president, Dhaka Chamber of Commerce and Industry; Sayeed Khokon, mayor, Dhaka South City Corporation; Zhao Qizheng, former vice mayor, Shanghai; Zhu Ruolin, former dean, Pudong Planning and

Design Institute; and Shao Yudong, former member, Pudong District Standing Committee.

The peer reviewers for the report were Gilles Duranton (Wharton School, University of Pennsylvania), Marc S. Forni (World Bank), Matias Herrera Dappe (World Bank), Somik V. Lall (World Bank) and Mustafizur Rahman (Center for Policy Dialogue, Bangladesh).

At the World Bank, the work greatly benefited from guidance and encouragement by Annette Dixon, former regional vice president for South Asia; Qimiao Fan, country director for Bangladesh, Bhutan and Nepal; and Karla González Carvajal and Catalina Marulanda, practice managers.

Funding by Australia's Department of Foreign Affairs and Trade and data and remote sensing support by the European Space Agency and GISAT are gratefully acknowledged.

The production of the report and the logistics supporting it were steered by Neelam Chowdhry from Washington, DC, and Mohammad Baharul Alam, Janet Bably Halder and Amani Haque from Dhaka, Bangladesh. Rajashree Paralkar guided the timing of local events related to the report.

The World Bank's former publishing program was in charge of the design, typesetting and dissemination of both the printed and electronic versions of the report. Special thanks are extended to Aziz Gokdemir and Jewel McFadden for coordinating the process and to Patricia Katayama for her advice. Sabra Ledent edited the report.

The team also thanks the World Bank's External Communication in South Asia Unit, including Alex Anthony Ferguson, Shilpa Banerji, Yann Doignon, Mehrin Ahmed Mahbub and Cheng (Joe) Qian, for their guidance and support.

About the Authors

Julia Bird is a postdoctoral researcher in economics at the University of Oxford. Her research seeks to explore the changing patterns of urbanization observed over recent decades, with a focus on Sub-Saharan Africa. In particular, she is interested in the location decisions of firms and people within and across urban areas, how they interact and generate agglomeration economies, and how these spatial patterns are impacted by policies such as infrastructure investments. She previously completed a PhD at Toulouse School of Economics, France.

Yue Li is a Senior Economist at the World Bank, working in the Office of the Chief Economist for the South Asia region. She has led the preparation of studies on regional issues, and contributed to country-level engagements. Prior to that, she coauthored the *World Development Report 2013: Jobs* and worked in the Sub-Saharan Africa, Europe and Central Asia, and East Asia and Pacific regions of the World Bank. Her research covers international trade, firm dynamics, economic geography, and urban economics. She holds a PhD in economics from Rutgers University, and master's degrees in Economics and Political Science from Syracuse University. Her bachelor's degree is from Peking University, China.

Hossain Zillur Rahman is the founder-chairman of the Dhaka-based think tank, Power and Participation Research Centre (PPRC). A leading civic and policy voice of Bangladesh, he currently leads the centre's work on urbanization, universal health coverage, social protection, and inclusive growth. His former positions include lead consultant for Poverty Reduction Strategy, member of the South Asian Association for Regional Cooperation (SAARC) Poverty Commission, and member of the Bangladesh Bank Board. He was appointed Advisor (cabinet minister) in charge of the Ministries of Commerce and Education in the Caretaker Government of Bangladesh (2007–08). He was awarded the Dr. John Meyer Global Citizenship Award by the Institute for Global Leadership of Tufts University, United States in 2009 and the Gold Medal 2013 by Rotary International Bangladesh.

Martin Rama is the Chief Economist for the South Asia region at the World Bank, where he promotes debate on difficult policy issues in the region, leads the preparation of major reports on regional issues, and oversees the quality of the Bank's analytical work in the region. His former positions include the Director of the *World Development Report 2013: Jobs*, and the Lead Economist for Vietnam. Prior to moving to operations, he spent 10 years with the research department of the World Bank and was visiting professor at the University of Paris. Back in his home country, Uruguay, he was a director of CINVE, the country's largest think tank. The main focus of his research is on labor issues.

Anthony J. Venables is Professor of Economics at Oxford University, where he directs a program of research on urbanization in developing countries and the Oxford Centre for the Analysis of Resource Rich Economies. He is a Fellow of the Econometric Society, the Regional Science Association, and the British Academy; a member of the steering group of the International Growth Centre; and Chair of the Scientific Advisory Committee of the IFO Institute. His former positions include Chief Economist at the UK Department for International Development and Professor at the London School of Economics. He has published extensively in the areas of international trade and spatial economics, including work on trade and imperfect competition, economic integration, multinational firms, economic geography, and natural resources.

Abbreviations

BBA	Bangladesh Bridge Authority
BBS	Bangladesh Bureau of Statistics
BIGD	BRAC Institute of Governance and Development
BRT	bus rapid transit
BRTA	Bangladesh Road Transport Authority
BRTC	Bangladesh Road Transport Corporation
BWDB	Bangladesh Water Development Board
CC	city corporation
CEGIS	Center for Environmental and Geographic Information Services
CEO	chief executive officer
CES	constant elasticity of substitution
DDM	Department of Disaster Management
DIT	Dhaka Improvement Trust
DITS	Dhaka Integrated Transport Study
DMDP	Dhaka Metropolitan Development Plan
DTCA	Dhaka Transport Coordination Authority
DUTP	Dhaka Urban Transport Project
DWASA	Dhaka Water and Sewerage Authority
EIU	Economist Intelligence Unit
FAP	Flood Action Plan
GDP	gross domestic product
ICT	information and communications technology
ISIC	International Standard Industrial Classification
IWM	Institute of Water Modelling
LGED	Local Government Engineering Department
MHPW	Ministry of Housing and Public Works
ML	Ministry of Land
MLGRDC	Ministry of Local Government, Rural Development and Cooperatives

MRT	mass rapid transit
MRTB	Ministry of Road Transport and Bridges
MWR	Ministry of Water Resources
NHA	National Housing Authority
PPP	purchasing power parity
PPRC	Power and Participation Research Centre
PWD	Public Works Department
RAJUK	Rajdhani Unnayan Kartripakkha (Capital Development Authority)
RHD	Roads and Highways Department
RSTP	Revised Strategic Transport Plan
SAARC	South Asian Association for Regional Cooperation
SAR	special administrative region
STP	Strategic Transport Plan
SWO	Special Works Organization
UN-Habitat	United Nations Human Settlements Programme
VAT	value-added tax
WARPO	Water Resources Planning Organization

Overview: Toward Great Dhaka

A unique opportunity beckons Bangladesh. Dhaka, central to the country's middle-income future, stands on the cusp of a decision to make itself more livable and more prosperous. Toward its east, where two major highway corridors will one day intersect, is a vast expanse of largely rural land. And much of it is within 6 kilometers of the most valuable parts of the city.

The time to act is now. Many parts of this area, hereafter called East Dhaka, are already being developed at an alarmingly rapid pace. Private developers are buying land and filling it with sand so they can build and sell new houses and apartments. This spontaneous and haphazard development could soon make East Dhaka look like the messy western part of the city, and retrofitting it later will be more difficult and costlier than planning and constructing it properly. Unless there is action soon, the opportunity represented by East Dhaka will be lost.

This study by the World Bank, with the participation of the University of Oxford and Bangladeshi experts, seeks to analyze how the opportunity of East Dhaka could be realized. Using state-of-the-art modeling techniques, this study simulates population, housing, economic activity and commuting times across the 266 unions that constitute Greater Dhaka. It does so under various scenarios for the development of East Dhaka, but always assessing the implications for the entire city.

The simulations used in this study suggest that a strategic approach to the development of East Dhaka must include three critically important interventions:

- *Building the eastern embankment along the Balu River.* Lower vulnerability to flooding would massively increase the amount of land available for urban development. In the simulations, the 119 square kilometers of East Dhaka can accommodate over 6 million people by 2035. This is fewer than the population of London, Paris or New York, but more than that of Berlin, Boston, or Rome. Importantly, a significant fraction of the additional population in East Dhaka comes from the existing urban core, effectively reducing its density.

- *Developing critically important transport infrastructure in this new area.* Such infrastructure is needed to enhance the quality of the additional urban land generated by the embankment. Several east-west axes in the spirit of the recently built 300 Feet Road can increase connectivity with the planned ring road and the Sylhet-Chittagong corridor. Two segments of mass rapid transit lines and one bus rapid transport line would make East Dhaka more accessible. In the simulations, density in the existing urban core is substantially eased.

- *Reducing the cost of doing business in the new area.* The shift of households and firms—especially those producing high-value-added services—toward East Dhaka is much stronger if a new central business district is developed there. However, this shift of economic activity cannot be taken for granted. Lower taxation and less red tape in the new business district would help overcome the "first mover" problem. In the simulations, success in doing so makes East Dhaka an area of high-value-added activities—such as banks, universities and logistics services—with more and better jobs, and much higher incomes.

The promise and pitfalls of urbanization

The proposed approach draws on the experience of Shanghai, China. The extraordinary growth of this city, from a population of 6 million in the 1980s to over 24 million today, was accompanied by far more economic activity, greater mobility through upgraded transportation, improved access to services, and better livability. Much of this success was due to China's strategic approach to the development of East Shanghai (Pudong) and to its integration with the rest of the city. The "Pudong miracle" transformed Shanghai into the connecting point between its hinterland and the rest of the world, and that in just 25 years. But this success required a clear vision—one that was embraced by government agencies, private investors and citizens—supported by careful planning and tight implementation.

For Dhaka, matching Shanghai's achievement will be a challenge. Dhaka has a myriad of overlapping and competing authorities. No effective coordination mechanisms are in place, and plans generated by different agencies are, at best, partially implemented. There are reasons for optimism, however. In the few cases in which mandates have been clear and strong coordination mechanisms have been established, an exceptional implementation capacity has emerged. The successful Hatirjheel Lake rehabilitation project is a stellar example.

Mobilizing the country's political leadership and creating the institutional arrangements to develop East Dhaka will pay off in greater prosperity for the people of Bangladesh. Urbanization is one of the most important drivers of economic and social development. In cities, markets have more buyers and sellers than in rural areas, new ideas spread faster, specialization is easier, and service delivery is cheaper.

From this perspective, the fact that almost 35 million Bangladeshis will become urban dwellers over the next two decades is excellent news. Dhaka itself illustrates the point. Building on strong economic fundamentals, Dhaka has experienced remarkable growth and become the economic powerhouse of the country. Its astonishing growth, from a population of 3 million in 1980 to 18 million today, represents the promise of a better life for its residents, offering them opportunities to lift themselves out of poverty and into the middle class.

But the benefits of urbanization can be easily lost if there is not enough high-quality land to accommodate the many new urban dwellers. With 29,000 inhabitants per square kilometer, Dhaka has already become one of the most densely populated cities in the world.

This mostly spontaneous urbanization has resulted in three serious challenges. Flooding and waterlogging are recurrent, with monsoon rains and river overflows often bringing the city to a standstill. Only 25 of the city's 43 canals are presently functional, severely reducing the city's water conveyance capacity. Meanwhile, the growth of the built-up surface has shrunk the natural water storage areas such as wetlands and ponds.

Dhaka is also one of the most congested cities in the world. The average driving speed has dropped from 21 kilometers an hour 10 years ago to less than 7 kilometers an hour today. Continuing current trends would result in a further slowdown to 4 kilometers an hour, or slower than walking speed. Congestion wastes about 3.2 million working hours each day and costs the economy billions of dollars every year.

The city is also messy in other ways. Many residents, including the 3.5 million people living in informal settlements, often lack access to basic services, infrastructure and amenities. Air, soil and water quality has deteriorated to alarming levels, and pollution is adversely affecting the lives of urban dwellers.

A South Asian hub

The urbanization of Bangladesh is now at a crossroads, as it will be much harder for the country to reach upper-middle-income status if its cities—and Dhaka in particular—do not realize their full potential. A new paradigm is needed before the compounded costs of flooding, congestion and messiness stall the country's economic and social development.

This new paradigm involves the massive creation of high-quality urban land both in Dhaka and in other cities, but in an interconnected way. The experience in South Asia, where the capacity for planning and implementation is not as strong as in East Asia, is that cities have developed well along vibrant transport corridors. The example of Delhi and the vast network of urban centers in its catchment area, especially along the Golden Quadrilateral, is highly relevant in this respect. Though Delhi itself has a population of 17 million, some 80 million people directly or indirectly benefit from its development. Indeed, Delhi-Jaipur has become an almost continuous urban space (if not always in name, for sure in practice). Seen from outer space, the entire area between Delhi and Amritsar is lit at night to various degrees.

Bangladesh is now on the cusp of a similar development. The envisioned Sylhet-Chittagong highway offers the prospect of connectivity to India's northeast and global markets. The almost-completed Padma Bridge will allow the establishment of an active link with Kolkata, continuing over time toward Myanmar and Southeast Asia more broadly. These two corridors intersect in Dhaka's east, across the Shitalakshya River. Bangladesh's rivers complement this emerging corridor network. The proposed rehabilitation of the Buriganga and Shitalakshya Rivers, together with the upgrading of river navigability more generally, is expected to boost the connectivity of inland waterways.

For both roads and rivers, Dhaka happens to be the hinge of this emerging network of economic corridors, much like Delhi is in India. Ensuring that Dhaka is vibrant and functional is therefore one of the most important development priorities for Bangladesh.

Depending on the metric used, Dhaka already contributes between a fifth and a third of the country's income. Its success as a city going forward would enhance this contribution. Directly, because Dhaka is more productive than the rest of Bangladesh, and therefore Bangladesh's aggregate output increases alongside Dhaka's share of the national population. Indirectly as well, due to the city's potential to spread prosperity and boost economic development along the emerging network of economic corridors, as Delhi does in India.

The cost of inaction

All of this may sound like wishful thinking given the difficulties faced so far in retrofitting and decongesting what is by any standard a very messy city. Most efforts and resources have focused on trying to fix Dhaka by building flyovers, developing mass transport, improving drainage and providing sanitation in the western part of the city. All of this is absolutely necessary. But retrofitting a crowded city is very expensive. And no matter how diligent the efforts, population growth always seems to outpace infrastructure development. For example, between 1995 and 2005 the road surface in the urban core of Dhaka increased by only 5 percent, while the population increased by 50 percent. With growing prosperity, traffic increased by a staggering 134 percent.

And yet seizing the opportunity to develop East Dhaka correctly would not only be less costly per unit of land surface, but also complement ongoing retrofitting efforts.

East Dhaka remains mainly rural because the eastern embankment foreseen by the Flood Action Plan of 1991 was never built. As a result, most of the land is flooded during the monsoon season. But the area is now urbanizing. Private developers are filling vast tracts of land with sand, and households and firms are encroaching the edges of the few roads there.

This spontaneous urban development eastward may create substantial risks.

One such risk is natural disasters. Existing Dhaka is built over the relatively stable Madhupur Tract, but East Dhaka is mostly off of it, which makes it more vulnerable to earthquakes than the western part of Dhaka. Sand filling is increasing even further the risk of soil liquefaction in the event of a major earthquake. And as more people move into this area, the human cost of a seismic shock will likely increase. Building the embankment, together with complementary soft interventions such as enforcing construction standards, is critically important to stop the sand filling, and keep natural disaster risks under control.

Another risk associated with the spontaneous development of East Dhaka is growing congestion. The population is densifying eastward, but the proper infrastructure has not yet been put in place. Once housing has been built around the relatively few narrow streets and axes that currently cross the area, enlargement of these streets and axes will become costly, as it is in the existing urban core today. Spontaneous development may also result in the encroachment of canals and ponds that are critically important for water overflow during times of heavy rainfall.

On the social front, risks are associated with weak land ownership rights. Urbanization results in large increases in land value, and how this economic surplus is distributed matters. An in-depth study of the *mouza* Purba Durgapur, which is arguably representative of the areas of East Dhaka that have not yet been targeted by private developers, has revealed much fewer land property titles than households living there. If land titling, appraisal and administration are not upgraded as part of a strategic approach to the development of East Dhaka, the current residents may lose. Much of the surplus value that should be distributed among lawful owners and the public may be appropriated by large developers.

As for infrastructure and services, the rapid expansion of the western part of Dhaka was partly associated with the construction of the western embankment along the Buriganga River after the massive flood of 1988. The resulting availability of land attracted large numbers of firms and households before adequate infrastructure could be built, social services could be made accessible, and transportation services could be developed. As a result, Dhaka lost many of its canals and retention ponds, saw its congestion spiral out of control, and became one of the least livable large cities in the world. The spontaneous development of East Dhaka could lead to a similar dynamic.

A more prosperous Bangladesh

The simulations in this study reveal how large the difference between continuing with business as usual versus pursuing a Pudong-like approach to the development of East Dhaka could be.

Based on current trends, Greater Dhaka would have a population of 25 million in 2035 and an income per capita of US$8,000 at 2015 prices. Building the eastern embankment would increase the overall population of the city by 1.5 million people and the number of jobs by half a million. Making critically important transportation investments would add another 1.5 million people and 0.6 million jobs. However, the population of existing Dhaka would actually decrease by 1 million compared with that in the business as usual scenario because many households and firms would choose to move eastward.

Completing the package by easing the cost of business in East Dhaka, thereby encouraging the eastward movement of high-value-added activities, would add another 2 million people and nearly 0.7 million jobs to the city. But it would be a more productive city, with an income per capita of more than US$9,200 at 2015 prices, or enough to put Dhaka on the map of global cities.

In summary, a strategic approach to the development of East Dhaka, similar in spirit to what China chose for Shanghai with the development of Pudong, would make Greater Dhaka a much more productive and livable city. With East Dhaka being the hinge of Bangladesh's emerging north-south and east-west corridors, this greater prosperity is likely to spread. Much like Delhi, Greater Dhaka could boost economic development over a vast catchment area. In doing so, it would help absorb the 35 million Bangladeshis who are expected to become urban dwellers over the next two decades.

While the returns of such an approach would be huge, the costs would be manageable. Building the eastern embankment could require around US$2 billion. Adding the critically important transport infrastructure for East Dhaka would take the total bill closer to US$10 billion. Reducing the cost of business in the new area would mainly require an institutional effort to coordinate across agencies and ensure leadership, but it may not be too costly in monetary terms. Providing comprehensive public services in East Dhaka would involve substantial spending and push the total bill to US$15 billion.

And yet the payoffs to the relatively modest spending needed to embrace a strategic approach to the development of East Dhaka would be enormous. What is at stake is not just Greater Dhaka itself—it is the chance for Bangladesh to become an upper-middle-income country over a couple of decades and in doing so meet the aspirations of its people.

CHAPTER 1

Dhaka: Dynamic but Messy

Urbanization drives economic development. In the words of Jane Jacobs, one of the greatest thinkers on urban development, "Whenever and wherever societies have flourished and prospered rather than stagnated and decayed, creative and workable cities have been at the core of the phenomenon." As households and firms concentrate in cities, they become more productive. And a more productive environment, in turn, attracts more households and firms (Jacobs 1992).

Making land available and suitable for urban use is of fundamental importance to supporting the development of cities. Economic activity does not take place in a vacuum. Firms need land for their factories, offices and shops. Human interaction does not take place in a vacuum either. People need accommodation and ways to commute to work and move around. Land is at the heart of the subsequent decisions made by firms and households on production, work and housing. Land availability and land use patterns are therefore crucial in determining how effectively, or ineffectively, cities function (Duranton and Puga 2015).

In South Asia, countries are urbanizing rapidly, and their spatial transformation over the last two decades has been extraordinary. A growing number of megacities have emerged in the process. Many of them are strategically located, serving as drivers of economic growth and lifting millions of people out of poverty. And yet urbanization has been messy in South Asia. The amount of urban land available has grown in a mostly organic way, with diseconomies happening naturally as firms and households concentrate in whatever areas are available. Countries in South Asia are thus missing out on some of the gains from agglomeration because of excessive congestion and low livability (Ellis and Roberts 2015).

Dhaka, the capital of Bangladesh, is a case in point. Building on strong economic fundamentals, it has experienced remarkable growth and has become the economic powerhouse of the country. As the saying goes, "You don't need to go to Dhaka: Dhaka will come to you." But the city is expanding in an unplanned and unchecked manner. Flood prevention measures have been introduced reactively in response to disasters and are inadequate. Rivers and canals are increasingly filled with solid waste, further reducing the storm water storage capacity. Roads have been built in a piecemeal fashion, leaving the connectivity network poorly established and road density not on a par with international standards. As for mass transit systems, they are almost nonexistent. Meanwhile, housing has developed in a haphazard manner, and services have not been well integrated with housing development. Large numbers of households lack access to the basic amenities, and many of them live in slums. Air, soil and water quality has deteriorated to alarming levels, and pollution is adversely affecting the lives of urban dwellers.

In summary, Dhaka's dynamism is increasingly constrained by flooding, congestion and messiness. But there is a growing realization that the organic version of urban land development on which Dhaka was built can deliver only to a certain point, which is why it is imperative to change the urban development paradigm now.

Disproportionally important

Dhaka is one of the largest and most densely populated cities in the world, regardless of how the boundaries of the city are delineated. Like other major metropolitan agglomerations, Dhaka has been the subject of a few competing definitions, with different implications for its exact area. The boundaries determined by the official master plan, the Dhaka Metropolitan Development Plan 1995–2015, are used in this report. They encompass an area of 1,528 square kilometers, which comprises an urban core but also several satellite cities, towns and villages (RAJUK 1995).

The urban core is under the purview of two local government authorities, the Dhaka North City Corporation (hereafter the Dhaka North CC) and the Dhaka South City Corporation (Dhaka South CC). This core is the most densely populated and the most vibrant part of the city. But satellite imagery of land cover and nighttime light intensity shows that the satellite cities, towns and villages surrounding the Dhaka CCs also have urban characteristics. That is not the case, however, for the areas immediately outside the boundaries of Greater Dhaka. It follows, then, that these boundaries are broad enough to encompass an urban continuum while clearly demarcating the city from the rest of the country.

Dhaka grew dramatically following Bangladesh's independence from Pakistan in 1971, and it has continued to expand rapidly until now. Between 1974 and 1981, its population growth rate was estimated at nearly 10 percent a year. Although it has stabilized at around 5 percent more recently, this is still a phenomenal expansion. The population of Greater Dhaka grew from 3.4 million in 1981 to nearly 18 million in 2015 (BBS 2011; Jahan 2011; Rahman 2017; RAJUK 2015).

With such vertiginous growth, Greater Dhaka is now the 11th-largest city in the world (UN 2015). Dhaka is also large in relation to Bangladesh, accounting for one-tenth of the country's population and over a third of its urban population. But it only occupies 1 percent of the country's land. About 9 million of Greater Dhaka's inhabitants live in the Dhaka CCs, of which 8 million in the western part. The average density of this central area of the city has reached a staggering 41,000 inhabitants per square kilometer.

The population of Greater Dhaka is projected to continue growing at a rate of about 3–4 percent a year, one of the highest rates among Asian cities (BBS 2011; UN 2015). Economic dynamism drives this phenomenal demographic growth. In addition to being Bangladesh's cultural and political center, Dhaka is the economic hub of the country.

Dhaka's regional primacy was already apparent during the Mughal period. Back then, it was a manufacturing center for a variety of cottage products and an important node in the worldwide muslin and silk trades. The easily washable cotton fabrics of the Dhaka region attracted European merchants, who settled in and established their factories and trading posts. Muslin was a coveted product. Contemporary royalties and nobilities became aware of the fabric, which came to them tagged with the place name "Dhaka" (Hasan 2008; Kabir and Parolin 2012; Mohsin 1989).

In modern times, Dhaka has become the growth engine of Bangladesh (figure 1.1). Greater Dhaka generates one-fifth of the country's gross domestic product (GDP) and almost half of its formal employment. Bangladesh's recent growth story has been associated with its export-oriented garment industry and the large number of salaried jobs it generates. A look at the spatial distribution of economic activity shows that Greater Dhaka hosts 80 percent of the country's export-oriented garment factories and creates over 30 percent of its formal manufacturing jobs. Therefore, whatever happens to Dhaka also

Figure 1.1 Greater Dhaka has an outsized share of Bangladesh's population and jobs

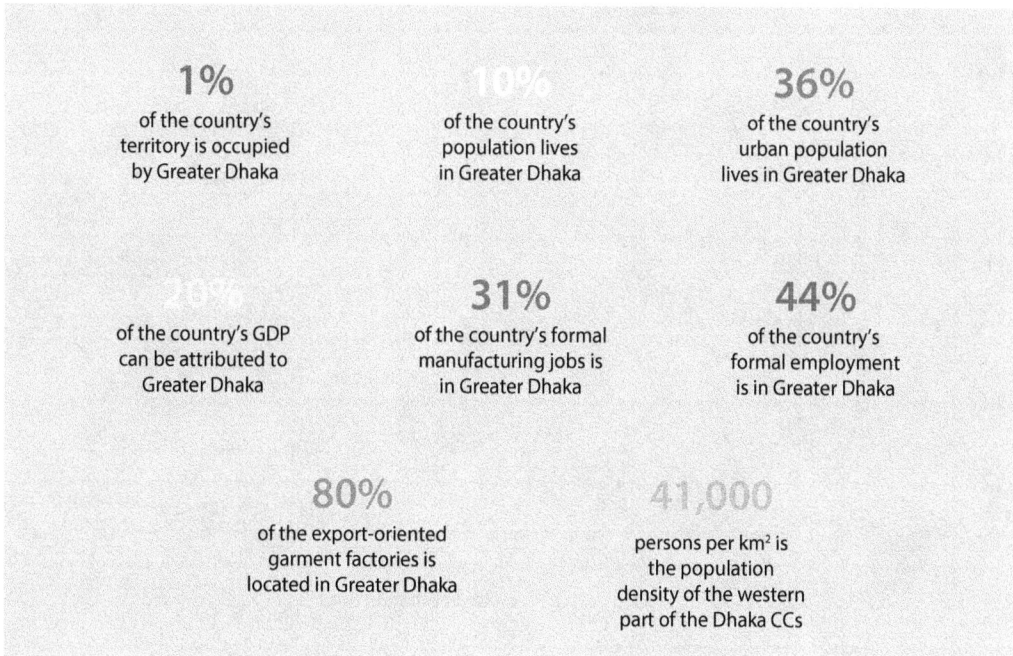

1% of the country's territory is occupied by Greater Dhaka	**10%** of the country's population lives in Greater Dhaka	**36%** of the country's urban population lives in Greater Dhaka
20% of the country's GDP can be attributed to Greater Dhaka	**31%** of the country's formal manufacturing jobs is in Greater Dhaka	**44%** of the country's formal employment is in Greater Dhaka
80% of the export-oriented garment factories is located in Greater Dhaka	**41,000** persons per km² is the population density of the western part of the Dhaka CCs	

Sources: Calculations based on BBS (2010, 2011, 2013); BGMEA (2017); Muzzini and Aparicio (2013).
Note: CC = city corporation; GDP = gross domestic product.

happens to Bangladesh. If Dhaka does not succeed, it will be very difficult for Bangladesh to do so.

Dhaka's primacy also derives from its role as Bangladesh's administrative capital, which requires specialized skills and support services. Moreover, the city is the country's main interlocutor in the international arena. Indeed, the economic dialogue between countries is increasingly carried out by global cities, even if they are not administrative capitals. New York and Shanghai are obvious examples, both having oversized financial and logistic sectors to interact with their global peers. Dhaka is the only city in Bangladesh able to play this global role.

The flip side of Dhaka's primacy is the shortage of sizable secondary cities. Across countries, the distribution of the urban population among cities of different sizes exhibits a common pattern. In statistical terms, the distribution of the largest cities by size approximately follows what is called Zipf's law: the population of a city is inversely proportional to its rank. In layman's terms, this law maintains that the second-largest city in a country should have half the population of the largest city, the third-largest city one-third that population, and so on (Gabaix 1999; Krugman 1995).

Zipf's law can be visualized through a simple relationship linking the rank of a city (first, second, third and so forth) to its population (Gabaix and Ioannides 2004). When both rank and population are measured in logs, the relationship is a straight line with a slope of –45 degrees (the dotted blue line in figure 1.2).

Figure 1.2 Bangladesh has few sizable secondary cities

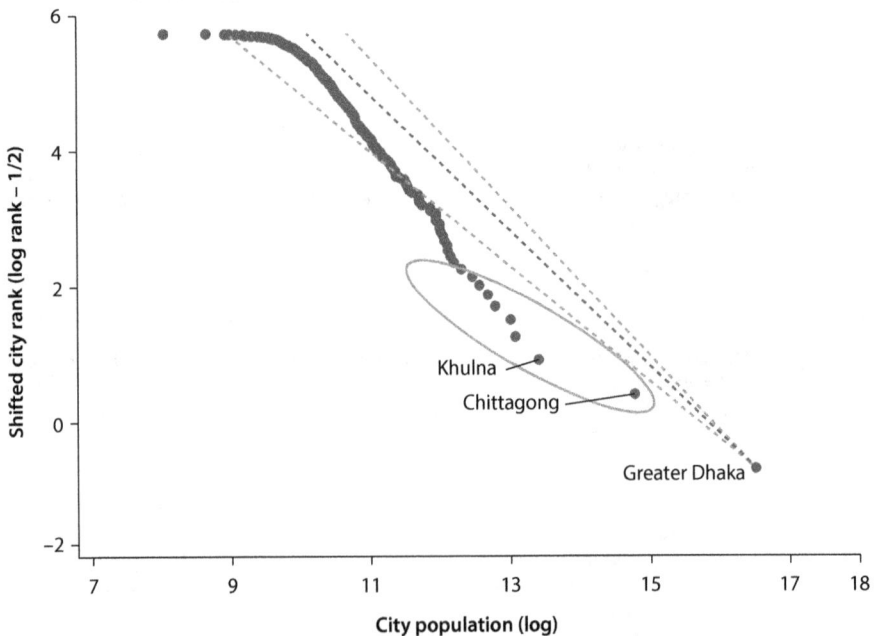

Source: Calculations based on BBS (2011).
Note: The y-axis is the log of shifted rank (rank—1/2) as per Gabaix and Ibragimov (2011). The slope of the dotted blue line is –1, corresponding to the case in which Zipf's law holds perfectly. The slopes of the dotted red lines are –0.85 and –1.10, which define the confidence interval when Zipf's law holds, as reported in Gabaix and Ioannides (2004).

In Bangladesh's case, Dhaka is the endpoint of the line, with a rank of 1 (–0.69 in log of shifted rank) and a population of 14.9 million (16.5 in log). If Zipf's law holds perfectly in Bangladesh's case, its secondary cities should be on the straight line with a slope of –45 degrees. If Zipf's holds as it does on average in other countries, then secondary cities should not be expected to be exactly on the line, but at least close to it (that is, in between the dotted red lines in figure 1.2). However, the largest secondary cities in Bangladesh are clearly outside the confidence interval around the straight line. The actual relationship between city rank and city size falls back into the expected interval only for cities with a rank above 34 (3.5 in log of shifted rank). This confirms that Bangladesh is an outlier in both the huge size of its biggest city and the relatively modest size of its secondary ones.

Strategically located

Several forces are generally believed to shape the size and productivity of cities. Among them, location advantages, agglomeration economies and self-selection stand out (Behrens and Robert-Nicoud 2015; Duranton and Puga 2004; Glaeser 2012). *Location advantages* refers to fundamentals such as geography and climate. Many highly productive cities, from New York to Singapore, developed around a strategically important transshipment point. Others, such as those in the U.S. Sun Belt, attract firms and households because of their relatively more favorable weather conditions. *Agglomeration economies* derive from better labor matching, greater product diversification and stronger knowledge spillovers. In this case, just being together makes everybody more productive, and the only reason cities do not keep growing indefinitely is that being together also gives rise to congestion costs. As for *self-selection*, both households and firms are diverse in their mixture of skills, energy and entrepreneurship, and the most productive ones often find themselves drawn to urban areas. There is much academic discussion about which of these three forces is more important in practice. But to varying degrees, all cities are influenced by location advantages, agglomeration economies and self-selection.

Location advantages

Dhaka's primacy derives in part from its strategic location. The history of the city dates to the first millennium, when the abundantly irrigated land no doubt attracted human settlement. The region was part of the district of Bikrampur under the Sena dynasty, and it later became part of Sonargaon, the regional administrative hub of the Delhi and Bengal Sultanates. The Mughals established their capital there in 1610, recognizing the benefit of being situated on higher ground in an otherwise low-lying area (Chowdhury and Faruqui 1989; Hasan 2008; Islam 2008; Kabir and Parolin 2012).

Indeed, topography makes Dhaka stand out relative to its surroundings. Bangladesh is located on a vast deltaic plain at the confluence of the Jamuna, Padma and Meghna Rivers—an area often submerged by water. Twice a day, the sea tide pushes a substantial portion of the country's territory below sea level, and only a vast network of dykes and embankments generally keeps the water out of inhabited areas. But staying dry is more difficult in the monsoon season. At times, three-quarters of the country's territory is inundated. As a result, any land area above the high-water mark attracts human activity. Historically, most of Dhaka sat on the southern part of the Madhupur Tract, a relatively firm surface above flood level (Alam 2014; Hasan 2008; Talukder 2006).

Dhaka also enjoys superior accessibility. Several navigable waterways flow to its south and east, including the Arial Kha, Buriganga, Dhaleswari, Padma, Lakkhya and Meghna Rivers. In choosing the area as their capital, the Mughals were keen to control the strategic water routes of the region.

Since its early days, Dhaka has also been well connected by land. The Grand Trunk Road passed through the region, connecting it with northern India, Central Asia and the southeastern port city of Chittagong. In the late 19th century, accessibility was further enhanced by the construction of railways, including the Dhaka-Narayanganj-Mymensingh and the Assam-Bengal. These rail lines, together with riverine and road networks, turned Dhaka into a nodal point connecting most of the important trading and commercial centers of the region (Hassan 2008).

Today, Dhaka is as strategically located as in its earliest days, and it is much better connected. It is the hinge linking secondary cities of Bangladesh, and it is bound to become a connecting node between South Asia and East Asia (map 1.1). The Asian Highway project foresees a corridor passing through Jessore and Kulna and connecting Dhaka to Kolkata, the region's wealthiest city. The almost-completed Padma Bridge will allow establishment of a more active link with Kolkata, continuing toward Delhi, Lahore, Mumbai and Chennai. To the northwest, the Jamuna Bridge connects Dhaka with Thimphu in Bhutan and Kathmandu in Nepal, two other South Asian capitals. And to the east, Dhaka sits in the Sylhet-Chittagong corridor, which offers the prospect of connectivity with East Asian cities such as Bangkok, Yangon and Kunming. With its central location and expanding connectivity, Dhaka has the potential to thrust the whole hinterland of Bangladesh into a new growth trajectory.

Agglomeration economies

Building on its favorable location, Dhaka has been able to reap the benefits of agglomeration economies. Political turmoil has stalled Dhaka's industries and businesses at times, but the city has always been able to regain its strength and thrive as a growth pole. Across countries, larger cities tend to be more productive. When a city's population doubles, its income per capita is estimated to grow 2–10 percent (Duranton 2015; Rosenthal and Strange 2004). Consistent with this global pattern, Dhaka is much wealthier than the rest of the country. On average, the annual household income in the Dhaka CCs was about US$4,284 in 2016, while in other city corporations it reached US$3,360. The average for the country as a whole was about US$2,448 (BBS 2016).

Map 1.1 Dhaka is at the intersection of emerging transport corridors

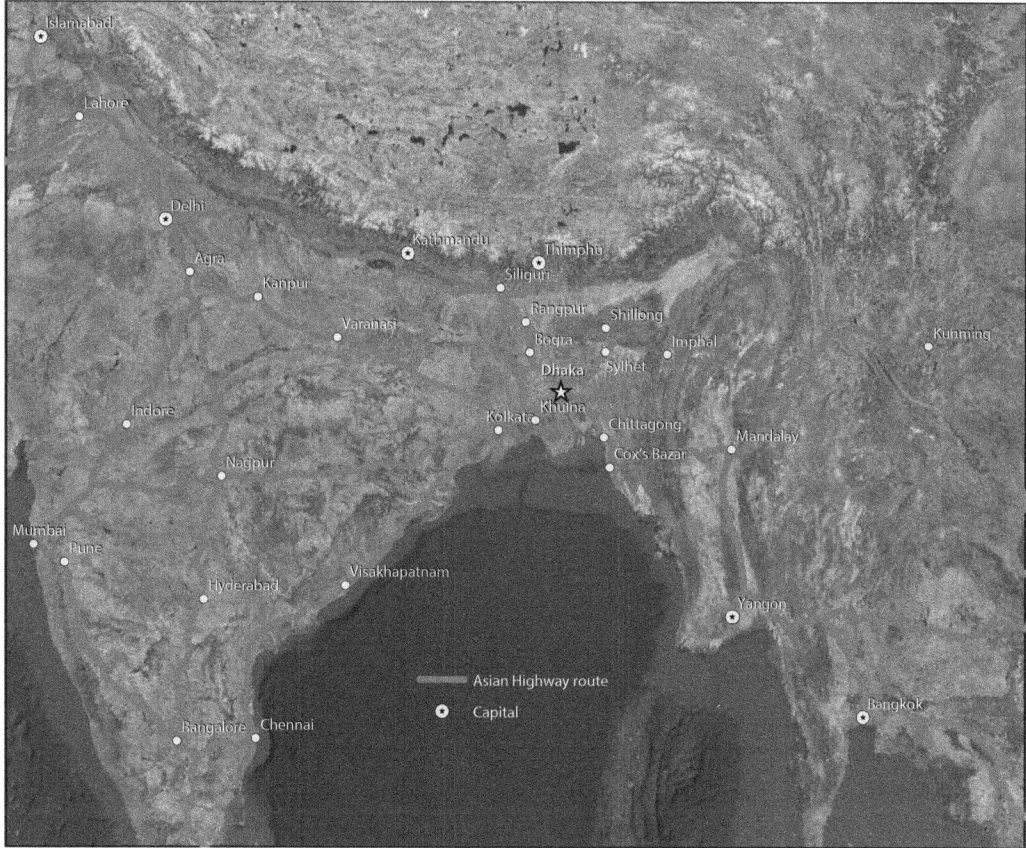

Sources: Mapping and visualization based on UN (2016) and Google Maps.

The spatial distribution of the ready-made garment industry has been strongly influenced by agglomeration economies as well. About 80 percent of the country's garment factories has been at some point located in Greater Dhaka. Labor pooling, input-output linkages and knowledge transfers have all been at work to support this strong geographical concentration.

Because of ever-increasing land prices, growing congestion and government policies, the garment industry has been gradually moving out of the city core (BGMEA 2017; RAJUK 2015). But tradable services—such as finance, consultancy, education, health care and logistics—have filled the gap. The Dhaka CCs are the seat of Bangladesh Bank and the Dhaka Stock Exchange. They also have one of the largest concentrations of multinational companies in South Asia. Tradable services account for 13 percent of their total formal employment (BBS 2013). Because of the city's diversifying economic structure, agglomeration economies may be gaining strength in Dhaka. Workers become more productive in Dhaka not by doing the same thing as in smaller cities. Instead, they are doing different things and doing them differently.

Toward Great Dhaka • http://dx.doi.org/10.1596/978-1-4648-1238-5

Self-selection

Dhaka's growth story is also shaped by the self-selection of households and firms across different parts of the country. Migrants accounted for 57 percent of the total population of the Dhaka CCs in 2011. Almost 90 percent of these migrants were from rural areas, and over 36 percent reported coming to Dhaka for jobs (BBS 2011). In that same year, one-third of the working-age population of the Dhaka CCs had a secondary education or above, whereas the national average was 16 percent (BBS 2011). Across countries, differences in worker characteristics explain up to half of the observed relationship between city income per capita and city size (Combes, Duranton and Gobillon 2008; Combes et al. 2010). And differences in worker characteristics are sizable in the case of Bangladesh.

It is more difficult to directly assess self-selection among entrepreneurs and firms, as their dynamism and productivity are not easy to measure. However, it is telling that more than one-third of Bangladesh's firms employing 20 workers or more and over half of the firms employing 100 workers or more are in Greater Dhaka (BBS 2013).

Successful on many counts

Dhaka's performance can be assessed on the basis of the amount and type of urban land it encompasses. Because cities are dominated by their built environment, the extent of built-up area has often been used as a proxy for the size of a city (Mumford 1937; Schneider, Friedl and Potere 2009). The extent of Dhaka's built-up area has expanded eightfold in barely seven decades. Its urban land surface increased from about 22 square kilometers after the Partition of the British Raj in 1947 to about 85 square kilometers at the time of Bangladesh's independence from Pakistan in 1971. Today, it is about 173 square kilometers (Pramanik and Stathakis 2016).

Data from outer space allow an even more granular analysis of this extraordinary spatial transformation. Images of land cover characteristics taken from satellites can be retrieved and processed to classify built-up areas and monitor their change over time. Based on high-resolution imagery of land cover, Greater Dhaka densified rapidly between 2003 and 2016 (map 1.2). The land surface characterized by high and medium built-up density grew by 4.8 percent a year, whereas the land surface with low built-up density declined by 9.6 percent a year. This densification process took place against the backdrop of a relatively modest increase in the extent of Dhaka's total built-up area, which grew by only 1.5 percent a year during this period.

Data from outer space can also be used to assess the economic vibrancy of urban areas. Artificial lights, especially stable and intense ones, correlate with human activity. For that reason, satellite imagery on nighttime light intensity is being used increasingly to measure the strength of an economy and its rate of growth (Henderson, Storeygard and Weil 2012). This approach reveals that Greater Dhaka registered remarkable economic dynamism between 2012 and 2016. The intensity of its nighttime light grew by 12 percent a year at a time when the

Map 1.2 Dhaka has rapidly densified while growing slowly in size

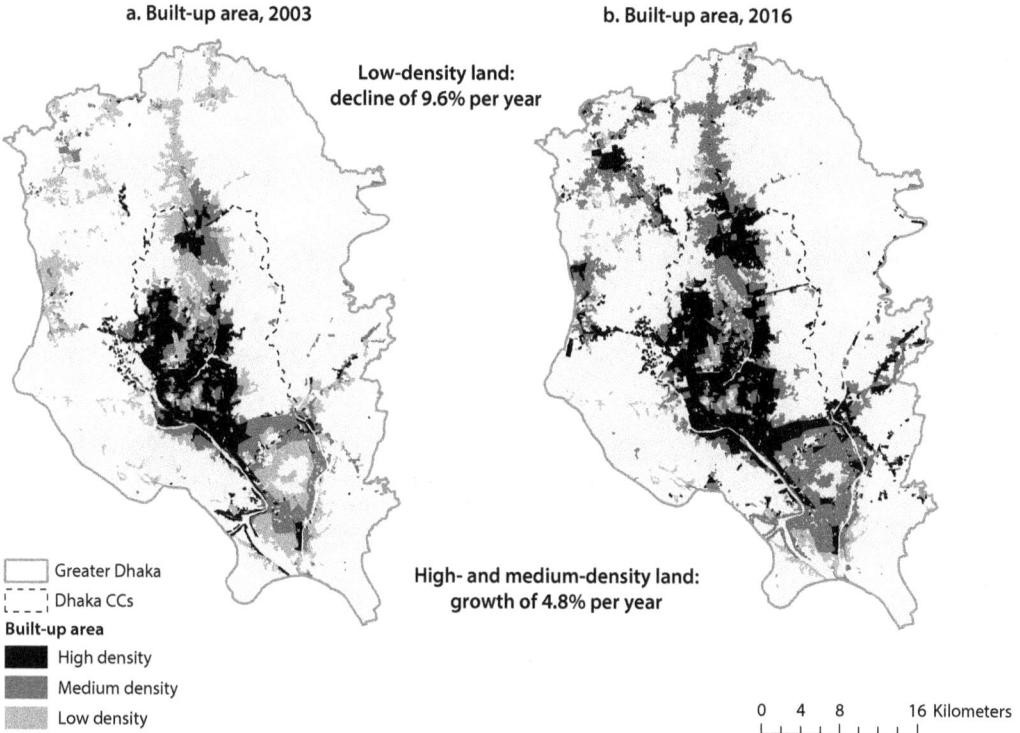

a. Built-up area, 2003

b. Built-up area, 2016

Low-density land:
decline of 9.6% per year

High- and medium-density land:
growth of 4.8% per year

Greater Dhaka

Dhaka CCs

Built-up area

High density

Medium density

Low density

0   4   8   16 Kilometers

Sources: Calculations and visualization based on land classification background work undertaken for this report (GISAT 2017); Li et al. (2015).
Note: The classification is based on 0.5- and 5-meter resolution satellite imagery. Land covered by 1–50 percent of continuous urban built-up area is low-density land. The corresponding figure for medium-density land is 50–80 percent and high-density land 80–100 percent. CC = city corporation.

GDP of Bangladesh was growing by 6–7 percent a year (map 1.3). Most notably, the intensity of the nighttime light in the Dhaka CCs grew by 13.4 percent a year, indicating the continued strength of the city's urban core.

Dhaka's success also lies in the contribution it makes to poverty reduction across Bangladesh. Three direct mechanisms are at play. First, people gain access to higher living standards by migrating to Dhaka from elsewhere in the country. Second, those who stay behind benefit from the remittances these urban migrants send back home. And third, large cities like Dhaka channel resources to the rest of the country through fiscal transfers operated by central government.

On the first mechanism, net migration into the Dhaka metropolitan area during the decade 2001–11 has been estimated at about 3.2 million people. More than half of this migration was directly from rural areas (World Bank 2017a). As for the other mechanisms, household surveys show that average household income exceeds average household consumption by 15 percent in the Dhaka CCs, but only by 7 percent in other city corporations. It is below average household consumption in rural areas. This finding is suggestive of transfers from richer to poorer areas. Rigorous impact evaluations find that even the families of

Map 1.3 Nighttime light intensity reveals remarkable economic dynamism

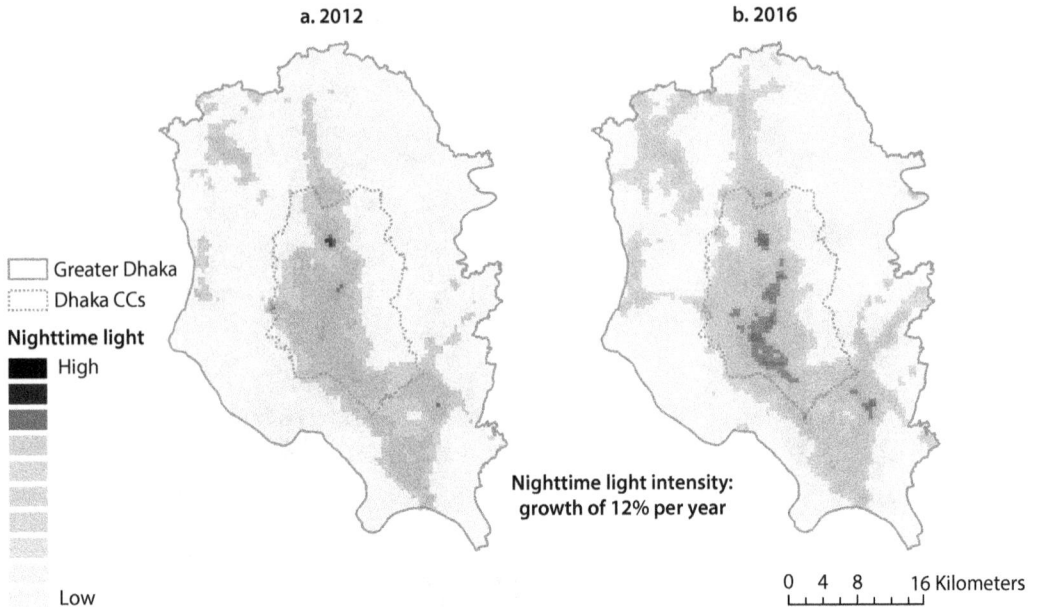

a. 2012   b. 2016

Greater Dhaka
Dhaka CCs

Nighttime light
High

Low

Nighttime light intensity:
growth of 12% per year

0   4   8   16 Kilometers

Sources: Calculations and visualization based on Li et al. (2015); NOAA (2017).
Note: Radiance values of nighttime light are expressed in nanowatts per square centimeter per steradian (nW/cm²/sr). CC = city corporation.

seasonal migrants fare better when those migrants move to Dhaka to work as short-term labor and send back remittances than when they stay in their home villages during the monsoon season (Aizenman 2017; Bryan, Chowdhury and Mobarak 2014).

Although many migrants end up living in slums, their living standards there may still be higher than those where they came from. A census and a survey of slum households recently conducted for Bangladesh (BBS 2014, 2016) revealed that the poverty rate in the Dhaka CCs is much lower than in the rest of the country, reaching 9 percent versus 19 percent in other cities and 26 percent in villages (figure 1.3). The poverty rate among slum dwellers is much higher than the average rate for the Dhaka CCs, as could be expected, but it is lower than that in rural areas (Arias-Granda et al. 2017).

A more detailed analysis suggests that the main disadvantage faced by slum dwellers is their limited access to basic services such as drinking water and sanitation. On both counts, households living in slums do worse than the average household in the Dhaka CCs. But the difference vanishes when it comes to the monetary dimensions of living standards. For example, the ownership of fans and mobile phones among slum dwellers and among other households in the Dhaka CCs is similar. And housing ownership is actually higher among slum dwellers. Those who own their housing face a lower poverty rate than those who rent it—16 versus 26 percent (Arias-Granda et al. 2017). This finding may explain why, despite the slums and the harsh living conditions, Dhaka's population keeps growing.

Figure 1.3 Slums are poorer than the rest of Dhaka, but less poor than rural areas

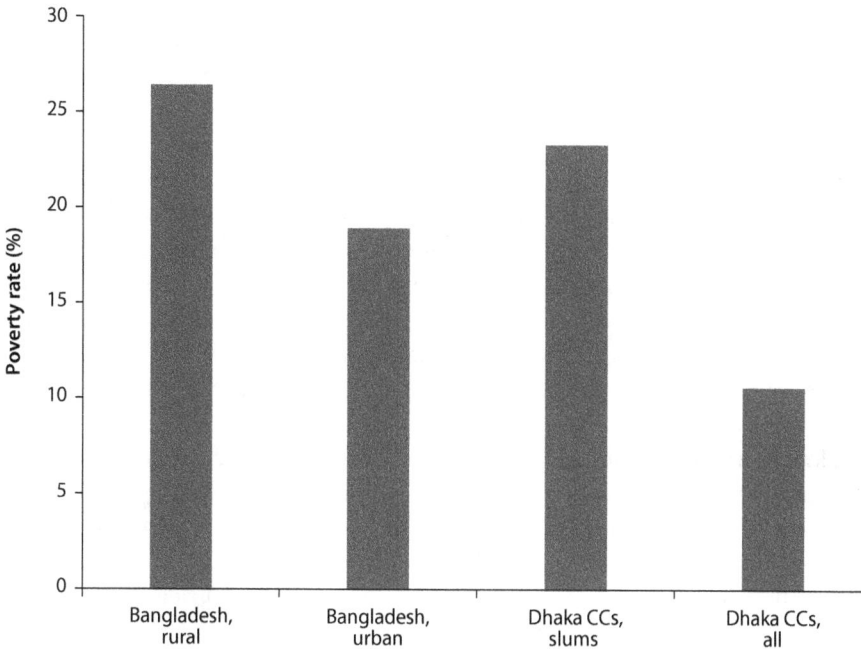

Source: Arias-Granda et al. 2017.
Note: CC = city corporation.

Three critical challenges

Dhaka's success in fostering economic growth and poverty reduction in Bangladesh suggests that a virtuous cycle exists among location advantages, agglomeration economies and self-selection. However, good fundamentals do not guarantee sustained growth over long periods of time. The experience of other cities indicates that their advantages can erode (Duranton 2015; Glaeser 2012). Continued innovation and job creation by the private sector are essential to sustain further productivity gains, while critical public interventions are needed to mitigate the unavoidable downsides of extremely high population density.

Despite its successes, there are areas in which Dhaka has not done particularly well. Flooding, congestion and messiness are three salient challenges to further urban growth. Flooding translates into a high probability that a land area will not be fully usable for extended periods of time. Congestion implies that many person-hours that could be devoted to work or leisure are wasted in traffic. And messiness refers to the inadequate coordination between different pieces of urban infrastructure and service delivery across various sectors. If the constraints that flooding, congestion and messiness impose are not relieved, the city will miss out on some of the gains from its otherwise virtuous circle of location advantages, agglomeration economies and self-selection.

Flooding

Owing to its climate, topography and proximity to rivers, Dhaka is prone to water-related hazards, including both river flooding and waterlogging. Dhaka is surrounded on three sides by rivers. Although historically most of it sat on relatively high ground, currently 40 percent of its land lies outside the Madhupur Tract, on low-elevation floodplains. When the water levels of the surrounding rivers are high, the city faces a higher probability of river flooding. Like the rest of Bangladesh, the city is affected by the monsoon. Its average annual rainfall is about 2,050 millimeters, and more than 70 percent of it occurs during three months. Intense rainfall over short periods of time increases both river and urban flood hazards. The clay of the city core is also impervious, not allowing rainwater to sink in and forcing it to run off, which causes ponding in contiguous low-lying areas (Ahmed and Bramley 2015; World Bank 2017a).

Flood management interventions have mostly emerged in response to disasters, and they have proven wholly inadequate for containing flooding and reducing the associated damage. The unplanned and unchecked expansion of the built-up area has exacerbated flood hazards. The western part of the Dhaka CCs is largely shielded from river flooding because a flood barrier—the western embankment—was built in response to the massive 1988 floods. But the eastern part of the city core remains vulnerable to rising water levels in the surrounding rivers because no similar infrastructure has been developed in that direction.

Dhaka's drainage system was designed for what is now its historical center. This aging infrastructure is inadequate to cope with the rapid densification within its reach, and its limited spatial coverage cannot handle the expansion of the city. It is encouraging that Dhaka has a network of canals, which play an important role in absorbing excess water in times of heavy rainfall. But over time many of these canals have been encroached by construction or filled with solid waste, especially in slum areas, where garbage is frequently dumped in the water. Only 25 of the city's 43 canals are functional at present, which severely reduces the water conveyance capacity. The growth of the built-up surface of the city has also shrunk natural water storage areas, such as wetlands and ponds, and aggravated the imperviousness of the soil (DWASA 2015; World Bank 2017b).

Over the years, the city has regularly experienced major floods, and the losses have been massive. The worst flooding in recent times was in 2004 and 2009. In the 2004 flood, 18 percent of the western part of the Dhaka CCs and 94 percent of the city's eastern part were inundated, directly affecting nearly 5 million people. Residents faced a severe shortage of drinking water, and the sewerage system failed across a wide area. In the 2009 flood, the Dhaka CCs once again collapsed, with the inundated area amounting to about three-quarters of the area affected in 2004 (Sayed and Huruyama 2017; World Bank 2017b).

In more recent years, even nonmajor floods have posed serious problems. In September 2015, the city's transport system came to a halt because of waterlogging, and this was after just 1 hour of heavy rainfall (photo 1.1). In 2016 streets

Photo 1.1 In Dhaka, flooding results from inadequate water management

Source: The Daily Star, 2015, http://www.thedailystar.net/frontpage/dhaka-deluged-136427. Used with permission. Further permission required for reuse.

were awash with bloodstained water because the heavy rainfall occurred while the Muslim community was sacrificing lambs to celebrate Eid al-Adha.

Congestion

Traffic congestion is the flip side of higher productivity when large numbers of people live and work in a relatively small area. This situation is actually the fundamental trade-off faced by cities (Fujita and Thisse 2002). The challenge for urban authorities is to find ways to handle congestion so that its costs do not grow faster than local productivity as the city's population increases (Combes, Duranton and Gobillon 2012). In Dhaka, this battle has mainly been a lost one.

Management of traffic congestion requires both hard infrastructure and soft interventions. For example, the segregation of lines by transportation mode is known to significantly improve the throughput of traffic on existing roads (World Bank 2017c). But Dhaka is notorious for its mixed traffic lane operation. All transportation modes—including buses, cars and rickshaws—use the full width of a road to circulate, stop, and even park. Driving in Dhaka qualifies as a contact sport because vehicles often push each other to get through, leaving their bodies colorfully scarred.

However, the fundamental bottleneck in Dhaka's case is hard infrastructure. To a large extent, the road network was developed in a disorganized manner, with construction driven by urgent considerations and opportunism rather than by clear thinking on connectivity. No continuous main road runs in the east-west direction; most traffic flows in the north-south direction, creating a major problem for the entire network. There is no ring road around Dhaka either, leading to hours of delays when entering or exiting the city. Under these circumstances, effective traffic management measures such as one-way operation, tidal flow operation and signal synchronization are difficult to implement (World Bank 2017c).

The road hierarchy is poorly established. The majority of transportation axes are disjointed, narrow and poorly aligned. Out of over 4,100 kilometers of paved roads, only about 500 kilometers (less than 12 percent) are of primary standard quality suitable for bus transportation. Many parts of Dhaka have been developed through individual initiatives, without proper roads to support them. These areas remain inaccessible to public transportation, even by minibus. This messy road network, characterized by poor alignment, sharp curves and lack of proper corner widening at intersections, is not well suited to accommodate more efficient modes of public transport. At present, despite protracted efforts, there is no bus rapid transit (BRT) system in operation. And there is no mass rapid transit (MRT) either (World Bank 2017c).

Although road length and road density are better in Dhaka than in the rest of Bangladesh, they are not on a par with international standards for large cities. Greater Dhaka and the Delhi Union Territory each occupy about 1,500 square kilometers of land. However, according to OpenStreetMap, total road length is only about 3,600 kilometers in Greater Dhaka, whereas it reaches 7,900 kilometers in Delhi. In practice, this gap translates into a much smaller area with high road density in Dhaka than in Delhi (map 1.4). The gap is equally wide in per capita terms, particularly in the urban cores—there are about 270 kilometers of roads per million people in the Dhaka CCs versus about 440 kilometers per million people in the Delhi municipal corporations. The gap is even wider for roads of secondary or higher standards—about 49 kilometers per million people in the Dhaka CCs versus 99 kilometers per million people in the Delhi municipal corporations (BBS 2011; Li et al. 2015; ORGI 2011; OSM 2014). It is telling that between 1995 and 2005 the road surface of the Dhaka CCs increased by a mere 5 percent, while its population grew by 50 percent and total traffic more than doubled (DTCA and JICA 2015; Rahman 2010; World Bank 2017c).

Not surprisingly, in Dhaka the average driving speed has declined from 21 kilometers per hour 10 years ago to 7 kilometers per hour today. People spend an average of 2.4 hours a day in traffic, of which 1.3 hours is in traffic jams. Continuing current trends would result in a further slowdown to 4 kilometers per hour, or slower than the average walking speed. Congestion currently consumes 3.2 million working hours each day and costs the economy billions of dollars every year. The result is a massive loss of income potential by the city and the country (DTCA and JICA 2015; MCCI and CMILT 2010).

Map 1.4 Congestion is a result of insufficient transportation infrastructure: comparing Dhaka and Delhi

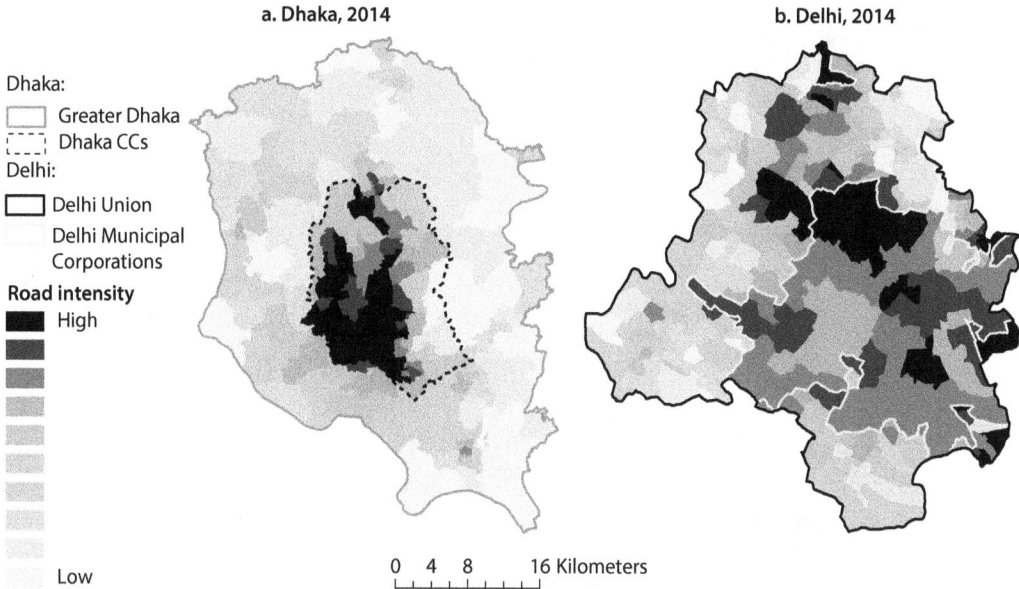

a. Dhaka, 2014   b. Delhi, 2014

Dhaka:
☐ Greater Dhaka
⌐‐⌐ Dhaka CCs
Delhi:
☐ Delhi Union
    Delhi Municipal
    Corporations

Road intensity
■ High

Low

0   4   8   16 Kilometers

Sources: Calculations and visualization based on BBS (2011); Li et al. (2015); ORGI (2011); OSM (2014).
Note: Road intensity is expressed in kilometer per 1,000 square kilometers (km/1,000 km²). CC = city corporation.

Messiness

The third challenge, and not the smallest one, is the exceptional messiness of Dhaka's urban development. What is meant by this is the irregularity of access to good services. Many parts of the city have emerged out of disconnected initiatives by both the public and the private sectors. Most of these developments preceded planning, or they paid little attention to the existing plans. Powerful interest groups have often ignored regulations or pushed disjointed projects. The newly created areas most often failed to ensure flood resilience, include proper transport connectivity, and foresee adequate utilities and service provision. Many residents, including the 3.5 million living in slums, often lack access to basic services, infrastructure and amenities. Thus, in addition to managing flooding and taming congestion, Dhaka also faces the critical challenge of sustaining its water supply, providing sanitation, managing solid waste, delivering education and health care services, and offering residential amenities to its rapidly growing population.

As a consequence of Dhaka's messiness, air, soil and water pollution have reached dangerous levels. Among Asian cities, Dhaka ranks second from the bottom on air quality. Fine particulate matter ($PM_{2.5}$) pollution is nine times higher than the safe limit of 10 micrograms per cubic meter. The level of coarser particulate matter (PM_{10}) is eight times higher than the safe concentration level of 20 micrograms per cubic meter (WHO 2016). In addition, more than 1.2 million people live in 87 polluted hotspots, accounting for one-tenth of all the people affected by soil pollution in South Asia. Of these hotspots, 58 are heavily

Figure 1.4 Messiness: Dhaka appears at the bottom of global livability rankings

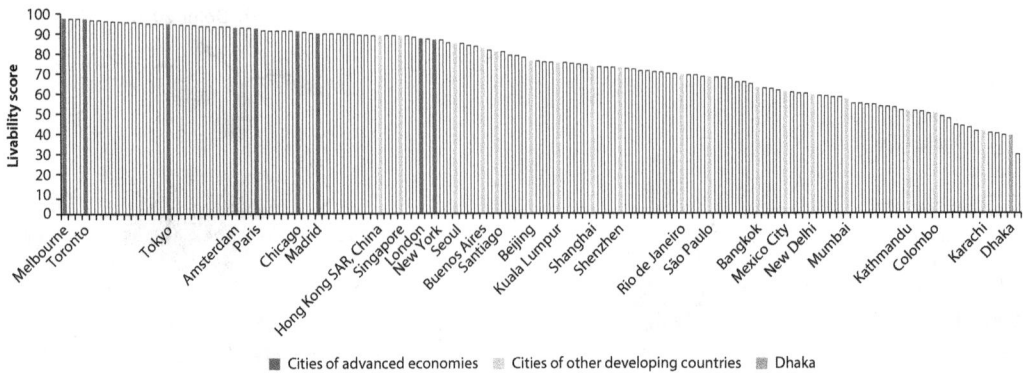

Source: EIU 2015.

contaminated with lead, 13 with chromium, 5 with arsenic and 2 with cadmium (Pure Earth 2017). The water quality of the rivers surrounding Dhaka has degraded at alarming rates as well. These rivers have extremely low concentrations of dissolved oxygen and high levels of chloride, total dissolved solids, biochemical oxygen demand and chemical oxygen demand (DOE 2015). Pollution can be so severe in certain sectors of these rivers that the supply of treatable water for human consumption is in decline (WRG 2015).

Dhaka now has the reputation of being one of the least livable major cities in the world (figure 1.4). This dubious distinction is to a large extent based on the livability index compiled by the Economist Intelligence Unit (EIU), which combines information on education, infrastructure, health and stability. The most recent EIU livability index (2015) ranks Dhaka 139th out of 140 cities, only ahead of Damascus, the Syrian Arab Republic. Dhaka not only falls behind cities in more advanced economies in Latin America and East Asia, but also lags behind all other major South Asian cities, including Delhi, Mumbai, Kathmandu, Colombo and Karachi. City livability rankings produced by other organizations corroborate this conclusion. For example, the most recent Mercer Quality of Living Survey places Dhaka 211th out of 230 cities (Mercer 2015).

Dhaka's failure to adequately address flooding, congestion and messiness has resulted in disproportionate urban costs. Although it dominates Bangladesh in terms of both its population and its economy, its international position is more unbalanced. Dhaka stands out globally by its population size, which makes it the 11th largest city in the world. But it is only the 78th largest city in terms of its GDP, measured in comparable purchasing power parity (PPP) terms (figure 1.5). This significant mismatch suggests that Dhaka is punching economically far below its population weight. But it also suggests that the city has an enormous potential to catch up in a process that could sustain economic growth for decades to come.

Figure 1.5 Dhaka's population is huge—its economy less so

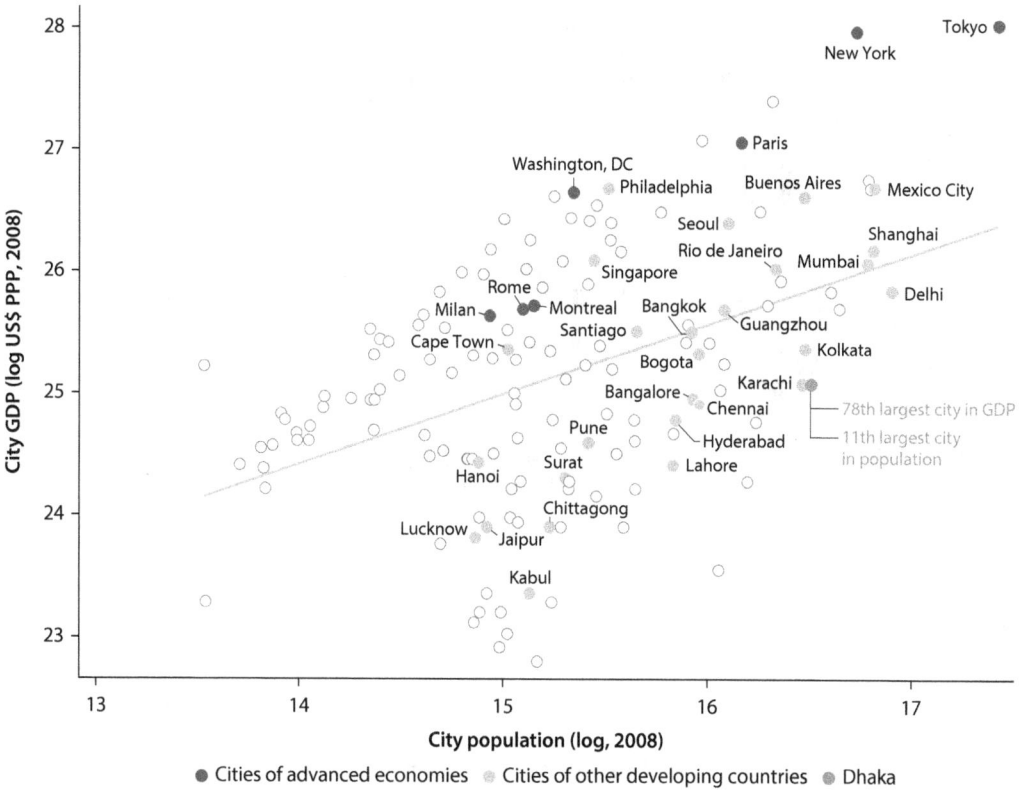

Sources: PWC 2009; UN 2015.
Note: GDP = gross domestic product; PPP = purchasing power parity.

Dhaka's economic size and density are also smaller than those of other South Asian cities when measured using the brightness of artificial lights in the evening. In the Dhaka CCs, where it is highest, the average nighttime light intensity is about 4.3 Digital Number per 1,000 persons. By comparison, the average nighttime light intensity of the Delhi municipal corporations is 24.6 Digital Number per 1,000 persons, or more than five times that of Dhaka. The nighttime light intensity is also much higher in Bangalore, Hyderabad, Kolkata and Mumbai.

Meanwhile, Dhaka spreads its prosperity to its surroundings to a much lesser extent than Delhi (map 1.5). Although Delhi itself has a population of 17 million, some 80 million people directly or indirectly benefit from its economic vibrancy. Today the broader region, comprising Gurgaon, Faridabad, Jaipur and cities all the way to the border with Pakistan, has become an almost continuous urban space (Li and Rama 2015). Seen from outer space, the entire area between Delhi and Amritsar is now lit at night to various degrees.

By contrast, areas outside of Dhaka remain mostly dark at night. Other urban agglomerations in the vicinity do not seem to benefit from economic spillovers from this megacity, nor do cities along the transport corridors connecting Dhaka with the rest of the country. The weakness of the linkages between the growth

Map 1.5 Dhaka spreads prosperity to a lesser extent than Delhi

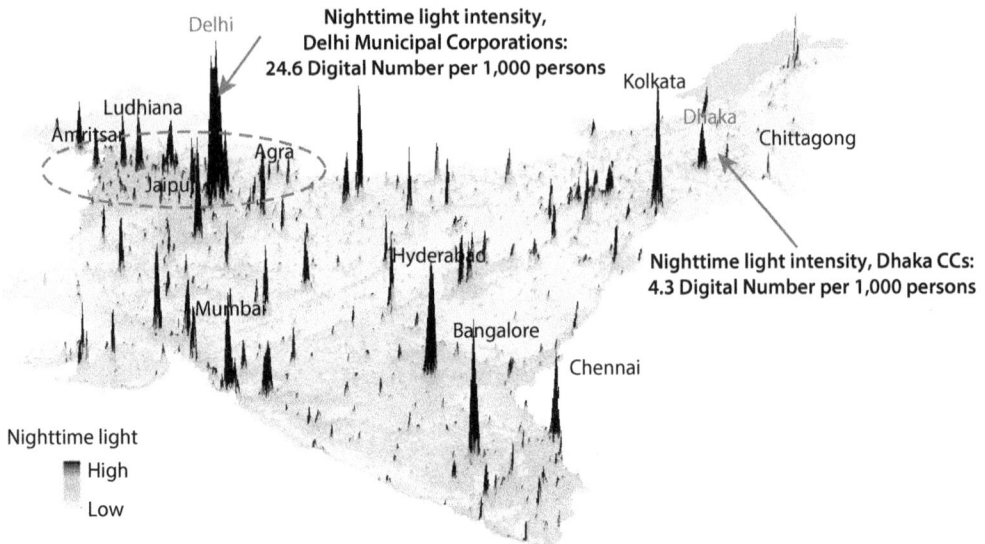

Nighttime light intensity, Delhi Municipal Corporations: 24.6 Digital Number per 1,000 persons

Nighttime light intensity, Dhaka CCs: 4.3 Digital Number per 1,000 persons

Nighttime light

High

Low

Sources: Calculations and visualization based on BBS (2011); Li et al. (2015); NOAA (2010); ORGI (2011).
Note: Radiance values of nighttime light are expressed in Digital Numbers. Digital Number is a positive integer assigned to the intensity of the electronic signal received by the sensor onboard satellites. CC = city corporation.

of Dhaka and that of its vicinity and other secondary cities may help explain its disproportionate primacy in Bangladesh.

A shortage of high-quality urban land

Dhaka's size and performance reflect strong economic forces that should be accompanied by change rather than opposed. There is a broad consensus that improving Dhaka's livability and harnessing its potential as a hub are critically important for the country's development. At the same time, Dhaka is only part of the effort needed for Bangladesh to reap the full benefits of urbanization. The development of secondary cities is also critical. Part of Dhaka's primacy is policy-induced. Bangladesh has a strong tendency toward centralization. Indeed, political, administrative and regulatory decision-making powers have increasingly been concentrated in the capital city. And this has further facilitated the disproportionate primacy of Dhaka. This policy bias needs to be corrected as well.

The process of urban development and rebalancing is bound to be accompanied by important changes in the structure of economic activity. The trend in many countries has been for manufacturing to move out of urban cores, first to remote urban peripheries and eventually to secondary cities and rural areas. Similarly, the development of Dhaka can be expected to lead to the relocation of jobs and economic activity—particularly in manufacturing—out of the city.

This relocation of economic activity should contribute to the development of secondary cities. The impact would be even greater if Dhaka became a richer city and its connectivity with the rest of country improved.

The big question is whether Dhaka can fulfill this potential. So far, building on strong economic fundamentals, it has been an engine of growth for Bangladesh. It also continues to serve as a magnet, attracting relatively more educated people from the rest of the country—especially those who are keen to succeed economically, for themselves and for their families. The mere fact that migrants continue to flock to the city suggests that for now the earnings opportunities it provides more than offset the undeniable costs of flooding, congestion and messiness. However, these costs are at unacceptably high levels and amount to the loss of billions of dollars every year.

Dhaka's rapid pace of expansion makes the problem even more acute. Continued urban growth requires more and better land to host firms and house people. Land is also needed to build transport and other infrastructure and to provide services and amenities. In fact, everything in a city is land-based. In comparison with other major agglomerations, including Delhi, Mumbai, Seoul and Shanghai, Dhaka's land use footprint stands out as the smallest, less than one-third that of other cities of comparable size (Pesaresi et al. 2015; World Bank 2017a).

To ensure continued economic growth and to spread its prosperity to its surroundings and to the secondary cities connected to it, Dhaka must expand the surface of its high-quality urban land. Incremental changes and improvements at the margin may not be sufficient to address this fundamental constraint. In this sense, Dhaka is reaching a crossroads. A change in the urban development paradigm is needed now, before the city becomes too dysfunctional to ever be fixed.

References

Ahmed, S., and G. Bramley. 2015. "How Will Dhaka Grow Spatially in Future? Modelling Its Urban Growth with a Near-Future Planning Scenario Perspective." *International Journal of Sustainable Built Environment* 4 (2): 359–77.

Aizenman, N. 2017. "Want to Help Someone in a Poor Village? Give Them a Bus Ticket Out." Goats and Soda: Stories of Life in a Changing World, National Public Radio, Washington, DC. December 28.

Alam, Jahangir. 2014. "The Organized Encroachment of Land Developers—Effects on Urban Flood Management in Greater Dhaka, Bangladesh." *Sustainable Cities and Society* 10: 49–58.

Arias-Granda, Yurani, Maria Eugenia Genoni, Ruth Hill, Monica Yanez-Pagans and Nobuo Yoshida. 2017. "Poverty in Dhaka: Evidence from the 2016 Bangladesh Informal Settlements Survey and the 2016/17 Household Income and Expenditure Survey." Background note prepared for Bangladesh Poverty Assessment, World Bank, Washington, DC.

BBS (Bangladesh Bureau of Statistics). 2010. "Household Income and Expenditure Survey (HIES)—2010/11." Statistics Division, Ministry of Planning, Government of the People's Republic of Bangladesh, Dhaka.

———. 2011. "Population and Housing Census 2011." Statistics and Informatics Division, Ministry of Planning, Government of the People's Republic of Bangladesh, Dhaka.

———. 2013. "Economic Census 2013." Statistics and Informatics Division, Ministry of Planning, Government of the People's Republic of Bangladesh, Dhaka.

———. 2014. "Census of Slum Areas and Floating Population 2014." Statistics and Informatics Division, Ministry of Planning, Government of the People's Republic of Bangladesh, Dhaka.

———. 2016. "Slum Survey 2016." Statistics and Informatics Division, Ministry of Planning, Government of the People's Republic of Bangladesh, Dhaka.

Behrens, K., and F. Robert-Nicoud. 2015. "Agglomeration Theory with Heterogeneous Agents." In *Handbook of Regional and Urban Economics*, vol. 5, edited by G. Duranton, J. V. Henderson and W. Strange, 175–245. Amsterdam: Elsevier, North-Holland.

BGMEA (Bangladesh Garments Manufacturers and Exporters Association). 2017. "Members List." Dhaka. http://www.bgmea.com.bd/member/memberlist.

Bryan, G., S. Chowdhury and A. M. Mobarak. 2014. "Underinvestment in a Profitable Technology: The Case of Seasonal Migration in Bangladesh." *Econometrica* 82 (5): 1671–748.

Chowdhury, A. M., and S. Faruqui. 1989. "Physical Growth of Dhaka City." In *Dhaka Past Present Future*, edited by Sharif Uddin Ahmed, 43–63. Dhaka: Asiatic Society of Bangladesh.

Combes, Pierre-Philippe, Gilles Duranton and Laurent Gobillon. 2008. "Spatial Wage Disparities: Sorting Matters!" *Journal of Urban Economics* 63 (2): 723–42.

———. 2012. "The Costs of Agglomeration: Land Prices in French Cities." CEPR Discussion Paper DP9240, Center for Economic and Policy Research, Washington, DC.

Combes, Pierre-Philippe, Gilles Duranton, Laurent Gobillon and Sébastien Roux. 2010. "Estimating Agglomeration Economies with History, Geology, and Worker Effects." In *Agglomeration Economics*, 15–66, edited by Edward L. Glaeser. Chicago: University of Chicago Press.

DOE (Department of Environment). 2015. "River Water Quality Report 2014." Ministry of Environment and Forest, Government of the People's Republic of Bangladesh, Dhaka.

DTCA (Dhaka Transport Coordination Authority) and JICA (Japan International Cooperation Agency). 2015. "Revised Strategic Transport Plan for Dhaka." Prepared by ALMEC Corporation, Oriental Consultants Global and Kathahira and Engineers International, Dhaka.

Duranton, G. 2015. "Growth through Cities in Developing Countries." *World Bank Research Observer* 30 (1): 39–73.

Duranton, G., and D. Puga. 2004. "Micro-foundations of Urban Agglomeration Economies." In *Handbook of Regional and Urban Economics*, vol. 4, edited by J. V. Henderson and J. F. Thisse, 2063–117. Amsterdam: Elsevier, North-Holland.

———. 2015. "Urban Land Use." In *Handbook of Regional and Urban Economics*, vol. 5, edited by J. V. Henderson and J. F. Thisse, 2063–117. Amsterdam: Elsevier, North-Holland.

DWASA (Dhaka Water and Sewerage Authority). 2015. *Annual Report 2014–15*. Dhaka: DWASA.

EIU (Economist Intelligence Unit). 2015. "Liveability Ranking Report." London.

Ellis, P., and M. Roberts. 2015. *Leveraging Urbanization in South Asia: Managing Spatial Transformation for Prosperity and Livability*. Washington, DC: World Bank.

Fujita, M., and J. F. Thisse. 2002. *Economics of Agglomeration: Cities, Industrial Location, and Regional Growth*. Cambridge: Cambridge University Press.

Gabaix, Xavier. 1999. "Zipf's Law for Cities: An Explanation." *Quarterly Journal of Economics* 114: 739–67.

Gabaix, Xavier, and R. Ibragimov. 2011. "Rank-1/2: A Simple Way to Improve the OLS Estimation of Tail Exponents." *Journal of Business and Economic Statistics* 29: 24–39.

Gabaix, Xavier, and Y. M. Ioannides. 2004. "The Evolution of City Size Distributions." In *Handbook of Regional and Urban Economics*, vol. 4, edited by J. V. Henderson and J. F. Thisse, 2341–78. Amsterdam: Elsevier, North-Holland.

GISAT. 2017. "Urban Land Use Update and Mapping for Greater Dhaka Region." Background paper prepared for this report. Prague, Czech Republic.

Glaeser, E. 2012. *Triumph of the City: How Our Greatest Invention Makes Us Richer, Smarter, Greener, Healthier, and Happier*. London: Penguin.

Hasan, Faruque. 2008. "From Jahangirnagar to Dhaka." *Forum: A Monthly Publication of the Daily Star*, August 3. http://archive.thedailystar.net/forum/2008/august/jahangirnagar.htm.

Hassan, Delwar. 2008. *Commercial History of Dhaka*. Dhaka: Dhaka Chamber of Commerce and Industry.

Henderson, Vernon, Adam Storeygard and David N. Weil. 2012. "Measuring Economic Growth from Outer Space." *American Economic Review* 102 (2): 994–1028.

Islam, I. 2008. "Wetlands of Dhaka Metro Area: A Study from Social, Economic and Institutional Perspectives." Ph.D. diss., Japan Society of Promotion of Science (JSPS), College of Policy Science, Ritsumeikan University, Kyoto.

Jacobs, Jane. 1992. *The Death and Life of Great American Cities*. 3rd ed. New York: Vintage.

Jahan, Sarwar. 2011. "Housing Infrastructure and Services." In *Urban Bangladesh: Challenges of Transition*, edited by H. Z. Rahman. Dhaka: Power and Participation Research Centre.

Kabir, Ahsanul, and Bruno Parolin. 2012. "Planning and Development of Dhaka—A Story of 400 Years." Paper presented at 15th Biennial International Planning History Society Conference: Cities, Nations and Regions in Planning History, São Paulo, July 15–18.

Krugman, Paul. 1995. "Innovation and Agglomeration: Two Parables Suggested by City-Size Distributions." *Japan and the World Economy* 7 (4): 371–90.

Li, Yue, and Martin Rama. 2015. "Households or Locations? Cities, Catchment Areas and Prosperity in India." Policy Research Working Paper 7473, World Bank, Washington, DC.

Li, Yue, Martin Rama, Virgilio Galdo and Maria Florencia Pinto. 2015. "A Spatial Database for South Asia." Working paper, World Bank, Washington, DC.

MCCI (Metropolitan Chamber of Commerce and Industry) and CMILT (Chartered Institute of Logistics and Transport). 2010. "Traffic Congestion in Dhaka City: Its Impact on Business and Some Remedial Measures." Dhaka.

Mercer. 2015. "2014 Quality of Living Worldwide City Rankings." *New York*, February 19. https://www.mercer.com/newsroom/2014-quality-of-living-survey.html.

Mohsin, K. M. 1989. "Commercial and Industrial Aspects of Dhaka in the Eighteenth Century." In *Dhaka Past Present Future*, edited by Sharif Uddin Ahmed. Dhaka: Asiatic Society of Bangladesh.

Mumford, Lewis. 1937. "What Is a City?" *Architectural Record* 82 (5): 59–62.

Muzzini, Elisa, and Gabriela Aparicio. 2013. *Bangladesh: The Path to Middle-Income Status from an Urban Perspective*. Washington, DC: World Bank.

NOAA (National Oceanic and Atmospheric Administration). 2010. "DSMP-OLS Radiance Calibrated Nighttime Lights." http://ngdc.noaa.gov/eog/dmsp/download _radcal.html.

———. 2017. "Version 1 VIIRS Day/Night Band Nighttime Lights." https://ngdc.noaa .gov/eog/viirs/download_dnb_composites.html.

ORGI (Office of the Registrar General and Census Commissioner). 2011. "Census of India 2011." Ministry of Home Affairs, Government of India. http://censusindia.gov .in/.

OSM (OpenStreetMap). 2014. "OpenStreetMap." https://www.openstreetmap.org.

Pesaresi, Martino, Daniele Ehrilch, Aneta J. Florczyk, Sergio Freire, Andreea Julea, Thomas Kemper, Pierre Soille and Vasileios Syrris. 2015. "GHS Built-Up Grid, Derived from Landsat, Multitemporal (1975, 1990, 2000, 2014)." Joint Research Centre (JRC), European Commission, Brussels.

Pramanik, Monjure A., and Demetris Stathakis. 2016. "Forecasting Urban Sprawl in Dhaka City of Bangladesh." *Environment and Planning B: Planning and Design* 43 (4): 756–71.

Pure Earth. 2017. "Toxic Sites Identification Program Global Database: TSIP." http:// www.contaminatedsites.org/TSIP/index.php.

PWC (PriceWaterhouseCoopers). 2009. "Global City GDP Rankings 2008–2025." http:// pwc.blogs.com/files/global-city-gdp-rankings-2008-2025.pdf.

Rahman, Hossain. 2017. "Transforming Dhaka East: A Political Economy Perspective on Opportunities and Challenges." Background paper prepared for this report, World Bank, Washington, DC.

Rahman, Saidur. 2010. "The Only Solution." *Forum: A Monthly Publication of the Daily Star*, March 3. http://archive.thedailystar.net/forum/2010/march/only.htm.

RAJUK (Rajdhani Unnayan Kartripakkha). 1995. "Dhaka Metropolitan Development Plan 1995–2015." Dhaka.

———. 2015. "Dhaka Structure Plan 2016–2035." Dhaka.

Rosenthal, Stewart, and William Strange. 2004. "Evidence on the Nature and Sources of Agglomeration Economies." In *Handbook of Regional and Urban Economics*, edited by J. V. Henderson and J. F. Thisse, 2119–71. Amsterdam: Elsevier, North-Holland.

Sayed, M. B., and S. Haruyama. 2017. "Flood Risk Measuring under the Flood Protection Embankment Construction in Dhaka Metropolitan Zone." *Journal of Geosciences and Geomatics* 5 (2): 46–58.

Schneider, A., M. A. Friedl and D. Potere. 2009. "A New Map of Global Urban Extent from MODIS Data." *Environmental Research Letters* 4.

Talukder, S. H. 2006. "Managing Megacities: A Case Study of Metropolitan Regional Governance for Dhaka." Ph.D. dissertation, Murdoch University, Dubai and Perth.

UN (United Nations). 2015. "World Urbanization Prospects: The 2014 Revision." Department of Economic and Social Affairs, Population Division, United Nations, New York.

———. 2016. "Asian Highway Route Map." Economic and Social Commission for Asia and the Pacific. http://www.unescap.org/resources/asian-highway-route-map.

WHO (World Health Organization). 2016. *WHO Global Urban Ambient Air Pollution Database*. Geneva: WHO.

World Bank. 2017a. "Dhaka Megacity: Development Issues, Plans and Prospects with Particular Reference to East Dhaka." Background paper prepared for this report, World Bank, Washington, DC.

———. 2017b. "Flood Risk Management in Dhaka: A Case for Eco-Engineering Approaches and Institutional Reform." Unpublished paper, World Bank, Washington, DC.

———. 2017c. "Urban Transport in Dhaka: Review of Plans and Institutional Set-up." Background paper prepared for this report, World Bank, Washington, DC.

WRG (Water Resources Group). 2015. "Consolidation and Analysis of Information on Water Resources Management in Bangladesh." World Bank, Washington, DC.

CHAPTER 2

Fragmented Responsibilities

Cities host millions of decision makers—households, firms and public agencies—and most of their choices and actions are coordinated by day-to-day market interactions. However, the market mechanism is not sufficient to ensure the most efficient operation of the city. The city government has to provide public goods and services and mitigate the costs of urban density. That government also has another essential role to play: providing a credible strategic vision of future development—a vision that informs and guides the individual decisions and investments on which urban development rests. Such a vision is necessary to ensure coherent development and thereby secure both the productivity and livability of the city in the longer term.

The quality of city governance is thus a central concern in urban development. The academic literature is still scarce on this topic, but recent studies have found that the fragmentation of city governance is associated with lower productivity across metropolitan areas. This is so in countries as diverse as Germany, Mexico, Spain, the United Kingdom and the United States (Ahrend et al. 2014; Ferranna, Gerolimetto and Magrini 2016). This relationship holds even after taking into account other factors that may affect city productivity.

Urban governance structures at the metropolitan level tend to be diverse because they are the outcome of specific historical and political circumstances. Although there is no consensus on which of these structures performs best, there is agreement on the need to abide by key principles such as autonomy, fiscal responsibility, accountability and transparency (Bahl 2013; National Research Council 2003; Sud and Yilmaz 2013; UN-Habitat 2007).

The reality of urban governance is often far from these ideals. Across South Asia, local urban governments face an empowerment deficit, a resource deficit and an accountability deficit (Ellis and Roberts 2016). Ill-structured and poorly financed urban authorities contribute little to city growth—and they may actually hinder it. In the long term, institutional reforms are something urban systems in these countries must deliver. But political economy factors make these reforms hard to implement. In the short term, alternative solutions may be needed so that countries do not miss out on the gains from urbanization.

Like many other cities in South Asia, Dhaka is characterized by fragmented institutional arrangements. Recent moves toward decentralization have strengthened and expanded the role of local governments in Bangladesh. However, Dhaka's city corporations (CCs) continue to face limited and overlapping functional assignments, and their capacity for revenue generation is weak. Meanwhile, a large number of central government agencies are mandated to work on almost every key functional area within the jurisdiction of the Dhaka CCs. No effective coordination mechanisms are in place across functional areas. Nor do they work well within each functional area.

Consequently, translating transformational ideas into reality in Dhaka is not easy. Numerous development plans and strategies, generated by different government ministries and departments, have appeared over time. However, these plans and strategies have often been at cross-purposes and only partially implemented, at best. Few have led to substantial improvements in the city.

And yet there are reasons for optimism. Where mandates have been clear and strong coordination mechanisms have been established, exceptional implementation capacities have emerged. These successful urban development examples, while few and far between, suggest an alternative way of thinking about solutions for Dhaka.

Weak urban authorities

The government of Bangladesh is highly centralized both administratively and fiscally. Articles 59 and 60 of its 1972 constitution established the legal foundation for subnational governments under the Ministry of Local Government, Rural Development and Cooperatives (MLGRDC). Since then, the structure, autonomy, roles and responsibilities of subnational governments have been adjusted several times.

Currently, there are two types of urban local governments: CCs for large urban centers and municipalities (*paurashavas*) for smaller cities. The system of rural local government consists of three tiers: district councils (*zila parishads*), subdistrict councils (*upazila parishads*) and union councils (*union parishads*). Each type of local government is guided by its own law and operational framework (Mollah 2007; Panday 2011; Rahman 2013).

Evolving responsibilities

The 1,528 square kilometers of Greater Dhaka encompass an urban core, as well as satellite cities and towns and villages. But almost 40 percent of this surface is still agricultural land, reflecting the rural character of the city's periphery (RAJUK 2015). Urban and rural government authorities therefore coexist in Greater Dhaka, each overseeing different areas. The urban local government authorities consist of four CCs—Dhaka North, Dhaka South, Gazipur and Narayanganj—and five municipalities. The rural government institutions consist of about 70 union councils (BBS 2011b).

Toward Great Dhaka • http://dx.doi.org/10.1596/978-1-4648-1238-5

Dhaka's urban local government arrangements have evolved over time, as shown by the rising status of the Dhaka CCs—at least on paper—and by the expansion of their jurisdictions (figure 2.1). The Dacca Municipality was created in 1864, under British rule, by the District Municipal Improvement Act. The city was elevated to the status of a corporation—a new form of urban local authority—in 1978, and it was expanded to include the adjoining Mirpur and Gulshan municipalities in 1982. The legal basis for its status as a corporation was provided in 1983 by the Dhaka Municipal Corporation Ordinance. The name was changed to Dhaka City Corporation in 1990, and further amendments were made to the ordinance, embracing a more democratic urban governance. The first direct election of a mayor and ward commissioners was held in 1994.

In 2011 the Local Government (City Corporation) Act 2009 Amendment Bill dissolved the Dhaka City Corporation. Two separate entities, the Dhaka North CC and the Dhaka South CC, replaced it. Both CCs are headed by directly elected mayors. In May 2016, the city's institutions experienced another important change when 16 new unions were brought under their jurisdiction, eight for each Dhaka CC. This expansion led to a doubling in the area of the Dhaka CCs, from 127 to 307 square kilometers. Out of the 16 unions added to the Dhaka CCs, 12 are in the eastern part of the city. Although they are geographically close to the urban core, these 12 unions remain largely rural and are still governed by their respective union councils (Dhaka North City Corporation, http://www.dncc.gov.bd/; Dhaka South City Corporation, http://www.dhakasouthcity.gov.bd/; Rahman 2017).

Figure 2.1 In Dhaka, urban institutions have been evolving

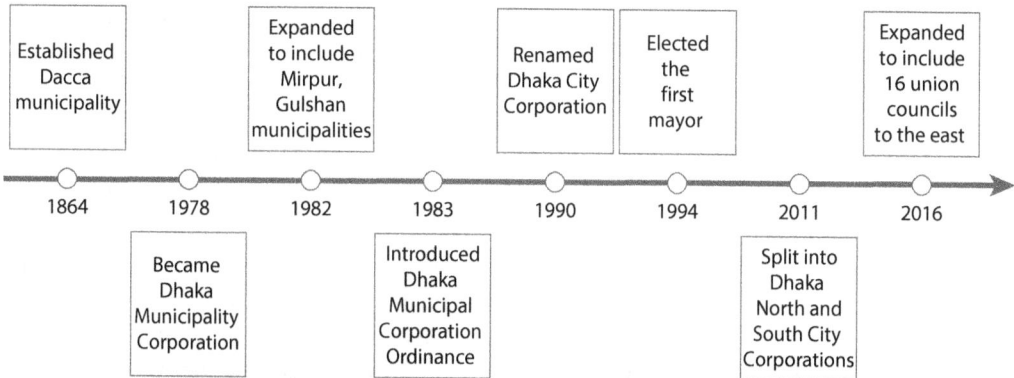

Dhaka North City Corporation	Dhaka South City Corporation
Previous area: 82 km²	Previous area: 45 km²
Added area: 115 km²	Added area: 64 km²
New unions: Beraid, Badda, Vatara, Satarkul, Harirampur, Uttarkhan, Dakshinkhan, Dumni	New unions: Shyampur, Dania, Matuail, Sarulia, Demra, Manda, Dakshingaon and Nasirabad

Sources: Based on Dhaka North City Corporation, http://www.dncc.gov.bd/; and Dhaka South City Corporation, http://www.dhakasouthcity.gov.bd/.

Despite their expanding jurisdictions and their rising status on paper, the Dhaka CCs have seen their effectiveness in governing the city undermined by friction and fragmentation.

Within each CC there are three administrative levels: the corporation at the top, zones in the middle, and wards at the bottom. At the corporation level, the mayor, the chief executive officer (CEO) and the secretary are the most senior officers. The mayor is elected by popular vote for a five-year term and operates under the leadership of MLGRDC. The CEO is appointed to assist the mayor as the principal administrative officer, who, in turn, is supported by the secretary and commands all other officers and employees. However, both the CEO and the secretary belong to the senior pool of the Bangladesh civil service cadre and are appointed by the central government. At the zone level, the zonal executive officers are the main forces of the administration. They, too, are appointed by the central government on deputation, and they are arguably more responsive to incentives from the central government than to the elected mayors (Islam et al. 2003; Talukder 2006).

This heavy reliance on the central government for key human resources also results in personnel shortages and limited technical capacity. Staff appointments by the central government may not be commensurate with the needs of the Dhaka CCs. For example, magistrates can play an important role in stopping the illegal occupation of public space. But the Dhaka CCs have only a handful of magistrates for the millions of people they serve. In fact, the Dhaka CCs were originally mandated to perform a large number of functions, ranging from town planning to drainage and transportation. But in part because of their weak capacity, they are limited in practice to maintenance functions such as street cleaning and lighting, and operation of markets. Even within these narrow functional areas, the Dhaka CCs often fall short in delivering public services to all residents (Islam et al. 2003; World Bank 2017a).

Limited resources

Effective local governments need a sound fiscal basis to meet their functional obligations, respond to the demands of their constituents, and support the development of their jurisdictions. Cities in South Asia are characterized by a sizable resource deficit. Dhaka's financial resources are inadequate even in comparison with other megacities in the region. The annual revenue of the North Delhi Municipal Corporation and the Kolkata Municipal Corporation was more than US$120 per resident in recent years. By contrast, the annual revenue of the Dhaka South CC was about US$66 per resident in fiscal 2015/16, and that of the Dhaka North CC was less than US$55 (figure 2.2).

Own-source revenue is even more constrained. In other countries, property-related taxes and charges are used as major revenue instruments for urban development and management. In Dhaka, they are barely sufficient to finance day-to-day operations. In fiscal 2014/15, the two Dhaka CCs together collected about US$50 million through holding tax, the main property-related tax instrument. That only amounted to about US$8 per resident per year. In fiscal 2015/16,

Figure 2.2 In Dhaka, the financial resources for urban development are very limited

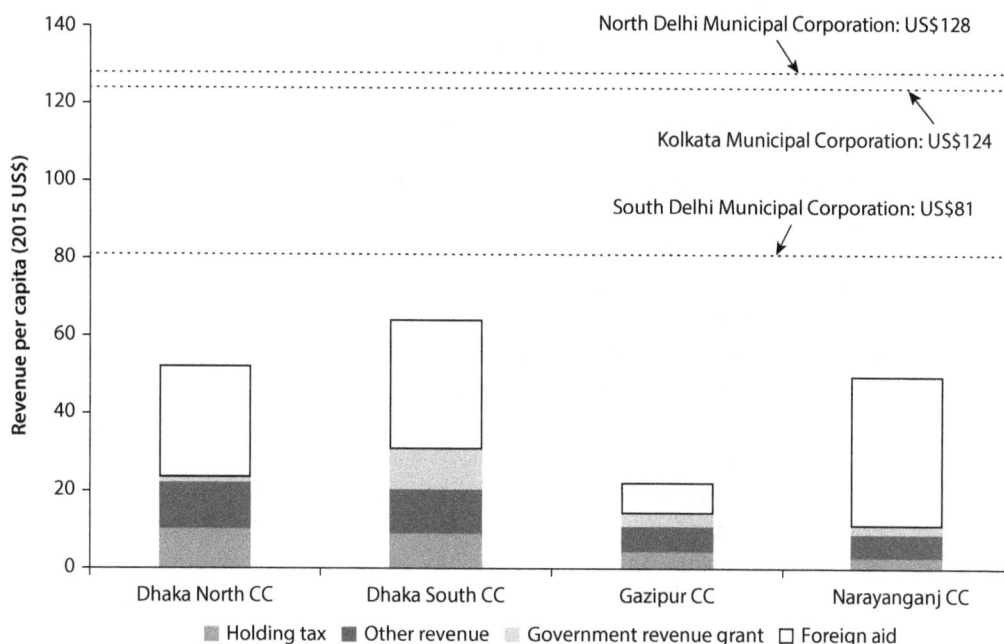

Sources: Calculations based on BBS (2011a) and World Bank (2017d).
Note: CC = city corporation.

holding tax revenue was budgeted to increase to about US$50 million in the Dhaka North CC and about US$36 million in the Dhaka South CC. However, this still amounts to an average of less than US$13 per resident per year.

The weak performance of holding tax stems partly from its low coverage. Only about 270,000 properties are on the tax rolls of the two Dhaka CCs, despite their combined population of about 9 million. For properties on the tax rolls, valuations have not been changed for 25 years. And of the modest tax revenue that should be raised, only about 60 percent is collected in practice. Both the assessment of property values and the tax collection process suffer from administrative irregularities and fraudulent behavior (Huda and Hasan 2009; World Bank 2017a).

In addition to their own-source revenue, the Dhaka CCs receive transfers from the central government. In doing so, they compete with the line ministries for public resources. In fiscal 2015/16, the Dhaka North CC received about US$6 million in transfers, accounting for 2 percent of its total revenue, or to less than US$2 per resident. The Dhaka South CC fared slightly better, with transfers reaching 16 percent of its revenue, or the equivalent of US$10 per resident. Transfers are also limited in the Gazipur and Narayanganj CCs.

Facing severe resource constraints domestically, the Dhaka CCs rely to a large extent on international development assistance, particularly for capital expenses. In fiscal 2015/16, the Dhaka North CC was budgeted to receive about US$140 million from development partners to finance urban development projects.

This amount represents over half of its total revenue. The situation was similar for the Dhaka South CC; its US$135 million in foreign aid also accounted for slightly more than half of its total revenue.

Ineffective coordination mechanisms

A number of central agencies are mandated to assume key urban management functions within the jurisdictions of the Dhaka CCs (figure 2.3). Some of these agencies are departments of the central government that have a metropolitan scope, such as the Dhaka Water and Sewerage Authority (DWASA) and the Dhaka Transport Coordination Authority (DTCA). Others are institutions with a national scope but with special relevance to Dhaka, such as the Bangladesh Water Development Board (BWDB) and the Roads and Highways Department (RHD). In taking up their mandates, these agencies rarely involve the Dhaka CCs or coordinate with each other.

The fragmentation of jurisdictions across sectors and functions is not unique to Dhaka. But the extent of confusion and overlapping, the weakness of coordination mechanisms, and the gaps in accountability are rather extraordinary. Coordination problems are not only pervasive across functional areas but also,

Figure 2.3 There is no shortage of urban institutions and actors in Dhaka

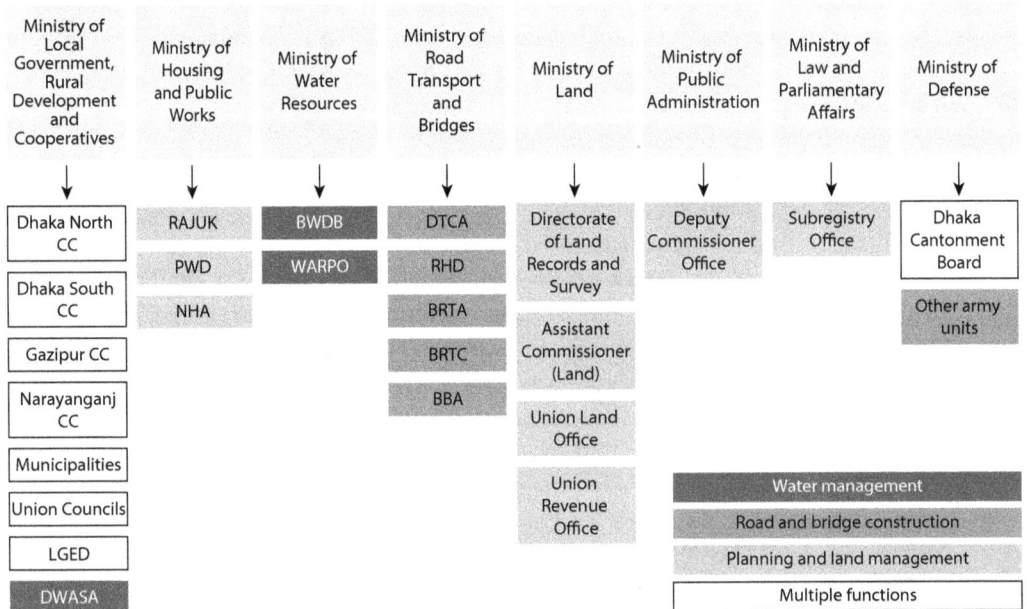

Sources: Based on Rahman (2017); Talukder (2006); World Bank (2017a, 2017b, 2017c, 2017d).
Note: BBA = Bangladesh Bridge Authority; BRTA = Bangladesh Road Transport Authority; BRTC = Bangladesh Road Transport Corporation; BWDB = Bangladesh Water Development Board; CC = city corporation; DTCA = Dhaka Transport Coordination Authority; DWASA = Dhaka Water and Sewerage Authority; LGED = Local Government Engineering Department; NHA = National Housing Authority; PWD = Public Works Department; RAJUK = Rajdhani Unnayan Kartripakkha (Capital Development Authority); RHD = Roads and Highways Department; WARPO = Water Resources Planning Organization.

more unusually, within each of them. Addressing key urban development issues requires the involvement of multiple institutions that have overlapping mandates but no effective mechanism to work together.

Studies have described and analyzed this institutional maze over time. One of them estimated that as of 1998 over 50 agencies were involved in urban development and the provision of services in the jurisdiction of the Dhaka CCs (ADB 1998). Another described the situation as a governance crisis (Siddiqui et al. 2000). This institutional fragmentation makes it difficult to address the three key challenges faced by Dhaka: flooding, congestion and messiness.

Institutions related to flooding

Flood control and drainage require a coherent approach, including the management of water bodies, the construction and maintenance of flood prevention infrastructure and storm water drainage systems, and the operation of early warning systems. Ideally, the agencies tasked with these functions are integrated or at least act in a concerted manner, but this is not so in Dhaka.

The responsibility for planning and executing flood prevention infrastructure is split between two central agencies: the BWDB under the Ministry of Water Resources (MWR) and the Local Government Engineering Department (LGED) under the MLGRDC. The BWDB is the principal agency for managing water resources and executing flood, drainage and irrigation projects in the country. In Greater Dhaka, it has undertaken major investments such as the construction of embankments. Meanwhile, LGED is mandated to develop, implement and maintain smaller-scale water projects, including small flood control embankments, sluice gates, culverts, rubber dams and canals. These two key agencies do not have an institutional interface and do not embark on joint planning processes (LGED 2014).

Building and maintaining storm water and sewerage drainage systems are similarly split among DWASA, which sits under the MLGRDC, and various local government institutions within the Greater Dhaka region. Since 1989, DWASA has assumed responsibility for supplying safe water and for building and maintaining storm water drainage lines and sewage systems. However, its jurisdiction includes only the Dhaka and Narayanganj CCs. Consequently, its storm water network covers only about 14 percent of Greater Dhaka, and its sewerage only covers a quarter of the metropolitan area (DWASA 2015). In parallel, the Dhaka and Narayanganj CCs are responsible for constructing and maintaining surface drains, but they are quite ineffective in fulfilling this mandate. In other areas of Greater Dhaka, the responsibility for storm water and sewerage drains lies with local government institutions, despite their even lower capacity (World Bank 2017b).

An important cause of flooding is the clogging of storm water drains and manholes by solid waste. The collection of solid waste is under the purview of local government institutions, but this function is poorly performed in the Dhaka CCs. An estimated 3,300 tons of solid waste are generated every day in the South Dhaka CC, but a full third of this amount goes uncollected. The situation is similar in the North Dhaka CC, and it is even worse in the rapidly growing out-skirts beyond the jurisdictions of the Dhaka CCs. The union councils that govern these areas are nominally in charge of waste management, but in most cases no formal solid waste collection system has been established (World Bank 2017b).

Institutions related to congestion

Transport is under the purview of an institutional network even more complex than that for flood control. Seven ministries and 13 agencies are involved in building transport infrastructure, managing traffic, regulating vehicles and pro-viding transport services. A case in point is the construction of roads, bridges and mass transit infrastructure, which is fragmented among central line ministries, parastatal metropolitan agencies and local government institutions (BIGD 2016; World Bank 2017d).

The Roads and Highways Department (RHD) within the Ministry of Road Transport and Bridges (MRTB) is the chief institution tasked with planning, con-structing and maintaining major roads and bridges in Bangladesh. It is responsible for national highways, regional highways and district roads in Greater Dhaka, and also for primary and secondary roads within the jurisdiction of the Dhaka CCs. LGED is in charge of transport infrastructure in rural areas, and it supposedly complements the RHD on subdistrict, union and village roads. It has mainly been involved in the planning and construction of primary and secondary roads and flyovers within the jurisdiction of the Dhaka CCs. The Rajdhani Unnayan Kartripakkha (RAJUK or Capital Development Authority), which sits under the Ministry of Housing and Public Works (MHPW), is also mandated to take a lead-ing role in transport infrastructure. But in practice it has focused on the construc-tion of roads linked to its own property development projects, with the maintenance of these roads being routinely transferred to the RHD, LGED or Dhaka CCs (BIGD 2016; World Bank 2017d).

The Dhaka CCs are solely responsible for planning and building connector and local roads within their jurisdictions. But their mandate also includes the maintenance of all roads, including lights and traffic signals. As a result, they are currently responsible for over 3,000 kilometers of roads of different categories.

Other agencies have played a role in the planning and construction of roads and bridges in Greater Dhaka on a case-by-case basis. Among them are the Bangladesh Bridge Authority under the MRTB, the Bangladesh Inland Water Transport Authority under the Ministry of Shipping and Inland Water Transport, and the Public Works Department (PWD) under the MHPW (World Bank 2017d).

Overlapping mandates and shared ownership have made the planning, con-struction and maintenance of roads more complex than it should be. Each agency formulates its own policies and conducts its own projects. For example, eight flyovers have been built in the Dhaka CCs over the last decades with the involvement of the five main agencies. Most of the flyovers were designed with-out paying sufficient attention to their integration in the surrounding road net-work and in ongoing and committed projects along the same corridors. Similarly, the Strategic Transport Plan (STP) envisioned that Dhaka's first mass rapid transit (MRT) line would end at Jatrabari. However, it was cut short, terminating at Motijheel instead because of a flyover being constructed by another agency (World Bank 2017d).

In an attempt to improve coordination, the DTCA was established within the MRTB in 2012. Its mandate includes formulating STPs, issuing urban transport policies, coordinating transport-related activities, and monitoring traffic. However, the DTCA does not have authority over the other agencies involved because they report to different ministries and are at the same or at an even higher administrative level. With inadequate human resources and limited enforcement power, the DTCA has so far been unable to play its assigned role as a coordinating agency (BIGD 2016; World Bank 2017d).

Institutions related to messiness

Messiness is to a large extent related to inadequate land use. In other countries, planning, land use zoning and land development functions often reside within local urban bodies, which are in principle more directly accountable to citizens. However, in Greater Dhaka multiple agencies are legally vested with planning and land development authority. The list includes RAJUK, the National Housing Authority (NHA) and the PWD under the MHPW, the Dhaka CCs and other urban local government bodies (World Bank 2016, 2017c).

Of these, RAJUK is the only agency with clear responsibilities at the metropolitan level. RAJUK derives its power from the Town Planning Act of 1953, which established its predecessor, the Dhaka Improvement Trust (DIT). According to the Town Planning Act, RAJUK's mandate encompasses land zoning and urban planning, land use clearance, the issuance of construction permits, the enforcement of zoning and plans, urban land development, and the design of the road network. However, RAJUK's capacity is limited, and planning activities have often been undertaken by external consultants. Its enforcement of land use, zoning and other development regulations has been inadequate. This has led to pervasive noncompliance, together with extensive complaints about regulatory complexity (World Bank 2017a, 2017b).

The NHA and PWD, also under the MHPW, have gained considerable influence over land acquisition and development in recent times. The NHA is responsible for preparing housing schemes for the population at large and for providing affordable housing for lower-paid government employees. It has wide powers to acquire land and distribute plots to private individuals, provided that the lots will benefit low-income groups. The PWD, in turn, is empowered to acquire land and construct buildings for government departments and their officers (Displacement Solutions and YPSA 2014).

Land titling is a critical part of land management. Land records that accurately reflect land ownership not only encourage private investment, but also enable improved governance in areas such as land use planning, land acquisition and disaster management (Sinha 2010). Land titles are particularly important in Greater Dhaka because they are needed to gain access to public services (Titumir and Hossain 2004). All tenancies enjoy ownership and use rights through settlement records, subject to payment of annual rents to the government. Land ownership and title—that is, the record of rights—can be transferred as long as the deed is registered (World Bank 2016, 2017c).

The Directorate of Land Records and Survey within the Ministry of Land (ML) is responsible for the record of rights, which is assembled by means of cadastral surveys. However, such surveys have been conducted at most once every decade. Land transfers inevitably take place in between, leading to land title changes that may or may not be reported in the record of rights.

Changing a title to establish new land property rights is a rather cumbersome process, involving multiple agencies under three central ministries. The Deputy Commissioner's Office at the district level is mandated to update land titles. The task is undertaken on its behalf by the Assistant Commissioner (Land) at the subdistrict level and by the Union Land Office at the union level. These three key actors report to both the ML and the Ministry of Public Administration. To complicate matters further, the Union Revenue Office under the ML is responsible for land revenue records, whereas the subregistry office under the Ministry of Law and Parliamentary Affairs is responsible for land transaction records (World Bank 2016, 2017c).

In parallel with this institutional complexity, an unconventional but important actor is the Ministry of Defense. Military complexes occupy significant amounts of land within the boundaries of the Dhaka North and Gazipur CCs. Cantonment boards are fully in charge of urban management within these complexes, taking responsibility for planning, infrastructure investment and the provision of services. Because cantonment boards have their own short-, medium- and long-term plans, their involvement adds to the fragmentation of urban management in Dhaka (Rahman 2017; World Bank 2017a).

Meanwhile, because of its strong expertise in engineering and logistics, the Special Works Organization (SWO-West) of the Bangladesh Army has been tasked with several important infrastructure projects in and around Dhaka. The most notable ones include the Mirpur-Airport flyover and the Hatirjheel Lake rehabilitation project. The Hatirjheel project was a major urban development undertaking, integrating the planning and construction of roads, bridges, drainage, green promenades and other amenities (Rahman 2017).

Partial implementation of plans

Dhaka's physical development—both its expansion and its densification—has been more organic than planned. But organic development is not caused by a shortage of plans. The first comprehensive master plan for the city, the Dacca Master Plan, was completed in 1959. And many have followed since then. Three of the plans, issued between 2013 and 2016, are supposed to chart the development of the city over the next two decades. They are the Storm-water Drainage Master Plan and Sewage Master Plan, issued by DWASA; the Revised Strategic Transportation Plan, launched by the DTCA; and the draft Dhaka Structure Plan

(2016–2035), shared by RAJUK as the first tier of a new master plan. According to international experts, each of these plans conveys a coherent long-term vision and is characterized by high technical quality (World Bank 2017a, 2017d).

However, the same problems that plague the institutional structure are at play in planning processes. Plans are designed largely in isolation, often by external consultants, with little input from the relevant stakeholders. There is weak ownership by urban authorities, defuse accountability for their implementation, and a limited capacity to take action on them. Potentially transformational ideas are either not adopted or progress in truncated versions (Rahman 2017). Consequently, plans only contribute partially to addressing the flooding, congestion and messiness challenges.

Plans to address flooding

Dhaka's vulnerability to floods has been addressed by both metropolitan master plans and more specific flood control plans aimed at increasing resilience (figure 2.4). Flood mitigation and control initiatives after independence date back to 1981, when the Dhaka Metropolitan Area Integrated Urban Development Project was prepared by the Planning Commission. This project sought to prepare a long-term development strategy for the city, with flood protection as its primary focus. However, the project was not formally approved by the cabinet and was never implemented in practice (Barua, Akther and Islam 2016; Islam 2009; Kabir and Parolin 2012).

Figure 2.4 Only one embankment was built and few canals were rehabilitated

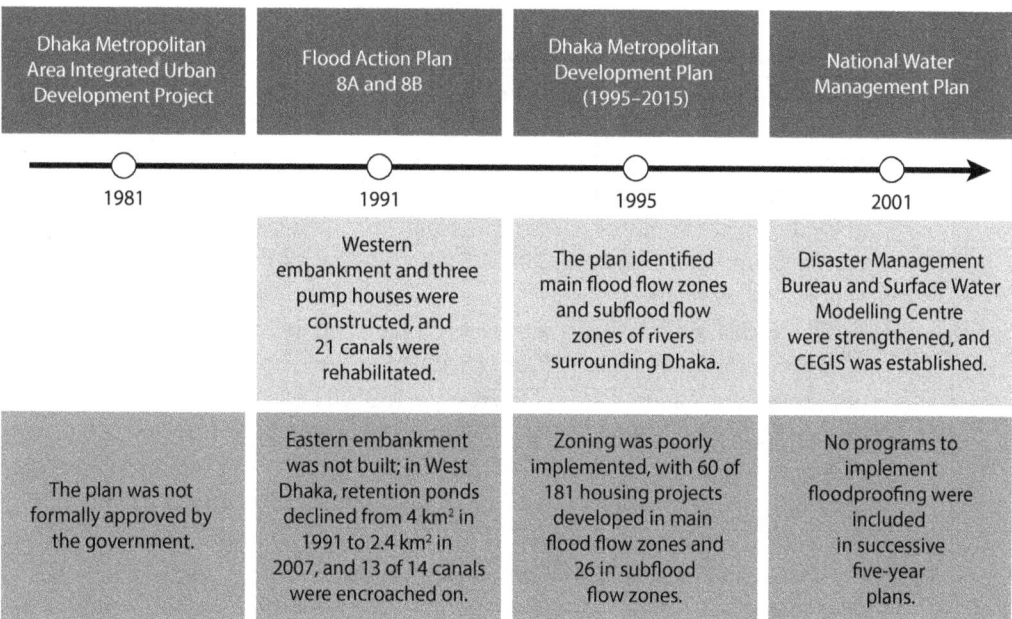

Dhaka Metropolitan Area Integrated Urban Development Project	Flood Action Plan 8A and 8B	Dhaka Metropolitan Development Plan (1995–2015)	National Water Management Plan
1981	**1991**	**1995**	**2001**
	Western embankment and three pump houses were constructed, and 21 canals were rehabilitated.	The plan identified main flood flow zones and subflood flow zones of rivers surrounding Dhaka.	Disaster Management Bureau and Surface Water Modelling Centre were strengthened, and CEGIS was established.
The plan was not formally approved by the government.	Eastern embankment was not built; in West Dhaka, retention ponds declined from 4 km² in 1991 to 2.4 km² in 2007, and 13 of 14 canals were encroached on.	Zoning was poorly implemented, with 60 of 181 housing projects developed in main flood flow zones and 26 in subflood flow zones.	No programs to implement floodproofing were included in successive five-year plans.

Sources: Based on Alam (2014); Brammer (2010); Das and Islam (2010); Lamb (2014).
Note: CEGIS = Center for Environmental and Geographic Information Services.

The first comprehensive flood management assessment of Dhaka was undertaken a decade later after the disastrous 1988 flooding, which inundated much of Dhaka and vast stretches of the nation. Based on studies carried out in 1988–89, a Flood Action Plan (FAP) was formulated, and its sections 8A and 8B were aimed at protecting the eastern and western portions of Dhaka, respectively. The most significant component of these two sections was to fully embank the rivers surrounding Dhaka. Both sections also included complementary measures for flood protection, drainage and environmental improvements (JICA 1992; Louis Berger Group 1991).

The Greater Dhaka Integrated Flood Protection Project was meant to implement sections 8A and 8B of the FAP with the support of multiple development agencies. On the western side of the city, the works foreseen by FAP section 8B were partially completed by the early 1990s. The main achievements included a 30-kilometer flood barrier from Tongi to Kellar Mor that fully embanked the western portion of Dhaka, three pumping stations, 20 sluice gates, a flood wall and an associated access road. The project also successfully reexcavated 21 canals (*khals*), including 14 in the western part of Dhaka (ADB 2002; Lamb 2014).

By 2007, 13 of the 14 reexcavated canals in the western part of Dhaka had been encroached on, and the area of retention ponds had declined to 2.4 square kilometers, down from 4 square kilometers in 1991. Despite these setbacks, the implementation of FAP section 8B has been largely successful in increasing flood resilience. Approximately 75 percent of the western part of the city was under water during the 1988 floods, whereas that share fell to 25 percent during the 1998 floods (Alam and Rabbani 2007; Brammer 2010; Das and Islam 2010; Lamb 2014).

By contrast, implementation of FAP section 8A never began, mainly because of lack of financial resources at the time. Given the budget constraints, this portion of the plan was deemed less urgent. The economic returns from protecting agricultural land against periodic damaging floods were estimated to be marginal (Brammer 2010; Das and Islam 2010; Lamb 2014). Even today, the eastern part of the city has a complex and hybrid urban morphology—part rural, part urban, part built-up, with high variability in economic density. But the economic returns may no longer be low.

The thrust of the FAP was partly embraced by the subsequent Dhaka Metropolitan Development Plan (DMDP), prepared with substantial international assistance and issued by RAJUK in 1995. The DMDP was a three-tiered master plan for Greater Dhaka, consisting of a structural plan, an urban area plan and a detailed area plan. The first tier adopted the proposals of FAP sections 8A and 8B envisioning development restrictions to protect the flood flow zones and retention ponds needed for flood control and drainage. The second tier also included these development restrictions. However, the third tier of the plan merged the main flood and subflood zones with urban residential areas. By 2008, 60 of 181 new housing projects were in the main flood flow zone, and 26 were in the subflood flow zones. Even RAJUK, a government agency, had chosen to develop its own major housing projects in a flood flow zone (Alam 2014; RAJUK 1995).

A new comprehensive review of national water policy was conducted in the late 1990s. It led to the adoption of the National Water Management Plan in 2001. As opposed to the FAP, this plan gave priority to small-scale floodproofing over major flood protection projects. The Disaster Management Bureau and the Surface Water Modelling Centre were strengthened, more cyclone shelters were built, and the Center for Environmental and Geographic Information Services (CEGIS) was established. However, no programs to implement the small-scale floodproofing proposals were included in successive five-year plans (Brammer 2004; WARPO 2001).

Plans to address congestion

A similar story could be told about congestion. Many studies and plans have emerged for upgrading Dhaka's transportation infrastructure and improving transport management, including metropolitan master plans and transport-specific plans. Early examples are the 1976 National Physical Planning Project and the 1981 Dhaka Metropolitan Area Integrated Development Project. The former looked at national physical planning, but in many aspects it was related to Dhaka. The latter was cross-sectoral, but it included components related to transportation.

A full-scale assessment of Dhaka's transportation challenges, the Dhaka Integrated Transport Study (DITS), was conducted by the Planning Commission in 1992. The DITS short-, medium- and long-term recommendations related to all aspects of transportation, infrastructure and management in Dhaka (Gallagher 2016).

The Dhaka Urban Transport Project (DUTP), supported by the World Bank, built on this assessment. This project was implemented in three phases from 1996 to 2005. The first phase reviewed DITS and led to the preliminary design of urgent transport improvements. The second phase focused on the feasibility and detailed design of project components, and the third phase moved on to developing urban transport management and strengthening related institutions (BIGD 2016; DTCA 2005).

The first comprehensive transport plan for Dhaka, the STP, was prepared in 2005 as a component of the DUTP. It set out a 20-year transport strategy (2005–25) for Dhaka, proposing long-term infrastructure investments as well as short-term management improvements. The STP envisioned spending US$5.5 billion on transport projects, including three MRT lines, three bus rapid transport (BRT) routes, an elevated expressway and numerous main road improvements (DTCA 2005).

An assessment of implementation of the STP was undertaken for this report in 2016. The methodology relied on a double-blind process. A local expert evaluated the status of routes proposed in the STP, relying on field trips and information obtained from implementation agencies, chiefly the RHD and the DTCA. In parallel, an international expert conducted a visual inspection of the same routes using high-resolution satellite imagery of land use, Google Earth imagery and crowd-sourced OpenStreetMap information. Both experts came to the same conclusion on all routes except three. The discrepancy was resolved by subsequent field trips and auxiliary satellite imagery with very high resolution. The final findings were also consistent with the qualitative assessment by another study (BIGD 2016).

The conclusion of the 2016 assessment was quite sobering. Substantial road upgrading had occurred and some new main roads had been built, but none of the major transport investments envisioned by the STP had been implemented during the first 10 years of the planning period.

A further exercise was conducted to convert this qualitative assessment of the implementation of the STP into a quantitative measure of the progress accomplished. Original paper maps of routes envisioned by the plan were digitized and georeferenced. Next, data from third-party sources—including satellite imagery and crowd-sourced information—were consolidated to generate maps of the STP routes actually implemented. A comparison of these two maps confirms that almost all ongoing road projects (about 90 kilometers) and about two-thirds of the proposed road upgrading (about 340 kilometers) were completed. Among the proposed new roads (about 780 kilometers), close to 40 percent was constructed. But no progress was made on the three MRT lines, the three BRT routes and the expressways envisioned by the STP (map 2.1).

Map 2.1 Few new roads were built and mass transport was not started

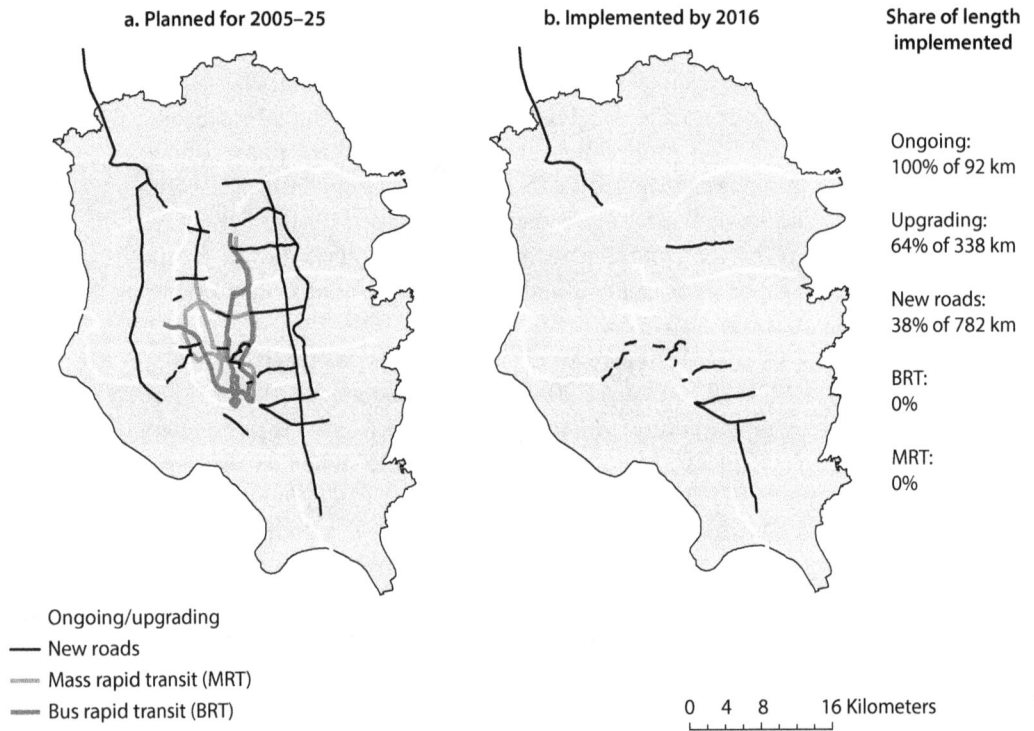

a. Planned for 2005–25   b. Implemented by 2016   Share of length
                                                                                        implemented

Ongoing:
100% of 92 km

Upgrading:
64% of 338 km

New roads:
38% of 782 km

BRT:
0%

MRT:
0%

Ongoing/upgrading
—— New roads
▭▭▭ Mass rapid transit (MRT)
▬▬▬ Bus rapid transit (BRT)

0   4   8   16 Kilometers

Sources: Calculations and visualization based on DTCA (2005); Google Earth imagery; Li et al. (2015); OpenStreetMap; Pleiades high-resolution satellite imagery (0.5 meters); and field research.
Note: BRT = bus rapid transit; MRT = mass rapid transit.

The lack of progress on MRT and BRT infrastructure is of particular concern. More than roads, public rapid transport is essential to address congestion and provide connectivity and mobility to the poor. Full BRTs are estimated to move 15,000 people per hour, and double-lane optimized BRTs such as the Transmilenio Bogota up to 40,000 people per hour. Rail-based MRT can help mobilize even larger numbers, in the range of 40,000–80,000 people per hour (World Bank 2017d). In the absence of this kind of transport infrastructure, addressing Dhaka's congestion challenge will be difficult.

Plans to address messiness

Dhaka has had several aspirational blueprints to address messiness. The first comprehensive design for the city, the Dacca Master Plan, was prepared in 1959 by a consortium of British firms under the supervision of DIT, the predecessor of RAJUK. The plan had a 20-year time horizon, covered an area equivalent to the jurisdictions of the current Dhaka CCs and the Narayanganj and Tongi munici-palities, and laid down principles for future development rather than a detailed and rigid scheme. However, the development proposals in the plan were only partially implemented.

The Dhaka Metropolitan Area Integrated Development Project of 1981 was a subsequent attempt by the Planning Commission to come up with a long-term vision for the city. However, this plan was never formally approved by the cabi-net and was thus inconsequential (RAJUK 2015).

In 1995 the DMDP 1995–2015 was prepared by RAJUK, with substantial international assistance. The DMDP also had a 20-year time horizon (1995–2015) and covered the entire Greater Dhaka area with a three-tiered structure consisting of a structure plan, an urban area plan and detailed area plans. None of them was followed closely. The structure plan proposed 31 policies under broad themes, such as spatial and environmental sector, socioeconomic sector and infrastructure sector. Of the policies, 23 were not implemented at all, and 8 were partially implemented. The urban area plan divided Greater Dhaka into 26 strategic planning zones and produced land use proposals for each of them. At best, about half of the proposals were implemented (RAJUK 2015).

More important perhaps, there was a significant delay in the preparation and approval of the detailed area plan. This tier aimed at containing free-for-all urban development by laying down a detailed framework, making detailed proposals for infrastructure and services, and setting land zoning for the city. However, the detailed area plan was only published in 2010, 15 years after issuance of the DMDP, at which point the time horizon was extended by one year, until 2016 (World Bank 2017b). But Dhaka's urban form had changed substantially by then.

It is not surprising that urban development has remained messy. Zoning crite-ria and building heights, critical components of any city master plan, have not been clearly spelled out or strictly enforced. To some extent, organic growth offered flexibility to accommodate Dhaka's vibrancy—no one seemed encum-bered by constraining regulations. But organic growth also allowed the encroach-ment and downgrading of public space, undermining efficiency and livability.

The transformation of Gulshan is a case in point. The Gulshan *thana* (subdistrict), with an area of about 9 square kilometers, was established in 1972 out of former wards 18 and 19. This area had been planned and developed in the early 1960s with the idea of supporting low-height residential accommodation for an emerging middle class. It included the Gulshan Model Town, established in 1961, and the Banani Model Town, established in 1964. But a rapidly growing population and a remarkable economic dynamism gradually changed the characteristics of the area (photo 2.1).

Ghulshan became keenly sought after by private businesses, foreign organizations and better-off households because its neat layout and abundance of amenities set it apart from the messiness prevailing elsewhere in Dhaka. Gulshan had wider roads, better access to services—including electricity and water—and scenic views of its lake. But as more firms, offices and people settled in, Gulshan gradually underwent a transformation from a low-height residential area to a high-rise area characterized by mixed land use. This transformation materialized through a still ongoing real estate boom (Ahmed, Hasan and Maniruzzaman 2014).

The densification of the Dhanmondi area is another illustration of the tension between zoning and dynamism. Dhanmondi was the first residential area planned by DIT, the predecessor of RAJUK. It covered about 5 square kilometers of what were mostly paddy fields in 1950. With an average plot size of 1,296 square meters, the area was envisioned as a neighborhood for higher-income groups. The height of residential buildings was not to exceed two stories.

During the 1970s and 1980s, however, urban regulations were not enforced. To increase their revenue from investments, landowners attracted foreign

Photo 2.1 In Gulshan, zoning regulations were weakly enforced and density evolved spontaneously

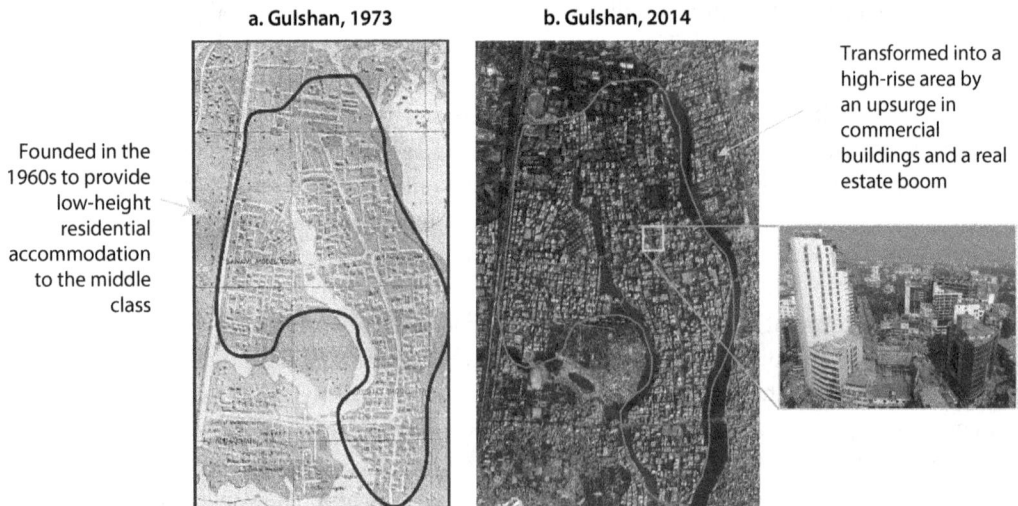

a. Gulshan, 1973   b. Gulshan, 2014

Founded in the 1960s to provide low-height residential accommodation to the middle class

Transformed into a high-rise area by an upsurge in commercial buildings and a real estate boom

Sources: Visualization based on Ahmed, Hasan and Maniruzzaman (2014); and Pleiades high-resolution satellite imagery (0.5 meters). Used with permission; further permission required for reuse. Photo far right: Reinhard Kroisenbrunner, Wikimedia Commons.

institutes and private companies on short-term leases, turning many low-density residential plots into high-density plots with mixed land use. This transformation was most evident on the edges of Dhanmondi, which had easier access by road. Land prices in the area increased from an estimated US$14 per square meter in 1974 to US$278 in 1989. Today, a large number of clinics and schools are operating in this "planned" area that was intended to be residential (Mahtab-uz-Zaman and Lau 2000; Seraj and Alam 2009; Siddiqui et al. 2016).

Weak enforcement of zoning regulations has supported economic dynamism, but it has also had adverse impacts, such as the encroachment on canals and retention ponds. The conversion of canals and ponds into built-up areas is common in the western part of the Dhaka CCs. About 73 percent of the encroached areas has been occupied for residential purposes, 10 percent for mixed land use, and the rest for other uses. Overall, about a third of the surface of the canals and ponds has disappeared, covered by illegal construction (Alam and Rabbani 2007; Brammer 2010; Das and Islam 2010; Lamb 2014).

A stellar exception

In sharp contrast with the fragmentation of responsibilities and the partial implementation of plans characterizing Dhaka's urban development, the rehabilitation of Hatirjheel Lake in 2013 stands out as an example of outstanding planning and remarkable execution. The somewhat unconventional player in this project was the Bangladesh Army's Special Works Organization (SWO-West). With strong political support from the central government and a clear mandate to restore the lake, SWO-West took an integrated approach that capitalized on its strong engineering expertise and logistical capacity. The Hatirjheel rehabilitation project is an illustration of both the difficulties faced by urban upgrading in Dhaka and the opportunities created by strategic interventions.

The Hatirjheel Lake area is located on the eastern edge of Dhaka's core, occupying an area of about 3 square kilometers. During the dry season, the lake can hold approximately 3 billion liters of water and during the rainy season about 5 billion liters, which makes it the largest water body inside Dhaka. Before the rehabilitation project, Hatirjheel Lake was heavily polluted by both sewage and solid waste, undermining its use as a natural retention area for storm water. The roads around the lake were narrow and unpaved, often congested and easily flooded. The surrounding *khash* (public land) was encroached for residential use, especially by informal settlements (SWO-West 2017).

The SWO-West approach spanned multiple objectives, from waste management to water drainage, from road infrastructure to traffic management, and from urban aesthetics to environmental protection. Most notably, the project addressed wastewater disposal and turned the low-lying areas into a storm water retention basin to improve water quality and minimize flood risk. The project also included a high-quality perimetral road, bridges and walkways around the lake. And it established a missing roadway link in the east-west direction to ease congestion and to protect the low-lying areas from further encroachment.

Public recreational facilities and water transportation services were established in parallel (Rahman 2017; SWO-West 2017).

The project fundamentally transformed the area (photo 2.2). Encroachment was removed, the waters of the lake became clear, and its surroundings became scenic. The bridges incorporate stylish architectural features, and at night they

Photo 2.2 Hatirjheel before and now

Source: © Hatirjheel Integrated Development Project. Used with the permission of the project director. Further permission required for reuse.

are illuminated. The area is decorated with shrubs and trees. There is also a garden around the lake, with benches and picnic facilities. Traffic on the 16-kilometer perimetral road behind this garden flows smoothly. Bus service and boat rides are readily accessible and well managed. Today, the area has become one of the most popular recreational places in Dhaka.

The Hatirjheel Lake rehabilitation project shows that transformational initiatives are possible in Dhaka, but a conjunction of multiple factors was needed for its success:

- The implementing agency was fully empowered. SWO-West was given the coordinating role among multiple agencies, backed up with the necessary political support from the highest quarters. In addition to this clear backing, SWO-West had credibility because of its technical expertise and implementation capacity.
- A clear division of responsibilities was established between all the involved agencies, a long list that included RAJUK, the LGED, the Dhaka CCs and the Bangladesh University of Engineering and Technology. The allocation of tasks was aligned with the comparative advantage of each of the agencies, and accountability was relatively well established.
- There was strong preparedness at key stages in the project. Some of the most important milestones were the removal of accumulated waste, the construction of roads and bridges, and the introduction of the traffic management system.

However, there is also a cautionary tale. For a period, the responsibility for routine maintenance of Hatirjheel Lake was transferred to RAJUK. But RAJUK was unable to prevent water pollution. The maintenance responsibility was subsequently given back to SWO-West until a more viable solution is found (Rahman 2017).

References

ADB (Asian Development Bank). 1998. *Asian Cities in the 21st Century: Contemporary Approaches to Municipal Management.* Vol. 3, Reforming Dhaka City Management. Mandaluyong, Philippines: ADB.

———. 2002. *Project Completion Report on the Dhaka Integrated Flood Protection Project in Bangladesh.* Mandaluyong, Philippines: ADB.

Ahmed, Bayes, R. Hasan and K. M. Maniruzzaman. 2014. "Urban Morphological Change Analysis of Dhaka City, Bangladesh, Using Space Syntax." *ISPRS International Journal of Geo-Information* 3: 1412–44.

Ahrend, R., I. Kaplanis, E. Farchy and A. Lembcke. 2014. "What Makes Cities More Productive? Evidence on the Role of Urban Governance from Five OECD Countries." OECD Regional Development Working Papers 2014/05, Organisation for Economic Co-operation and Development, Paris. http://dx.doi.org/10.1787/5jz432cf2d8p-en.

Alam, Jahangir. 2014. "The Organized Encroachment of Land Developers—Effects on Urban Flood Management in Greater Dhaka, Bangladesh." *Sustainable Cities and Society* 10: 49–58.

Alam, M., and M. G. Rabbani. 2007. "Vulnerabilities and Responses to Climate Change for Dhaka." *Environment and Urbanization* 19 (1): 81–97.

Bahl, R. 2013. "The Decentralization of Governance in Metropolitan Areas." In *Financing Metropolitan Governments in Developing Countries*, edited by Roy W. Bahl, Johannes F. Linn and Deborah L. Wetzel, 85. Cambridge, MA: Lincoln Institute of Land Policy.

Barua, U., M. S. Akther and I. Islam. 2016. "Flood Risk Reduction Approaches in Dhaka, Bangladesh." *Urban Disasters and Resilience in Asia*, edited by Rajib Shaw, Atta-Ur-Rahman, Akhilesh Surjan and Gulsan Ara Parvin, 209. Amsterdam: Elsevier.

BBS (Bangladesh Bureau of Statistics). 2011a. *Annual Report of Dhaka North CC, Dhaka South CC, Gazipur CC, and Narayanganj CC*. Public Finance India. http://publicfinance.in/advancedsearch/index?title=&documentname=Delhi&description=&date_after=&date_before=&categoryid=&report=Search.

———. 2011b. "Household Income and Expenditure Survey (HIES)—2010/11." Statistics Division, Ministry of Planning, Government of the People's Republic of Bangladesh.

BIGD (BRAC Institute of Governance and Development). 2016. "State of Cities 2016—Traffic Congestion in Dhaka City Governance Perspectives." BIGD, BRAC University, Dhaka.

Brammer, H. 2004. *Can Bangladesh Be Protected from Floods?* Dhaka: University Press.

———. 2010. "After the Bangladesh Flood Action Plan: Looking to the Future." *Environmental Hazards* 9 (1): 118–30.

Das, B., and I. Islam. 2010. "Analyzing the Proposals of FAP 8B Project of Dhaka and Present Context of Retention Pond Areas and Canals." *Journal of Bangladesh Institute of Planners* I2075: 9363.

Displacement Solutions and YPSA (Young Power in Social Action). 2014. "Climate Displacement in Bangladesh: Stakeholders, Laws and Policies—Mapping the Existing Institutional Framework." Geneva.

DTCA (Dhaka Transport Coordination Authority). 2005. "Strategic Transport Plan for Dhaka." Prepared by Louis Berger Group and Bangladesh Consultant Ltd., Dhaka.

DTCA (Dhaka Transport Coordination Authority) and JICA (Japan International Cooperation Agency). 2015. "Revised Strategic Transport Plan for Dhaka." Prepared by ALMEC Corporation, Oriental Consultants Global and Kathahira and Engineers International, Dhaka.

DWASA (Dhaka Water and Sewerage Authority). 2015. *DWASA Annual Report 2014–15*. Dhaka: DWASA.

Ellis, Peter, and Mark Roberts. 2016. *Leveraging Urbanization in South Asia: Managing Spatial Transformation for Prosperity and Livability*. Washington, DC: World Bank.

Ferranna, Licia, Margherita Gerolimetto and Stefano Magrini. 2016. "Urban Governance Structure and Wage Disparities across US Metropolitan Areas." Department of Economics Research Paper Series 26/WP/2016, Ca Foscari University of Venice, October 12. https://ssrn.com/abstract=2862534 or http://dx.doi.org/10.2139/ssrn.2862534.

Gallagher, R. 2016. "Dhaka's Future Urban Transport: Costs and Benefits of Investment in Public and Private Transport." Copenhagen Consensus Center.

Huda, M. S., and M. R. Hasan. 2009. "Problems and Prospects of Municipal Holding Taxation System: A Study on Bhairab Pourashava." *Journal of Bangladesh Institute of Planners* 2: 126–35.

Islam, I. 2009. *Wetlands of Dhaka Metro Area: A Study from Social Economic and Institutional Perspectives*. Dhaka: A. H. Development Publishing House.

Islam, N., M. M. Khan, N. I. Nazem and H. M. Rahman. 2003. "Reforming Governance in Dhaka, Bangladesh." In *Governance on the Ground: Innovations and Discontinuities in Cities of the Developing World*, edited by P. McCarney and R. Stren, 194–220. London: Johns Hopkins University Press.

JICA (Japan International Cooperation Agency). 1992. "Feasibility Study on Greater Dhaka Protection Project (Study in Dhaka Metropolitan Area) of Bangladesh Flood Action Plan No. 8A." JICA, Tokyo.

Kabir, A.H.S.A.N.U.L., and B. Parolin. 2012. "Planning and Development of Dhaka—A Story of 400 Years." Paper presented at 15th International Planning History Society Conference, Cities, Nations and Regions in Planning History, São Paulo.

Lamb, Zachary. 2014. "Embanked: Climate Vulnerability and the Paradoxes of Flood Protection in Dhaka." Department of Urban Studies and Planning, Massachusetts Institute of Technology, Cambridge, MA.

LGED (Local Government Engineering Department). 2014. "LGED Annual Report 2014–15." LGED, Dhaka.

Louis Berger Group. 1991. "Dhaka Integrated Flood Protection (Flood Action Plan 8B), Final Report." Dhaka.

Mahtab-uz-Zaman, Q. M., and S. S. Lau. 2000. *City Expansion Policy versus Compact City Demand: The Case of Dhaka. Compact Cities: Sustainable Urban Forms for Developing Countries*. London: Spon Press.

Mollah, M. A. H. 2007. "Administrative Decentralization in Bangladesh: Theory and Practice." *International Journal of Organization Theory and Behavior* 10 (1): 1.

National Research Council. 2003. *Cities Transformed: Demographic Change and Its Implications in the Developing World*. Washington, DC: National Academies Press. https://doi.org/10.17226/10693.

Panday, P. K. 2011. "Local Government System in Bangladesh: How Far Is It Decentralised?" *Lex Localis—Journal of Local Self-Government* 9 (3).

Rahman, Hossain. 2017. "Transforming Dhaka East: A Political Economy Perspective on Opportunities and Challenges." Background paper prepared for this report.

Rahman, M. S. 2013. "Role of the Members of Parliament in the Local Government of Bangladesh: Views and Perceptions of Grassroots in the Case of Upazila Administration." *Public Organization Review* 13 (1): 71–88.

RAJUK (Rajdhani Unnayan Kartripakkha). 1995. "Dhaka Metropolitan Development Plan 1995–2015." Dhaka.

———. 2015. "Draft Dhaka Structure Plan Report 2016–2035." Dhaka.

Seraj, T. M., and M. S. Alam. 2009. *Housing Problem and Apartment Development in Dhaka City. Dhaka: Past Present Future*. Dhaka: Asiatic Society of Bangladesh.

Siddiqui, Kamal, Jamshed Ahmed, Abdul Awal and Mustaque Ahmed. 2000. *Overcoming the Governance Crisis in Dhaka City*. Dhaka: University Press.

Siddiqui, Kamal, Jamshed Ahmed, Kaniz Siddique, Sayeedul Huq, Abul Hossain, Shah Nazimud-Doula and Nahid Rezawana. 2016. *Social Formation in Dhaka, 1985–2005:*

A Longitudinal Study of Society in a Third World Megacity. Abingdon-on-Thames, UK: Routledge.

Sinha, Rita. 2010. "Moving towards Clear Land Titles in India: Potential Benefits, a Roadmap, and Remaining Challenges." In *Innovations in Land Rights Recognition, Administration, and Governance*, edited by Klaus Deininger, Clarissa Augustinus, Stig Enemark and Paul Munro-Faure. Washington, DC: World Bank.

Sud, Inder, and Serdar Yilmaz. 2013. "Institutions and Politics of Metropolitan Management." In *Financing Metropolitan Governments in Developing Countries*, edited by Roy W. Bahl, Johannes F. Linn and Deborah L. Wetzel, 107–34. Cambridge, MA: Lincoln Institute of Land Policy.

SWO-West (Special Works Organization of Bangladesh Army). 2017. "Integrated Development of Hatirjheel Area Including Begunbari Khal Project." Presentation to World Bank, Washington, DC, February 25.

Talukder, S. H. 2006. "Managing Megacities: A Case Study of Metropolitan Regional Governance for Dhaka." Ph.D. dissertation, Murdoch University, Dubai and Perth.

Titumir, R. A. M., and J. Hossain. 2004. "Barriers to Access to Public Services for the Urban Poor: An Enquiry into Dhaka Slums." *Journal of the Institute of Bangladesh Studies* 27: 28.

UN-Habitat (United Nations Human Settlements Programme). 2007. *Enhancing Urban Safety and Security: Global Report on Human Settlement, 2007.* Abdingdon-on-Thames, UK: Routledge.

WARPO (Water Resources Planning Organization). 2001. *National Water Management Plan.* Dhaka.

World Bank. 2016. "Unlocking Disaster Resilient: Urbanization of Dhaka East." Unpublished paper, Disaster and Risk Management Team, World Bank, Washington, DC.

———. 2017a. "Dhaka Megacity: Development Issues, Plans and Prospects with Particular Reference to East Dhaka." Background paper prepared for this report, World Bank, Washington, DC.

———. 2017b. "Flood Risk Management in Dhaka: A Case for Eco-Engineering Approaches and Institutional Reform." Unpublished paper, World Bank, Washington, DC.

———. 2017c. "Land and Legal Diagnostic: Proposed Embankment on Balu-River/Eastern Bypass Project." Unpublished paper, Disaster and Risk Management Team, World Bank, Washington, DC.

———. 2017d. "Urban Transport in Dhaka: Review of Plans and Institutional Set-Up." Background paper prepared for this report, World Bank, Washington, DC.

CHAPTER 3

East and West

Dynamic cities grow. At the beginning of the 19th century, New York City was not much more than a toehold on the southern tip of a large island called Manhattan. Beyond the settled town lay a patchwork of farms and meadows, ponds and marshes, laced with country roads. Yet in 1811 the commissioners of New York boldly projected the city's extension from the southern end of the island all the way to its northern shore. They laid down a conceptual grid of 155 streets over what was then rural land, hypothetically corresponding to a seven-fold increase in the built-up area. They predicted that the city would grow from 100,000 inhabitants in 1810 to 400,000 in 1860, which was a remarkably bullish projection. And they painstakingly marked down the property lines, adhering to the grid over the years despite strong objections from influential people (Angel 2012; Ballon 2012).

Today, Manhattan is framed by this grid, now upheld by vibrant streets and boosted by skyscrapers. And New York City has arguably become the economic, financial, cultural and entertainment center of the world. Currently home to over 8.5 million people, it still gained more residents than any other U.S. city over the last five years. Its expansion matches the dreams of its commissioners more than two centuries ago. As former mayor Michael Bloomberg put it, "The Commissioner's Plan of 1811 was one of the earliest and boldest manifestations of our city's incessant drive to build, to grow—to reach beyond our grasp" (Bloomberg 2012; U.S. Census Bureau 2017).

Like New York, Dhaka is growing. Born on the southern tip of the Madhupur Tract, nature dictated its expansion toward the north and the northwest, where most often the land stood above water. This development pattern was enhanced by the construction of the western embankment, which further reduced the risk of floods. Growing in an organic and messy way, Dhaka has seen its population, businesses, buildings, roads, economic vibrancy and day-to-day life gravitate toward its western part. And this messy area has not been made much more orderly by retrofitting efforts, aimed at building and enlarging the roads and avenues that were missing from the very beginning.

Meanwhile, the eastern part of Dhaka has remained largely rural, with a mix of low-lying land prone to floods and patchworks of rice and vegetable fields. But large private developers have now begun to invest in the area, prompted by rising population pressures and spiraling land prices in the western part. Without the protection of an embankment, as in the west, the low-lying plains in the east have to be filled in with sand and elevated above water level before they can be converted to urban uses. The eastward expansion of Dhaka is therefore characterized by a multiplication of sand-filled parcels, many of which are rapidly becoming construction sites.

This private-led expansion of Dhaka is a testimony to the vitality of market forces in Bangladesh. However, it is taking place without the sort of public interventions that could be expected as a city develops. In the eastern part of the city, there are few new roads, canals are not maintained, and service delivery is very limited. Because of this tension between private sector dynamism and government detachment, it is difficult to tell what kind of urbanization the eastern part of Dhaka will experience. The answer will very much depend on today's vision for the city and on the actions taken as a result of it (Fuller and Romer 2014). To make the most of this opportunity, Dhaka needs leaders who think and act now, and who can turn the eastward expansion into a new urban development paradigm, just as the commissioners of New York did two centuries ago.

Dhaka's western part

There is an explanation for Dhaka's west-east imbalance, and water is at the core of it. The city is situated in the central region of a common deltaic plain for three major rivers—that is, an area defined by water. The current jurisdictions of the Dhaka city corporations (CCs) are surrounded by the Tongi Khal (canal) to the north, the Turag River to the west, the Buriganga River to the south, and the Balu-Shitalakshya River system to the east. Within and around the Dhaka CCs are swamps and depressions. During the monsoon season, when water levels are high, low-lying areas are easily submerged.

Historically, the combination of fertile soils and access to waterways made the area attractive as the site of a city, but topographic characteristics have also made it vulnerable to flooding. Urban development initially took place in the elevated parts that were less likely to be inundated. But once all these elevated parts were occupied, the rising demand for urban land was met increasingly through the conversion of low-lying floodplains, vegetated areas and wetlands (Dewan and Yamaguchi 2009). This relatively spontaneous land conversion process has been an integral part of Dhaka's development.

Organic development
During the Mughal period (1610–1757), Dhaka's physical extension was limited to the north bank of the Buriganga River, with the city remaining very close to its port on this waterway. Land was divided into functional areas for markets, cottage industries and residential uses. A real road system was absent because

back then rivers and canals were used as the main means of transportation (Ahmed, Hasan and Maniruzzaman 2014; Islam 1996; Kabir and Parolin 2012; Nilufar 2010; Pramanik and Stathakis 2016).

Dhaka began to expand beyond the old Mughal town boundaries during the British period (1757–1947). This time, roads were built, but their construction was not part of any explicit plan, and the roads that were built did not follow a strategic pattern. The city reached the current area of old Dhaka—about 22 square kilometers—at the end of the British period. By then, Dhaka was already characterized by a high-density, mixed-use pattern, with very compact low-rise buildings and narrow roads (Ahmed, Hasan and Maniruzzaman 2014; Islam 1996; Kabir and Parolin 2012; Nilufar 2010; Pramanik and Stathakis 2016).

During Bangladesh's union with Pakistan (1947–71), Dhaka experienced a major northward expansion. Most of the new areas used to be paddy fields, marshes and swamps, but they were still on relatively high land (Kabir and Parolin 2012; World Bank and EMI 2014). The public sector took a leading role in this expansion. A handful of model towns were planned and built for the upper-middle class, including Dhanmondi, Ghulsan, Banani, Uttara and Baridhara. Several areas, such as Mirpur and Tejgaon, were carved out to accommodate migrants and new businesses. And new commercial areas—among them, Motijheel—were established as well.

The road infrastructure network gradually expanded. The Mirpur road emerged as the city's main north-south axis. Meanwhile, a gridiron pattern with some semicircular segments was chosen as the street layout of the new model town areas. Riding on this improved infrastructure network, the city's built-up area had almost quadrupled—to 85 square kilometers—by the time of independence in 1971 (Ahmed, Hasan and Maniruzzaman 2014; Kabir and Parolin 2012; Pramanik and Stathakis 2016; Shankland Cox Partnership et al. 1981; World Bank and EMI 2014).

Constrained by low-lying, flood-prone land on both its eastern and its western fringes, the city continued to expand northward after independence. The highlands spreading in that direction were reclaimed and built up, and the intervening valleys, swamps and marshes were gradually filled (Kabir and Parolin 2012; World Bank and EMI 2014). But unlike during the previous phase, this time the expansion was dominated by spontaneous development. Although the government continued to contemplate aspirational development patterns and to formally issue plans, actual housing developments and infrastructure investments did not seem to bow to any official guidance.

The main force behind Dhaka's development during the post-independence phase was indeed the private sector. Many landowners turned their low-density residential land plots into high-density, mixed-use land. Other plots were squatted, and low-quality informal housing emerged, forming slums. Private developers began to conceive their own housing projects in the government's footsteps. Meanwhile, many planned areas were modified, at times deviating radically from their original morphologies. With this new round of expansion, Dhaka's built-up area increased by an additional

52 square kilometers (Ahmed, Hasan and Maniruzzaman 2014; GISAT 2011; Kabir and Parolin 2012; World Bank and EMI 2014).

The unprecedented flood of 1988 convinced the government to be more proactive on urban matters. A western embankment was built in 1991 to protect the city, largely following the recommendations of the Flood Action Plan (FAP) for Bangladesh. This embankment suddenly created an opportunity for development of the low-lying lands to the west and northwest of the city.

Because it was quite close to the existing city center, land within the embankment saw its price skyrocket, alongside the rapid growth of built-up areas. The ensuing development was, again, mostly spontaneous and often chaotic. Because major floods have been rare since 2009, the western embankment has even become the spine for urban development on its outer side (Lamb 2014). As a result of this intense wave of organic building and infilling, Dhaka has expanded by another 36 square kilometers. There are now 173 square kilometers of built-up area in the jurisdiction of the Dhaka CCs. But the lion's share—147 square kilometers—lays in the western part of the city.

Ineffective retrofitting

The haphazard private sector investments in real estate were not coordinated with transportation infrastructure and did not integrate the provision of basic services. Private developers were understandably reluctant to spend money on these two critically important components of urban development. Instead, they favored high-density investments around the major thoroughfares, where infrastructure and social services were more readily available.

In the same spirit, individual owners increased building heights closer to the main roads so they could maximize the return on their investments. The Rajdhani Unnayan Kartripakkha (RAJUK, Capital Development Authority) even revised regulations to encourage such development. Owners of all plots facing the main roads were allowed to convert their holdings to commercial uses, with buildings up to 20 stories high, provided they paid conversion fees (Mahtab-uz-Zaman and Lau 2000). This may have been an effective way for the city to adjust to market forces in the short term. But uncoordinated investments made it difficult to recalibrate the road network and transportation services to the city's changing scale and density.

Meanwhile, attempts to retrofit the western part of Dhaka have proven costly and ineffective (photo 3.1). The year 1996 saw the launch of the Dhaka Urban Transport Project (DUTP), the first comprehensive effort by the government to tackle the city's congestion problems. Implementation of this initiative was supported by the World Bank through a US$234 million credit. The components of this ambitious project included road upgrading, bus route improvements, rehabilitation of bus terminals, provision of pedestrian facilities and traffic management. However, the project was cut to only US$140 million in 2002 and was closed in 2005. Components such as the Jatrabari Flyover were dropped, and the almost US$80 million earmarked for the alleviation of *Janjot* (gridlock) was

Photo 3.1 Urban retrofitting in the western part of Dhaka has been costly and ineffective

Source: Mehedi Hasan © *Dhaka Tribune.* Used with the permission of *Dhaka Tribune.* Further permission required for reuse.

never utilized. The estimated economic rate of return for the implemented components was declining. By the midlife of the project, none of these components was delivering the promised level of services.

The Strategic Transport Plan (STP) adopted in 2005 was the leading initiative to improve transport infrastructure in Dhaka during the following decade (DTCA 2005). However, implementation was rather limited. Only 85 lane-kilometers of primary roads and 66 lane-kilometers of secondary roads were built in the western part of the city between 2005 and 2016. Assuming that the width of the lanes is the same for the two types of roads, they represented a meager 17 percent increase in road surface. Moreover, the construction of new primary roads was concentrated in areas with relatively low density, presumably because land prices were higher and land reclamation was more difficult in more central areas. Unsurprisingly, congestion did not ease.

The fragmentation of urban management responsibilities is partially responsible for the failure of retrofitting efforts. For example, realignment of transport infrastructure requires not only acquiring land, but also adjusting existing infrastructure such as drainage facilities, sewerage pipes, water pipes and utility lines. Joint work by all concerned actors is indispensable. In the absence of an empowered local government or an effective coordination mechanism, implementation of the STP and its successor, the Revised Strategic Transport Plan (RSTP), turned out to be impractical in the west (DTCA and JICA 2015).

The development of mass rapid transit (MRT) line 6 illustrates the difficulties faced. Utility lines had to be shifted before construction could start. A budget was eventually allocated to the relevant agencies so they could undertake the task, but all sorts of unforeseen circumstances hampered the work. In some cases, the Dhaka Transport Coordination Authority (DTCA) had to come forward to resolve the issues on behalf of Dhaka Mass Transit Company Ltd., the implementing entity. In the end, the schedule to shift the utility lines was seriously hampered, and project costs increased substantially. Similarly, the development of MRT line 5 requires clearance by the Cantonment Board because the planned layout cuts through the military-managed area of the Dhaka CCs (World Bank 2017). That clearance is still pending.

Dhaka's eastern part

The construction of an eastern embankment along the Balu River was recommended in the FAP for Bangladesh, prepared after the devastating floods of 1988. Because this embankment was expected to make the eastern part of Dhaka less prone to inundation, in 1992 the entire area was earmarked for future urban development. In 1995 the Dhaka Metropolitan Development Plan (DMDP) further assumed that low-lying areas in both the east and the west would become flood-free and could accommodate further urban expansion. However, no effective flood mitigation measures were adopted, and the proposed eastern embankment was never built.

Rural but urbanizing

The eastern part of the Dhaka CCs remains largely rural (Lamb 2014; Nilufar 2010). On high-resolution satellite imagery, the contrast with the western part is stark (map 3.1). The Pragati Sarani Airport Road and the Dhaka-Narayanganj-Demra drainage improvement project could serve as the dividing line between east and west because they were the boundary of the Dhaka CCs before their 2016 expansion. In the west, formal built-up areas account for over 75 percent of the surface. Moreover, 65 percent of the surface is characterized as high and medium density, meaning that over half of the land is covered by continuous construction. Water bodies take up another 6 percent of the land, leaving only 18 percent for agriculture, wetlands and forests. The picture is almost the opposite in the east. Built-up areas account for only 35 percent of the surface, and almost a third of them is made up of scattered rural settlements. Water bodies, agricultural land and forests occupy almost two-thirds of the area.

In 2011 the western part of Dhaka was home to about 8 million residents, with an average density of 41,000 persons per square kilometer. By contrast, the eastern part had a total population of only 0.9 million, with an average density of 8,800 persons per square kilometer. Even areas very close to the west were

Map 3.1 Dhaka's western part is dense, but its eastern part is still mainly rural

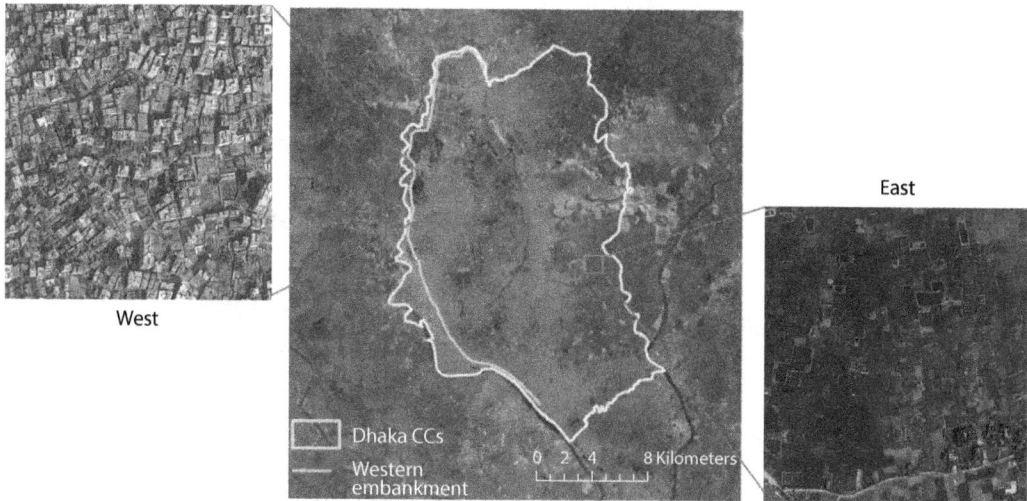

West

East

Dhaka CCs

Western embankment

0 2 4   8 Kilometers

Sources: Visualization based on land classification background work carried out for this report (GISAT 2017); and Li et al. (2015).
Note: CCs = city corporations.

characterized by low population density. For example, union Dumni had only 150 inhabitants per square kilometer (BBS 2011).

However, because of the tightening of land markets and the lack of high-quality land in the west, Dhaka is growing rapidly toward the east. And this is despite the absence of an embankment along the Balu River. Ever-rising land prices have prompted large private developers and individual property owners to reclaim flood-prone land to build on it for residential and commercial purposes. But without the protection of a flood barrier, the low-lying plains in the east need to be filled and elevated above water level before they can be converted to urban use.

The expansion of sand-filled areas and construction sites reveals the direction of Dhaka's current physical expansion (map 3.2). Such areas and sites were scattered in 2003. Since then, the surface of construction sites has increased sixfold, from less than 7 square kilometers in 2003 to 50 square kilometers in 2016. Expansion has been even more vertiginous for sand-filled areas, which grew from a little more than 1 square kilometer in 2003 to almost 40 square kilometers in 2016. Most of these areas and sites are either inside the Dhaka CCs or within a 5-kilometer band outside their boundaries. Expansion has been fastest to the east of the Pragati Sarani Airport Road and above the Dhaka-Narayanganj-Demra drainage improvement project area.

Rapid sand filling

To support a rigorous analysis, it is useful to clearly delineate what is meant by the eastern part of Dhaka, or East Dhaka for short. Section 8A of the FAP for

Map 3.2 Dhaka is now growing rapidly toward the east

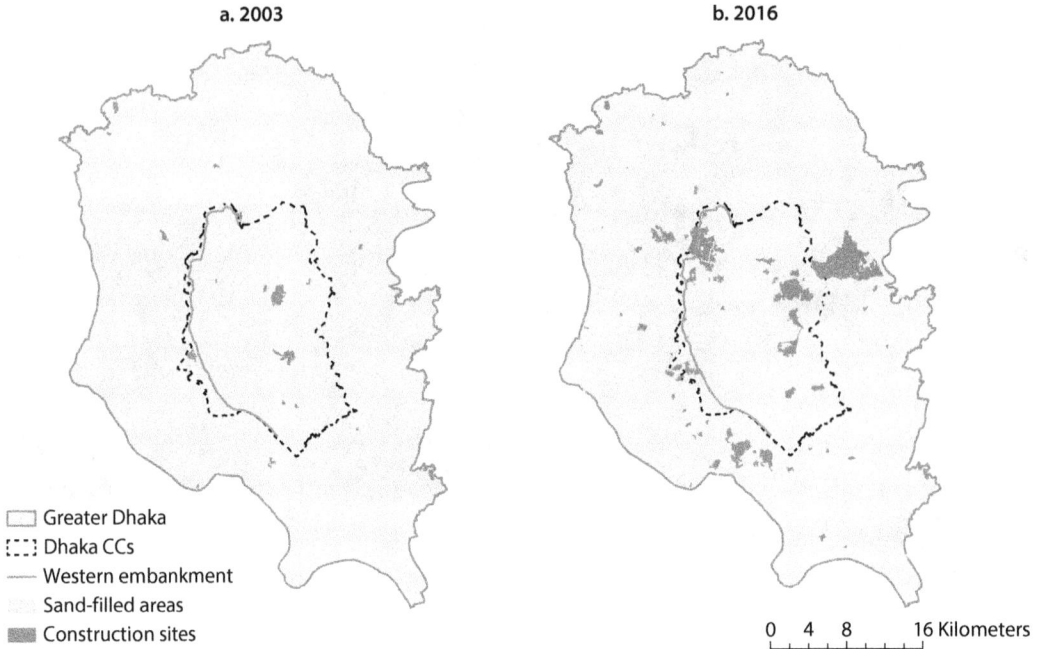

a. 2003   b. 2016

Greater Dhaka
Dhaka CCs
Western embankment
Sand-filled areas
Construction sites

0   4   8   16 Kilometers

Sources: Visualization based on land classification background work carried out for this report (GISAT 2017); and Li et al. (2015).
Note: The classification is based on 0.5- and 5-meter resolution satellite imagery. CCs = city corporations.

Bangladesh defined the eastern part of Dhaka in relation to the surface to be protected from floods by the eastern embankment (JICA 1992). Subsequent work to update and extend FAP section 8A continued to adhere to this notion (BWDB 2017; Halcrow Group Limited 2006). Master plans were less specific in demarcating the boundaries of the area. Both the DMDP and the Dhaka Structure Plan (2016–35)—the first tier of the new master plan—referred to this area as simply the eastern fringe of Dhaka (RAJUK 1995, 2015).

Given the close link between the geographic area of East Dhaka and flooding risks that are dependent on the eastern embankment, the definition used by FAP section 8A is retained in what follows. East Dhaka is thus the area delimited by the Tongi Khal to the north, by the Balu River to the east, by the Dhaka-Narayanganj-Demra drainage improvement project to the south, and by the Pragati Sarani Airport Road to the west (map 3.3). This area includes 12 of the 16 unions that were incorporated into the Dhaka CCs in 2016. The remainder of the Dhaka CCs is hereafter called West Dhaka.

The built-up areas of East Dhaka can be classified into three broad categories: rural settlements, urban built-up areas on relatively high land, and construction sites and sand-filled areas on low-lying land.

Rural settlements are concentrated in the higher land in the north of East Dhaka, along the east bank of the Balu River, as well as on the banks of the canals

Map 3.3 The boundaries of East Dhaka can be clearly outlined

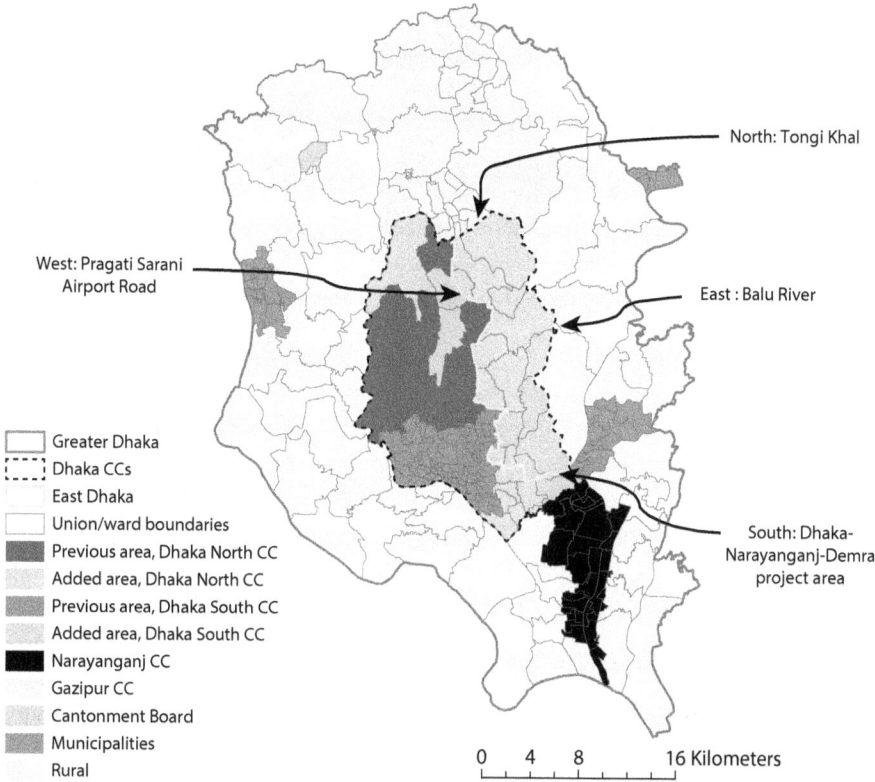

North: Tongi Khal

West: Pragati Sarani
Airport Road

East : Balu River

Greater Dhaka
Dhaka CCs
East Dhaka
Union/ward boundaries
Previous area, Dhaka North CC
Added area, Dhaka North CC
Previous area, Dhaka South CC
Added area, Dhaka South CC
Narayanganj CC
Gazipur CC
Cantonment Board
Municipalities
Rural

South: Dhaka-
Narayanganj-Demra
project area

0   4   8   16 Kilometers

Sources: Classification and visualization based on BBS (2011); and Li et al. (2015).
Note: CC = city corporation.

that crisscross it. Residents take advantage of the higher elevation of these places, their greater connectivity, and their accessibility through water to support their livelihoods. High-resolution satellite imagery reveals that over the last decade the overall surface covered by these rural settlements has remained relatively stable at about 12 percent of East Dhaka's total.

The urban built-up area on higher land covers a narrow band along the eastern side of the Pragati Sarani Airport Road. Located where east meets west, this band is a natural spillover of the rapid urbanization in Dhaka's western portion. The overflow is governed by market forces rather than by the administrative definition of what is urban and what is rural. The Pragati Sarani Airport Road is on relatively high ground, which is why it evolved from an urban-rural divide into a spine of urban expansion. As part of the organic urban development wave after independence, individuals, private developers and public institutions took advantage of the land toward the east of this line, turning it into a dense urban zone that is from 1 to 3 kilometers wide. When riding on the Pragati Sarani Airport

Road, there is no way to tell which side is urban and which side is rural. However, the expansion of this band has somewhat stabilized over the last decade.

Most of the action these days is in the low-lying areas. Large sections of these flood-prone fields are being filled with sand and developed for sale. Fleets of barges and legions of dredgers are hired to pump sand from the river into paddy lands and canals to raise them above high-water levels. The ground is pushed up by 3–12 meters. Construction is under way in these sand-filled areas, whereas many other sites are kept idle for now. These sand-filled areas and construction sites are easy to detect using satellite imagery because of their distinct spectral pattern. By now, the sand-filled areas may be occupying about 11 square kilometers and the construction sites 10 square kilometers (map 3.4).

Powerful private groups

Behind the rapid sand filling under way are many large-scale real estate development projects (map 3.5). The public sector led the initial charge as part of planned interventions to ease housing pressure. However, the private sector has become the dominant force in the transformation of the eastern part of Dhaka.

The most significant public development project, Purbachal New Town, is being led by RAJUK. The project is located immediately to the east of East

Map 3.4 Flood-prone areas in East Dhaka are rapidly being filled with sand

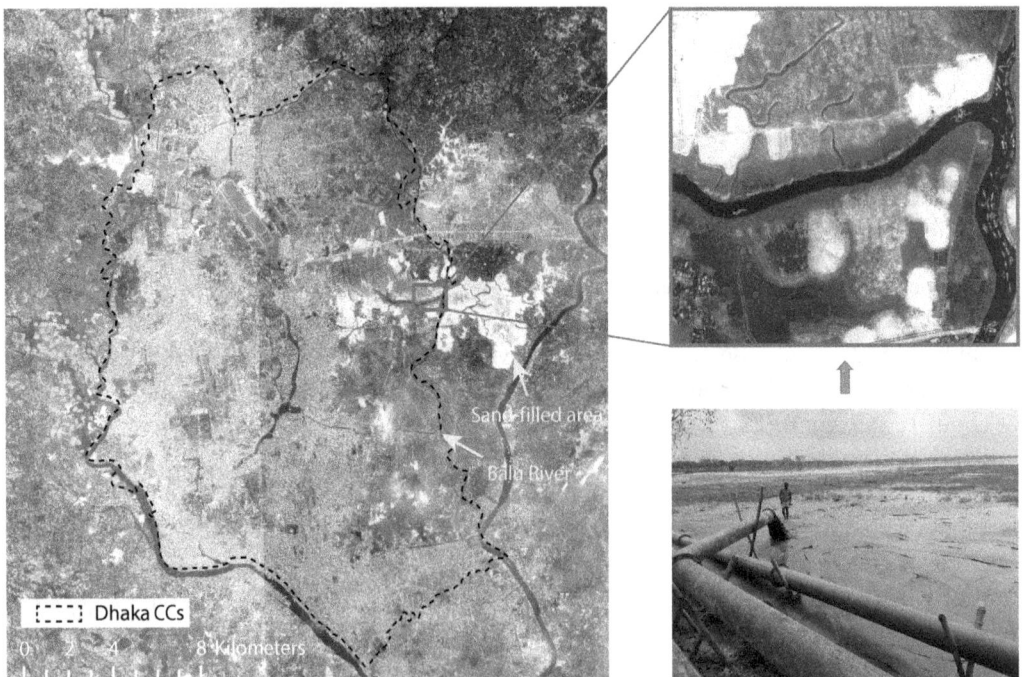

Sources: Visualization based on land classification background work carried out for this report (GISAT 2017). Photo bottom right: © Infratech Construction Company Ltd. Used with the permission of Infratech Construction Company Ltd. Further permission required for reuse.
Note: The classification is based on 0.5- and 5-meter resolution satellite imagery. CCs = city corporations.

Map 3.5 Many real estate development projects are under way in East Dhaka and beyond

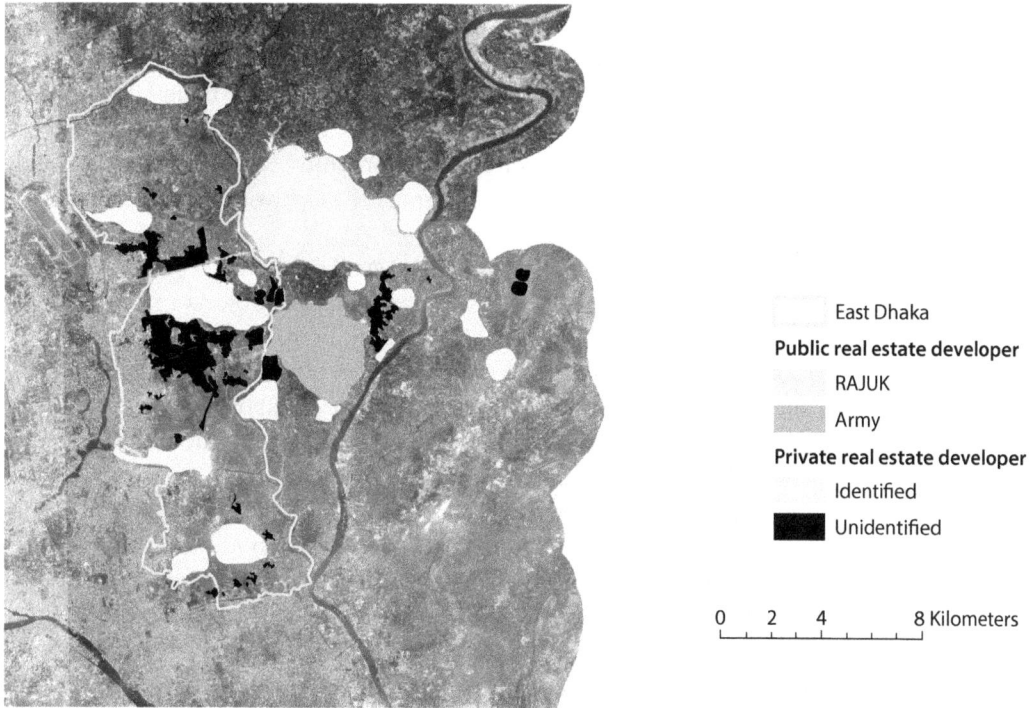

Legend:
- East Dhaka
- **Public real estate developer**
  - RAJUK
  - Army
- **Private real estate developer**
  - Identified
  - Unidentified

0　2　4　　　　8 Kilometers

Sources: Visualization based on land classification background work carried out for this report (GISAT 2017) and private developers' websites.
Note: The classification is based on 0.5- and 5-meter resolution satellite imagery. RAJUK = Rajdhani Unnayan Kartripakkha.

Dhaka, between the Balu and Shitalakshya Rivers, with a designed area of about 25 square kilometers. Despite having been formally inaugurated in 2002 and scheduled for completion in 2018, implementation has been slow. Seven of the 30 sectors originally foreseen are still undergoing basic site development, and 14 require substantive road construction work. In all, 29 sectors are still waiting for the installation of electric substations, and none has a dedicated water supply. A feasibility study of sewage treatment and solid waste management remains under way (Rahman 2017; RAJUK 2017).

In contrast with this slow progress, the transport corridor that connects the Purbachal township project with West Dhaka has been fully established. A highway officially named the Purbachal Link Road, but more often called the 300 Feet Road because of its width, has been constructed. It includes a massive 3-kilometer multilane flyover that connects with the Dhaka-Mymensingh Highway, as well as service roads, underpasses and sluice gates (Rahman 2017; RAJUK 2017).

The Purbachal township project and the 300 Feet Road have had a dramatic impact on East Dhaka. Private investors saw the potential value of these otherwise flood-prone areas, and they were quick to acquire land on the eastern portion of the city for their real estate projects (Rahman 2017). There have been some attempts to assess how much land is already in the hands of these private real estate developers. One example is the 2006 update of FAP section 8A (Halcrow Group Limited 2006). However, this estimate is clearly outdated, and private real estate developers rarely publicize how much land they control.

To address this gap, a detailed quantitative exercise was undertaken for this report. It involved identifying the name of each real estate development project, its location and the name of its owner. The information was gathered from media articles and real estate websites. Project-specific maps were compiled and geo-referenced based on this information.

Overall, 19 real estate development projects by 18 major private investors were identified. In some cases, the boundaries of the projects match well the sand-filled areas identified using satellite imagery. In others, the areas covered by these projects are still rural settlements or agricultural land, indicating little action on the ground. These 19 projects account for about 70 percent of the sand-filled areas and construction sites in East Dhaka and to the east of the Balu River. The rest are occupied by unidentified owners.

The identified private developers have massively acquired land not only around the Purbachal township project, but also on both sides of 300 Feet Road. By now, they occupy more than 10 square kilometers of land contiguous to this new major thoroughfare, which shows their determination to take full advantage of public investment on road infrastructure. Moreover, private developers are also occupying a growing number of areas inside East Dhaka, some of which are close to the developed urban land east of Pragati Sarani Airport Road.

According to the information compiled, large private sector investors have overtaken the public sector in East Dhaka in terms of both number of housing projects and total area these projects cover (figure 3.1). By 2016 large private sector investors had purchased or developed about 28 square kilometers of land within East Dhaka, amounting to about one-quarter of its total surface. Some 60 percent of this surface belongs to 8 out of the 19 real estate development projects identified for this study. Among them, the Bashundhara Group stands out as the dominant player, occupying 7 square kilometers of land immediately to the south of 300 Feet Road.

Potential and risks

Private-led real estate development in East Dhaka holds substantial potential for the city as a whole. But in the absence of measures to address flooding, congestion and messiness, it could also lead to challenges like those confronting the western part of the city. New risks may also emerge in relation to natural disasters and land value capture.

Functioning neighborhoods

The potential of private-led urban development is best illustrated by the Bashundhara Residential Area—also known as the Bashundhara Baridhara

Figure 3.1 Privately developed land already covers one-quarter of East Dhaka

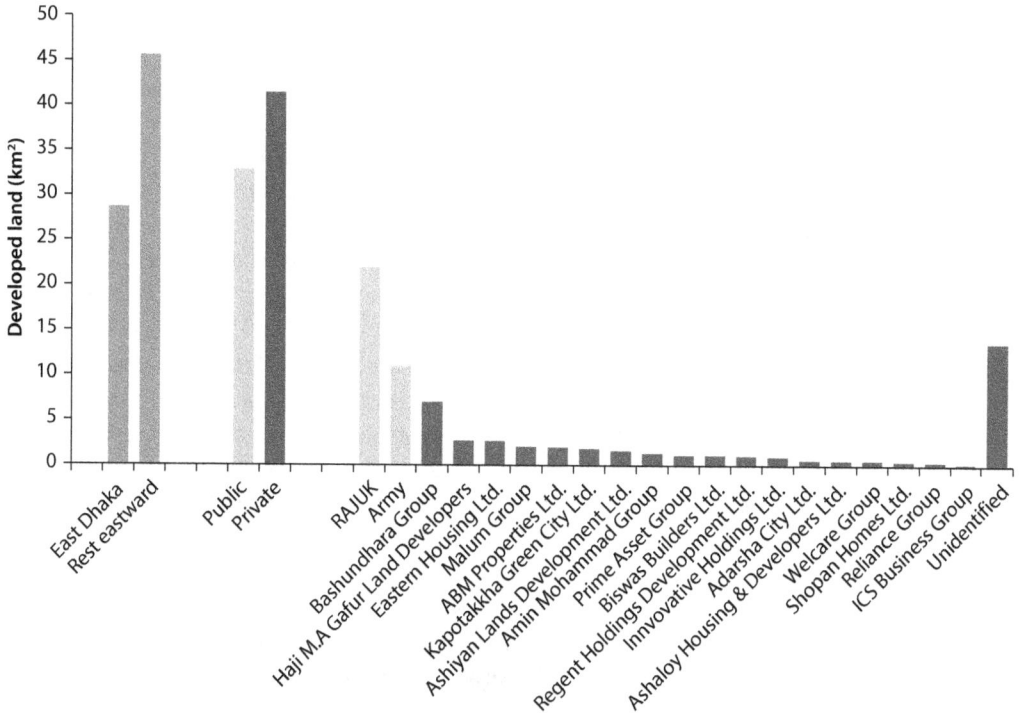

Sources: Calculations based on land classification background work carried out for this report (GISAT 2017) and private developers' websites.
Note: Rest eastward represents the developed land to the east of the Balu River and above the Dhaka-Narayanganj-Demra drainage improvement project area within the boundary of Greater Dhaka. The classification is based on 0.5- and 5-meter resolution satellite imagery. RAJUK = Rajdhani Unnayan Kartripakkha.

Housing Project or Baridhara Project (box 3.1). This undertaking was initiated in late 1988 and consists of 11 blocks. Work on blocks A to F, located along Pragati Sarani Airport Road, was under way even before the Purbachal township project. They are now completed and have evolved into a mature neighborhood. Other segments such as blocks G to L, which align more closely with 300 Feet Road, only received approval after 2014. Auxiliary roads and facilities are under construction, and the allocation of plots is still under way (Rahman 2017).

The Bashundhara Residential Area has become a city inside a city, home to primarily upper-middle-class and high-income residents. Beyond providing planned land use allocation, decent housing and open spaces, the Bashundhara Residential Area also offers basic urban services. A four-lane, well-maintained road runs north-south through the established neighborhood made up of blocks A to F. Auxiliary roads link to all apartment buildings. Private security guards manage traffic and ensure law and order inside the area. Gas and some solid waste management are provided. Schools, hospitals, mosques, restaurants and shopping malls are conveniently located. Not surprisingly, residents voice their

Box 3.1 Bashundhara Residential Area: A modern town with its own rules

The Bashundhara Residential Area is the largest private real estate project in Greater Dhaka. It is owned and operated by East West Property Development Pvt. Ltd., the real estate arm of the Bashundhara Group.

Delivering the project required filling low-lying marshland and flood zones that covered roughly 7 square kilometers in East Dhaka. Although the initiative was conceived in 1988, some significant areas of the project lacked legal regularization as late as in 2011. In 2014 the project became fully legal after the government allowed private housing initiatives on these low-lying areas if they included provisions for sewerage and drainage. However, it is not clear this requirement is being met.

The project seeks to satisfy the growing demand for residential housing and less congested living space. Its master plan envisions connectivity to wide streets; access to electricity, gas and water networks; and designated space for commercial activity. Modern amenities are essential components of the project. Its general layout also includes educational institutions, health facilities, banks, police barracks, playgrounds, parks and shopping malls.

Located at the heart of the Dhaka CCs, the Bashundhara Residential Area stands out for its prime location and its good connection to access roads. Established neighborhoods such as Gulshan, the Baridhara Diplomatic Zone, Nikunja and Uttara are in the vicinity, and major roads, such as 300 Feet Road, the Kuril Flyover and Pragati Sarani Airport Road, connect the project not only to the core of Dhaka but also to other major surrounding cities.

The area has established its own regulatory framework, focusing on security and traffic control. A system of resident identification is in place. Residents and frequent visitors receive car stickers upon approval by the residents' "welfare society office." They are also required to strictly abide by the traffic rules imposed by the security personnel within the area.

As the project has developed and matured, modern amenities have emerged as planned. The area hosts the Apollo Hospital, a tertiary care hospital providing comprehensive health care services in a modern facility and using state-of-the-art technology. Two major universities have set down roots in the area, serving about 25,000 students on campuses covering more than 35,000 square meters. At the primary and secondary levels, four major schools are also on hand, one of them offering a comprehensive international baccalaureate program.

The largest shopping mall in the country sits near the entry gate to the area, offering access to more than 510 stores scattered across 150,000 square meters of leasable space. Access to financial institutions was ensured when major banks such Eastern Bank Limited, Southeast Bank Limited, Prime Bank Limited and Bank Asia Limited opened branches there. About 72 food establishments provide the neighborhood with a large array of options from biryani to burgers to Mexican food.

The area's potential has not gone unnoticed by the private sector. Some large economic groups have established their headquarters in the area. Some notable examples are the Bashundhara Group, one of the country's largest industrial conglomerates; BDG-Magura Group, a diversified holding with interests in the manufacturing and service sectors; East West Media Group Ltd., the largest media house of Bangladesh; Grameenphone, a leading telecommunications service operator; and Walton, the country's largest electronics exporter.

Sources: Ali 2014; East West Property Development 2017.

general satisfaction with the livability of this city inside a city. Meanwhile, high-value-added services and activities such as information communications technology, hospitals, media and universities have also settled in the area, giving it an unmistakable dynamism.

Not all private housing projects have been this successful, however. Field visits were conducted for this report in the completed segments of four of them: Bashundhara Residential Area, Aftab Nagar, Banasree and Maddhya Badda (Rahman 2017). The Bashundhara Residential Area stands out as a functional neighborhood, whereas Maddhya Badda lies at the other end of the spectrum. Built for lower- and lower-middle-income groups, the layout does not appear to follow a planned land use allocation, and the area is congested and poorly equipped. Even in Banasree—where residents are primarily middle- and upper-middle-income—congestion is prevalent. The assessment is also mixed for Aftab Nagar.

Uneven service delivery

Beyond their differences in quality and livability, all private housing projects rely on the public sector for basic infrastructure and social services, including drainage, sewerage and transportation. Except for the well-functioning Bashundhara Residential Area, the field visits conducted for this report revealed substantial gaps in service delivery. And the interface between the private and the public spheres is often inadequate. Even in the otherwise well-functioning Bashundhara Residential Area, the internal road network connects with outside transport infrastructure only at three points.

The government has certainly invested significant resources in building roads and bridges in East Dhaka (Lamb 2014). But despite these efforts, transportation infrastructure is falling behind population growth, and is progressing significantly more slowly than construction sites and sand-filled areas. Assuming the same lane width across road types, total road surface in East Dhaka grew by about 5.7 percent a year between 2005 and 2016. Meanwhile, the population grew by more than 7.4 percent a year between 2001 and 2011, and most likely vehicle traffic grew even faster (figure 3.2).

Moreover, there is no public disclosure of the boundaries of private real estate sites and their connections—if any—to existing master plans such as the RSTP and the Dhaka Structure Plan. Consequently, land originally envisioned for mass transit routes, road corridors and key services may already be occupied. There is also anecdotal evidence suggesting that the alignment of the roads has been altered from land use plans to meet the needs of private developers (Lamb 2014).

High disaster risk

East Dhaka suffers from recurrent flooding and waterlogging during the monsoon season. An embankment is a first-best option to reduce flooding risks, particularly river flooding. Water drainage capacity is also critical to mitigate the impact of flooding and reduce losses. However, these infrastructures are public

Figure 3.2 Road building is falling behind population growth and sand filling in East Dhaka

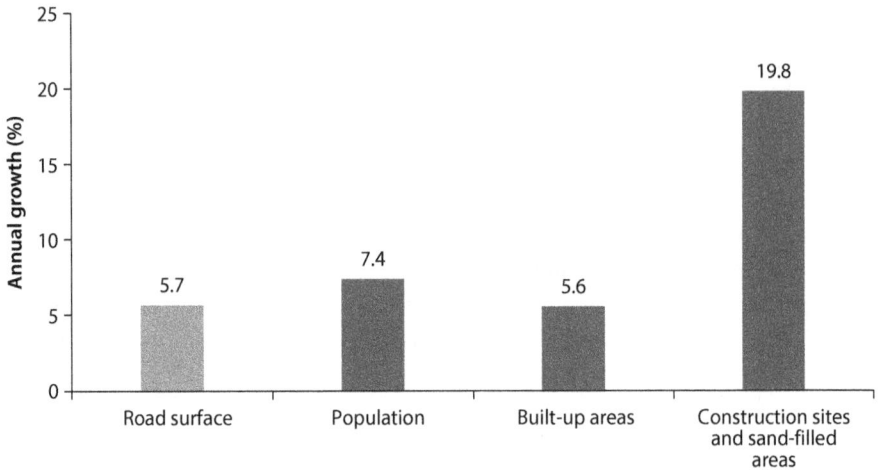

Sources: Calculations based on BBS (2001, 2011); DTCA (2005); DTCA and JICA (2015); Google Earth imagery; OpenStreetMap; and land classification background work carried out for this report (GISAT 2017).
Note: The classification is based on 0.5- and 5-meter resolution satellite imagery.

goods and private investors have limited incentive to supply them. Furthermore, private projects do not consider future drainage needs, instead relying almost fully on the public sector to address the issue. It is also reported that improper solid waste disposal by private developers led to the clogging of existing drainage pipes, thereby contributing to waterlogging in existing residential areas in East Dhaka. In the absence of public infrastructure in the area, the lack of investment in basic flood protection, the lack of proper waste collection and disposal, and the unplanned and uncoordinated growth by the private sector will likely compound the impacts of flood disasters. Indeed, they will lead to even higher losses than what East Dhaka has experienced during the monsoon season. Most of these losses will be related to business interruptions as well as flood-related costs.

Disaster risk is high as well in the event of an earthquake. Most of Greater Dhaka is located within 60 kilometers of the Madhupur fault line and thus is exposed to seismic activity. But the level of risk varies across land parcels, with the nature of the soil determining whether ground shaking is cushioned or amplified. In extreme cases, ground vibration can convert soils with specific properties from a solid to a liquid state. This process, known as liquefaction, causes severe damage to built-up structures. Housing can sink and fall over, bridges can float away, pipe systems can rupture, and roads can be destroyed (CDMP 2009; GSB and BGR 2014; World Bank and EMI 2014).

About 40 percent of the surface of East Dhaka lies outside the Madhupur Tract (map 3.6). This area is mainly low floodplains and marshy lands. Its soil

Map 3.6 Mostly off the Madhupur Tract, East Dhaka is vulnerable to earthquakes

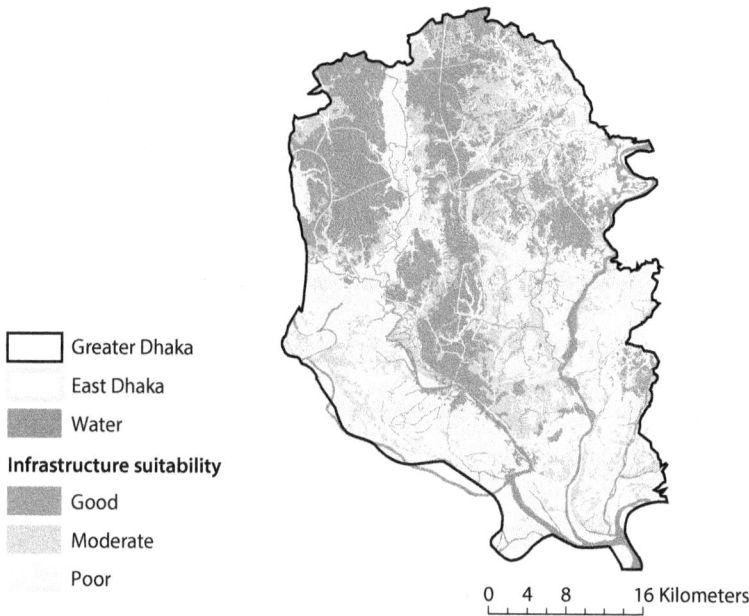

Greater Dhaka

East Dhaka

Water

Infrastructure suitability

Good

Moderate

Poor

0   4   8   16 Kilometers

Source: Visualization based on GSB and BGR (2014).
Note: Good includes Madhupur terrace high and middle, and old natural levee. Moderate covers Madhupur terrace low, younger natural levee, and high floodplain. Poor is for road valley, channelbar, low floodplain, and marshy land.

tends to be soft, and so ground shaking may be amplified in the event of an earthquake. Liquefaction is more likely in loose to moderate saturated granular soils with poor drainage. A high groundwater table makes this type of soil common in East Dhaka (CDMP 2009; GSB and BGR 2014; World Bank and EMI 2014).

A number of private real estate projects are located in these particularly vulnerable areas. And many of these projects have relied on hydraulic filling to reclaim their sites. As dredged materials are pumped in slurry form after being mixed with water, hydraulic filling makes the soil structure become loose and segregated (Ahamed 2005; Hore 2013; Hossain 2009; Islam et al. 2010; World Bank and EMI 2014; Youd and Perkins 1987).

Site-specific studies have found that some private real estate projects are indeed susceptible to liquefaction in the event of a severe earthquake. Among them are the Banasree housing project, the Bashundhara Residential Area and United City. These studies have advised more in-depth evaluations to determine the most adequate treatment for building on these parcels. Potential treatment includes soil engineering and restructuring. However, no action has been taken so far in response to this advice (Ahamed 2005; Hore 2013; Hossain 2009; Islam et al. 2010).

Irreversible environmental losses
The irreversible loss of wetlands presents another important risk of unchecked private-led development, with implications for Dhaka's flood mitigation capacity and beyond. Wetlands are productive ecosystems, providing benefits such as biodiversity support, water purification, flood mitigation, carbon sequestration and climate stabilization. Because of their public good nature, their conservation is often inadequate.

Unfortunately, wetland resources have been declining in Bangladesh for many reasons, including conversion to agricultural use and urban development. Permanent wetlands (or perennial wetlands) include canals, lakes, ponds and rivers that retain water year-round with seasonal expansion and reduction. Permanent wetland areas in Greater Dhaka were estimated to be 55–83 square kilometers in the 2010s, down from 207 square kilometers in 1967. Even the remaining ones are suffering from severe degradation. The four rivers surrounding the Dhaka CCs (Turag, Buriganga, Balu and Shitalakshya) have been polluted by unregulated industrial and land developments to the point that they can no longer sustain any form of life (CEGIS 2012; Karim 2014; World Bank 2018).

In East Dhaka, wetlands include the Balu River, the Tongi Kahl and other canals that crisscross East Dhaka and ponds along the Balu River and scattered in the area. They are critically important to the provision of natural flood water drainage, retention and storage capacity for East Dhaka, among other functions (World Bank 2018).

However, land filling by private developers has been threatening the very existence of these wetlands. As early as 2006, the update of FAP section 8A had already reported that private developers were encroaching on the retention pond areas. It also identified 10 canals as being fully filled and four as being partially filled. In 2010 RAJUK designated 13.9 square kilometers of the area as retention ponds. By 2017 private developers had encroached on about 27 percent (or 3.8 square kilometers) of retention areas. Only about 2 square kilometers of permanent wetlands can still be found in East Dhaka (Halcrow Group Limited 2006; World Bank 2018).

Land value capture
On the social front, urbanization results in large increases in land value, and how this economic surplus is distributed matters. Even if private owners do little to upgrade their property, land value often increases steeply following the concentration of businesses and households in the area. The rise in land value is reinforced by public investment in infrastructure and services. Thus it is fair for the government to retain part of land value appreciation to fund public investment and distribute the benefits of urban development across the population more broadly.

Risks are also associated with weak land ownership rights. Depending on how large private investors acquire land for their urban development projects, current residents may stand to lose. Surges in land prices invite appropriation by powerful interest groups when the rights of the current occupants are not well defined and protected.

With the ever-rising population pressure in West Dhaka, land and housing prices have surged in East Dhaka. For example, in 2000 the price of a square meter of land in the Bashundhara Residential Area ranged from US$24 to US$83. As of 2016, the price had increased to US$94 to US$120 per square meter. The prices of ready-to-occupy apartments have experienced the biggest appreciation, even if their quality has not improved much. In 2000 the price of an apartment ranged from US$19,000 to US$63,000. By 2016, it had climbed to US$123,000–$164,000 (Masum et al. 2016).

Private real estate developers acquire property from farmers and individual owners through negotiations. But the process is at times opaque. Reportedly, some individual landowners have been threatened into selling to developers. It is also said that land filling results in blurred demarcation lines during the monsoon season, and the resulting uncertainty may have been used by private real estate developers to extend the area they control (Halcrow Group Limited 2006; Lamb 2014). Meanwhile, the weakness of land titling information (records of rights) undermines the public sector's ability to prevent illegal land appropriation and to offer mechanisms of redress.

Comprehensive data on land records are not available, but an in-depth study of a single *mouza* (a subunit of a union in rural areas) for this report illustrates the concern. The *mouza* Purba Durgapur is arguably representative of the areas in East Dhaka that have not yet been targeted by private developers. It is located in the south of East Dhaka and sits between the Balu River and the Dhaka-Narayanganj-Demra project. Situated in low-lying, flood-prone areas, it consists predominantly of agricultural land and small-scale rural settlements. A manual review of local files for this *mouza* revealed a significant gap between the number of land titles (records of rights) and the number of households living in the area (figure 3.3).

Admittedly, some households may not own land, while others may own land plots registered under multiple titles. Members of the same household may also hold multiple titles for the same plot. But despite these caveats, this review suggests that the property rights of a number of households may not be protected by registered land titles. These households, and many others in East Dhaka, may therefore be deprived of fair compensation for their land assets.

Furthermore, a large portion of East Dhaka is public land. Particularly, many plots falling into the category of *khas* land—water bodies and low-lying floodplains that do not support permanent human settlements. *Khas* land is owned by the government and held under the Ministry of Land. Some of the government titles of *mouza* Purba Durgapur are *khas* land. There will be a strong pressure to develop this and other public land in East Dhaka for urban uses, making it vulnerable to illegal capture as well.

Figure 3.3 There are few land property titles for the growing population of the *mouza* Purba Durgapur

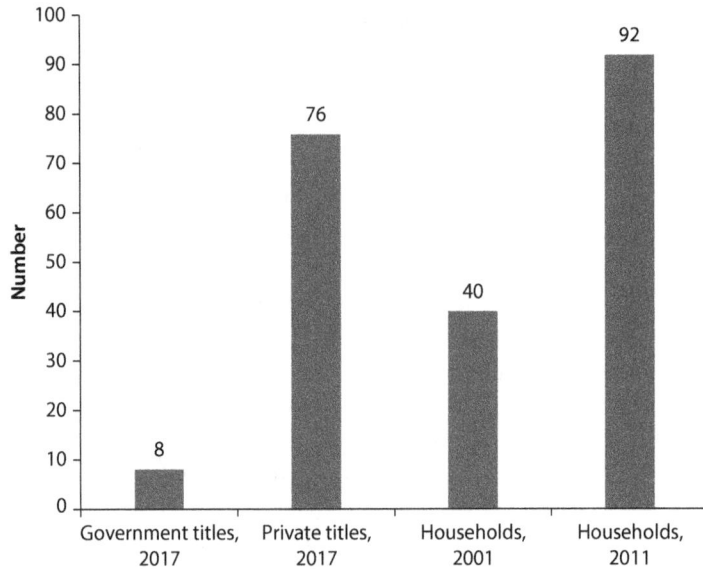

Sources: Calculations based on BBS (2001, 2011) and *Khatian* book (records of rights) of the *mouza* Purba Durgapur.

References

Ahamed, Selim. 2005. "Soil Characteristics and Liquefaction Potential of Selected Reclaimed Areas of Dhaka City." M.Sc. Engg. thesis, Department of Civil Engineering, Bangladesh University of Engineering and Technology, Dhaka.

Ahmed, B., R. Hasan and K. M. Maniruzzaman. 2014. "Urban Morphological Change Analysis of Dhaka City, Bangladesh, Using Space Syntax." *ISPRS International Journal of Geo-Information* 3 (4): 1412–44.

Ali, Tawfique. 2014. "Goodbye to City's Flood Flow Zones." *Daily Star*, June 5. http://www.thedailystar.net/goodbye-to-citys-flood-flow-zones-27105.

Angel, Shlomo. 2012. *Planet of Cities.* Cambridge, MA: Lincoln Institute of Land Policy.

Ballon, Hilary. 2012. *The Greatest Grid: The Master Plan of Manhattan 1811–2011.* New York: Museum of the City of New York and Columbia University Press.

BBS (Bangladesh Bureau of Statistics). 2001. "Population and Housing Census 2001." Statistics Division, Ministry of Planning, Government of the People's Republic of Bangladesh.

———. 2011. "Population and Housing Census 2011." Statistics Division, Ministry of Planning, Government of the People's Republic of Bangladesh.

Bloomberg, Michael. 2012. "Reflection: Michael R. Bloomberg." In *The Greatest Grid: The Master Plan of Manhattan 1811–2011*, edited by Hilary Ballon. New York: Museum of the City of New York and Columbia University Press.

BWDB (Bangladesh Water Development Board). 2017. "Technical Study of Flood Control and Drainage Development at Dhaka Circular Road (Dhaka Eastern Bypass) Project, conducted by IWM (Institute of Water Modelling)." Dhaka.

CDMP (Comprehensive Disaster Management Programme). 2009. "Seismic Hazard Assessment of Dhaka, Chittagong and Sylhet City Corporation Area of Bangladesh." Ministry of Disaster Management and Relief, Dhaka.

CEGIS (Center for Environmental and Geographic Information Services). 2012. "Bangladesh." Dhaka.

Dewan, A. M., and Y. Yamaguchi. 2009. "Land Use and Land Cover Change in Greater Dhaka, Bangladesh: Using Remote Sensing to Promote Sustainable Urbanization." *Applied Geography* 29 (3): 390–401.

DTCA (Dhaka Transport Coordination Authority). 2005. "Strategic Transport Plan for Dhaka." Prepared by Louis Berger Group and Bangladesh Consultant Ltd., Dhaka.

DTCA (Dhaka Transport Coordination Authority) and JICA (Japan International Cooperation Agency). 2015. "Revised Strategic Transport Plan for Dhaka." Prepared by ALMEC Corporation, Oriental Consultants Global and Kathahira and Engineers International, Dhaka.

East West Property Development. 2017. "Bashundhara Baridhara Land Project." http://www.ewpd.com.bd/bashundhara-baridhara/bd-brochure.

Fuller, Brandon, and Paul Romer. 2014. "Urbanization as Opportunity." In *Rethinking Cities: A Roadmap Towards Better Urbanization for Development*, edited by Edward Glaeser and Abha Joshi-Ghani. Washington, DC: World Bank.

GISAT. 2011. "Historical Assessment of Spatial Growth of Built-Ups in Metropolitan Areas of Delhi and Mumbai in India and Dhaka in Bangladesh." Technical Note and GIS Maps, World Bank, Washington, DC, and European Space Agency, Earth Observation for Development, Paris.

———. 2017. "Urban Land Use Update and Mapping for Greater Dhaka Region." Background paper prepared for this report. Prague, Czech Republic.

GSB (Geological Survey of Bangladesh) and BGR (Bundesanstalt für Geowissenschaften und Rohstoffe). 2014. "Infrastructure Suitability for Shallow Foundation of Dhaka Metropolitan City, Bangladesh." Printed map issued by GSB, Dhaka.

Halcrow Group Limited. 2006. "Updating/Upgrading the Feasibility Study of Dhaka Integrated Flood Control Embankment cum Eastern Bypass Road Multipurpose Project." London.

Hore, Ripon. 2013 "Liquefaction Potential of Selected Reclaimed Areas of Dhaka City Based on Cone Penetration Test." M.Sc. Engg. thesis, Department of Civil Engineering, Bangladesh University of Engineering and Technology, Dhaka.

Hossain, T. 2009. "Estimation of Earthquake Induced Liquefaction Potential of Selected Reclaimed Areas of Dhaka City Based on Shear Wave Velocity." M.Sc. Engg. thesis, Department of Civil Engineering, Bangladesh University of Engineering and Technology, Dhaka.

Islam, Mohammad Shariful, Md Tanvir Hossain, Syed Fakhrul Ameen, Eqramul Hoque and Selim Ahamed. 2010. "Earthquake Induced Liquefaction Vulnerability of Reclaimed Areas of Dhaka." *Journal of Civil Engineering* (Institution of Engineers, Bangladesh) 38 (1): 65–80.

Islam, N. 1996. "Dhaka: From City to Megacity: Perspectives on People, Places, Planning, and Development Issues (No. 1)." Urban Studies Programme, Department of Geography, University of Dhaka.

JICA (Japan International Cooperation Agency). 1992. "Feasibility Study on Greater Dhaka Protection Project (Study in Dhaka Metropolitan Area) of Bangladesh Flood Action Plan No. 8A." JICA, Tokyo.

Kabir, A., and B. Parolin. 2012. "Planning and Development of Dhaka—A Story of 400 Years." Paper presented at 15th International Planning History Society Conference, "Cities, Nations and Regions in Planning History," São Paulo.

Karim, K. R. 2014. "Trends of Permanent Wetland Change in Detailed Area Plan of Dhaka." *American Journal of Water Resources* 2 (5): 106–09.

Lamb, Zachary. 2014. "Embanked: Climate Vulnerability and the Paradoxes of Flood Protection in Dhaka." Department of Urban Studies and Planning, Massachusetts Institute of Technology, Cambridge, MA.

Mahtab-uz-Zaman, Q. M., and S. S. Lau. 2000. "City Expansion Policy versus Compact City Demand: The Case of Dhaka." In *Compact Cities: Sustainable Urban Forms for Developing Countries*, edited by Mike Jenks and Rod Burgess, 141–52. London: Spon Press.

Masum, F., U. E. Chugbu, J. Espiniza and C. Graffen. 2016. "The Limitations of Formal Land Delivery System: Need for a Pro-Poor Urban Land Development Policy in Dhaka, Bangladesh." Paper presented at World Bank Land and Poverty Conference.

Nilufar, F. 2010. "Urban Morphology of Dhaka City: Spatial Dynamics of Growing City and the Urban Core." In the International Seminar on The History, Heritage and Urban Issues of Capital Dhaka, on the occasion of the Celebration of 400 years of the Capital Dhaka, organized by the Asiatic Society of Bangladesh, 17–19 February 2010.

Pramanik, M. M. A., and D. Stathakis. 2016. "Forecasting Urban Sprawl in Dhaka City of Bangladesh." *Environment and Planning B: Planning and Design* 43 (4): 756–71.

Rahman, Hossain. 2017. "Transforming Dhaka East: A Political Economy Perspective on Opportunities and Challenges." Background paper prepared for this report.

Rahman, Saidur. 2010. "The Only Solution." *Forum A*, March 3. http://archive.thedailystar .net/forum/2010/march/only.htm.

RAJUK (Rajdhani Unnayan Kartripakkha). 1995. "Dhaka Metropolitan Development Plan 1995–2015." Dhaka.

———. 2015. "Dhaka Structure Plan 2016–2035." Dhaka.

———. 2017. "Purbachal New Town." http://www.rajukdhaka.gov.bd/rajuk/projectsHome ?type=purbachal.

Reza, Abu. 2017. "WB's Proposal to Develop Dhaka Eastward—A Critique." *Financial Express*, August 22. http://thefinancialexpress.com.bd/print/wbs-proposal-to-develop -dhaka-eastward-a-critique-1503378071.

Shankland Cox Partnership et al. 1981. "Dhaka Metropolitan Area Integrated Urban Development Project." Planning Commission, Government of Bangladesh, Dhaka.

U.S. Census Bureau. 2017. "Population and Housing Unit Estimates Datasets." https:// www.census.gov/programs-surveys/popest/data/data-sets.2017.html.

World Bank. 2017. "Urban Transport in Dhaka: Review of Plans and Institutional Set-Up." Background paper prepared for this report, World Bank, Washington, DC.

———. 2018. "Unlocking Opportunities for Clean and Resilient Growth—Bangladesh Country Environmental Analysis." Powerpoint presentation, World Bank, Washington, DC.

World Bank and EMI (Earthquakes and Megacities Initiative). 2014. "The Dhaka Profile and Earthquake Risk Atlas." Manila, Philippines.

Youd, T. Leslie, and David M. Perkins. 1987. "Mapping of Liquefaction Severity Index." *Journal of Geotechnical Engineering* 113 (11): 1374–92.

CHAPTER 4

Urban Development Scenarios

A city can follow multiple growth paths, and what the city becomes in the long run very much depends on the path it chooses. In analytical terms, the dynamics of agglomeration and congestion imply that there are multiple possible equilibria (Baldwin et al. 2011; Fujita, Krugman and Venables 1999; Krugman 1991; Krugman and Venables 1995; Venables 2017). The fate of a city is therefore not predetermined, and just being in a strategic location is not enough to succeed. The vision of city leaders, their credibility with the private sector, and their implementation capacity can make an enormous difference. If a suboptimal growth path is chosen, market forces alone may not be sufficient to "grow" the city later on.

However, moving a city from one growth path to another may require bold decisions and actions. Marginal changes in urban policies are most likely insufficient to escape a suboptimal growth path and put the city on a better trajectory. Minor departures from business as usual may fail to reach the critical threshold required to change the expectations and behaviors of the private sector. The scope of potentially effective policy changes ranges from investing in critically important infrastructure, to addressing coordination failures that lead to congestion, to improving service delivery to make the city more attractive. Bold changes of this sort can reinforce each other, so that the city continues on a strong trajectory even after the big push is over.

There is growing recognition that Dhaka's current organic development path can deliver only up to a point, and multiple ideas have emerged for putting the city on a better growth path. These ideas include revitalizing old Dhaka, retrofitting West Dhaka, and building satellite towns on the outskirts of the current Dhaka city corporations (CCs). All these ideas have merit. But in an environment in which resources and implementation capacity are constrained, the key question is which interventions would reach the critical threshold to trigger a change in the city's growth trajectory. The answer may well lie in thinking outside the box.

Dhaka is fortunate in this respect, as it has a unique opportunity not often available to other megacities in the developing world. Toward its east, where two major regional highway corridors will one day intersect, there is a vast expanse of mostly rural land. Most of the plots in this area are within a few kilometers of the most valuable parts of the city; many are within walking distance. The availability of a massive amount of vacant land so close to the core of the city is reminiscent of Pudong in Shanghai a quarter of a century ago. Which is why, when thinking about a new growth paradigm for Dhaka, an obvious reference is Shanghai.

The decision to develop Pudong as the best path for the development of Shanghai was made in the early 1990s, when the level of development of the city was similar to that of Dhaka today. In the mere two and half decades since then, Pudong has become a vibrant hub for finance, trade and high-tech industries. And along the way, Shanghai has become an affluent global city, recognized as China's main international gateway.

Taking Dhaka from its current, organic development path into a strategic growth trajectory inspired by the experience of Shanghai would amount to a bold change in urban policy. Although governance constraints may impede fully replicating the Pudong experience, its spirit can nonetheless serve as an aspirational reference. To ensure realism, the options considered for Dhaka in what follows are firmly anchored in master plans and technical studies developed in Bangladesh. Combining key elements of these plans and studies, this study considers four different scenarios to simulate Greater Dhaka's development toward 2035. The most ambitious of them somewhat mimics the Pudong approach.

At one extreme, there is the business as usual scenario, in which private-led real estate development toward the east continues unabated. At the other extreme is a strategic approach scenario inspired by the Pudong approach but acknowledging Dhaka's institutional constraints. This strategic approach scenario brings together three concrete interventions: (1) building the eastern embankment and setting up auxiliary measures; (2) laying out a modern transportation network before East Dhaka densifies; and (3) adopting soft reforms to boost the creation of good jobs, improve amenities and protect the environment. In between these two extreme scenarios, only one or two of the three concrete interventions are retained.

Multiple proposals

Proposals to improve Dhaka's development path have proliferated in recent times (table 4.1). Some of them focus on making West Dhaka a better place in which to live and work. Because of the challenges faced by the western part of the city in terms of flooding, congestion and messiness, these proposals are worth considering, and progress in their implementation should be assessed. Other proposals focus on fostering urbanization in low-density areas outside the boundaries of the Dhaka CCs. Location and connectivity are the key issues in evaluating these proposals.

Retrofitting West Dhaka
Waterfront revitalization has been embraced by many great cities to reconnect with their history, preserve their cultural heritage and promote their local identity.

Table 4.1 Urban development ideas for Dhaka have proliferated in recent years

Area	Location	Land use development
West Dhaka	Waterfront in Old Dhaka	Waterfront revitalization and heritage conservation
	Hazaribagh tannery area	Brownfield regeneration
	Tejgaon industrial area	Retrofitting and redevelopment
	Gulshan, Banani and Baridhara lake area	Retrofitting and lake conservation
Outside Dhaka CCs	Gazipur CC, Tongi town	Satellite town development
	Narayanganj CC	Satellite town development
	Savar municipality	Satellite town development
	Tarabo municipality	Satellite town development

Sources: Based on Fatemi and Rahman (2015); Rahman and Ara (2016); Rahman and Imon (2017); RAJUK (2015).
Note: CC = city corporation.

Dhaka was born on the eastern shore of the Buriganga River. This was once a sought-after residential area with magnificent views. The waterfront still hosts some of the most valuable architectural heritage of the city, including the Ahsan Manzil palace, the Lalbag fort and the Satgambudj Masjid mosque. However, the area has also suffered from haphazard growth, illegal encroachment, detrimental uses and heavy pollution (Rahman and Ara 2016; Rahman and Imon 2017).

The Dhaka Structure Plan 2016–2035 rightfully lists revitalization of the old town as one of its objectives. Awareness campaigns, adoption of measures for heritage protection, and river dredging had already been attempted to support this objective. But the efforts were too fragmented and short-lived to make a substantial difference. Realizing their limitations, experts are now proposing a holistic approach toward waterfront revitalization and heritage conservation, which is commendable. At the same time, international experience has revealed that institutional capacity and long-term commitments are vital for such initiatives to reach fruition, even in advanced economies (Rahman and Ara 2016; Rahman and Imon 2017; RAJUK 2015).

The regeneration of the Hazaribagh tannery area is another important retrofitting proposal for West Dhaka. Leather processing has played a significant role in Bangladesh's economy, accounting at some point for a large share of exports. Over 90 percent of the country's tanneries is located in Hazaribagh, occupying a mere 0.25 square kilometers of land.

Hazaribagh literally means "a thousand gardens." But the use of outdated technologies, coupled with the absence of proper industrial waste management and waste treatment facilities, have destroyed the ecology of the area and badly affected its surroundings. Hazaribagh is rated as one of the world's most polluted places. Soil contamination and air and water pollution have made the area unlivable (Ahmed 2016; Blacksmith Institute 2013; Fatemi and Rahman 2015; UNIDO 2006). Undoing this damage is, understandably, another key urban development priority for Dhaka.

Despite its potentially large environmental and socioeconomic benefits, regeneration of the Hazaribagh tannery area has faced serious challenges. As early as 2001, in accordance with the Bangladesh Environment Conservation Act 1995 and the Environment Conservation Rules 1997, the Bangladesh High Court had asked the government to ensure that the tanneries would install adequate means of treating their waste. The request, however, was inconsequential. A decade later, the High Court asked the government to relocate tanneries outside of Dhaka or close them down, setting a six-month deadline for compliance. In 2016 it ordered the government to shut down all the tanneries, and in 2017 it instructed the government to cut off their power supply. And yet as of May 2017, only about 35 percent of tanneries had relocated, and some of the closed ones had managed to resume operations (Ahmed 2016; *Dhaka Tribune* 2017; Khan 2016; Ovi and Islam 2017; Shaon 2017).

Even if the tannery relocation were complete, the regeneration initiative would consume another 15 years. This is the time required to treat the soil with suitable remediation techniques. But treatment cannot start before the current homeowners are relocated to other areas. Such massive resettlement may be as impractical, and face as much resistance, as the relocation of the tanneries (Bhowmik 2013; Fatemi and Rahman 2015; Roy 2009; Ruhani 2017).

Other retrofitting ideas have been proposed in addition to these two salient examples. One idea is to redevelop the Tejgaon industrial area, tapping into its existing concentration of business activities. Another is to upgrade the infrastructure of the Gulshan, Banani and Baridhara neighborhoods to meet current demands and to conserve their lakes for drainage and recreation purposes. These proposals are critically important too, but they face challenges. For example, in Gulshan, Banani and Baridhara encroachment clearance and lake conservation were initiated in 2010, but little progress has been made in practice, despite repeated High Court rulings (Ali 2007; Banglanews24 2015; *Daily Star* 2016; Mahmud 2013; New Age 2016).

Overall, retrofitting initiatives for West Dhaka have proven to be expensive and ineffective. Waterfront revitalization, brownfield rehabilitation and population resettlement require considerable resources and strong institutional capacity. Land reclamation is challenging everywhere, and financial resources are limited in Bangladesh. But, in addition, the fragmented urban institutional arrangements that characterize Dhaka have severely undermined the city's ability to take action.

Densifying farther out

In light of the difficulties faced by retrofitting, starting anew is potentially more promising. In greenfield development, there is less need for land reclamation, and resource requirements are lower. More important, the scope for action is likely higher as there are fewer vested interests to overcome.

Starting anew should not be interpreted as abandoning the existing urban core. As defined by the Dhaka Metropolitan Development Plan 1995–2016 (DMDP), Greater Dhaka covers a metropolitan area consisting of an urban core, suburbs and exurbs. Within this metropolitan area, all business activities are intrinsically linked, forming one economic ecosystem. The interaction between locations varies with their physical distance and with the input-output relationships between sectors. Because of these linkages, starting anew in one part of Greater Dhaka can release population and traffic pressure elsewhere in the city.

At a first glance, there are multiple options for starting anew. They range from the densification of northern Dhaka beyond Gazipur to the construction of more distant satellite cities around Greater Dhaka. In deciding which of these options to favor, a key element to consider is their potential contribution to city growth. And distance to the city core is critically important in this respect.

The urban economics literature finds that agglomeration effects decline sharply with distance and travel time. This is particularly so for knowledge spillovers. In the United States, employment concentration and wage rates are much higher within an 8-kilometer ring of the urban core than out of it (Rosenthal and Strange 2008). In the United Kingdom, the positive effect of proximity on labor productivity declines steeply with distance and becomes insignificant beyond 80 minutes of travel time (Rice, Venables and Patacchini 2006). In Berlin, both productivity and residential externalities fall to zero beyond 10 minutes of traveling—the equivalent of about 1 kilometer by foot or 4 kilometers by mass rapid transit (MRT) (Ahlfeldt et al. 2015). And in New York, productivity externalities are very large for high-value-added services such as advertising, but they dissipate quickly with distance and become nil beyond 0.75 kilometers (Arzaghi and Henderson 2008).

In Dhaka, some of these satellite towns have the potential to become significant economic centers and to accommodate the manufacturing activities that move out of the urban core. Tongi and Gazipur on the north and Narayanganj on the south have both emerged as new centers for garment industries. Savar is designated as the center for tanneries being relocated out of Hazaribagh area and to be equipped with the proper industrial waste management and water treatment facilities. These satellite towns have seen rapid population growth in recent years as well (RAJUK 2015).

However, distance and travel times between the proposed satellite towns and the most vibrant parts of the city are substantial. Gazipur, Narayanganj, Savar, Tarabo and Tongi are between 12 and 23 kilometers away from the center of Gulshan. According to Google Maps, commuting from these locations to Gulshan currently takes between 40 and 80 minutes by bus or car. The densification of these satellite towns may accommodate a growing population and facilitate the restructuring of the city's economy. But given the lengthy travel times to the city center, suburban densification alone may not be sufficient to put Dhaka on a different growth trajectory.

A unique opportunity

The imbalance between the eastern and western parts of Dhaka offers an opportunity to increase the amount of high-quality urban land that few other megacities have. West Dhaka is overcrowded. East Dhaka, which remains largely rural, covers an area in excess of 100 square kilometers, shares a 26-kilometer boundary with West Dhaka, and is close to some of the most valuable land in the city (map 4.1). Just across Pragati Sarani Airport Road are some of the most vibrant and affluent parts of Dhaka—and of Bangladesh—such as Gulshan and the Tejgaon industrial area. The minimum distance between the center of Gulshan and the edge of East Dhaka is less than 1 kilometer, and the average

Map 4.1 East Dhaka is close to the most valuable land in Bangladesh

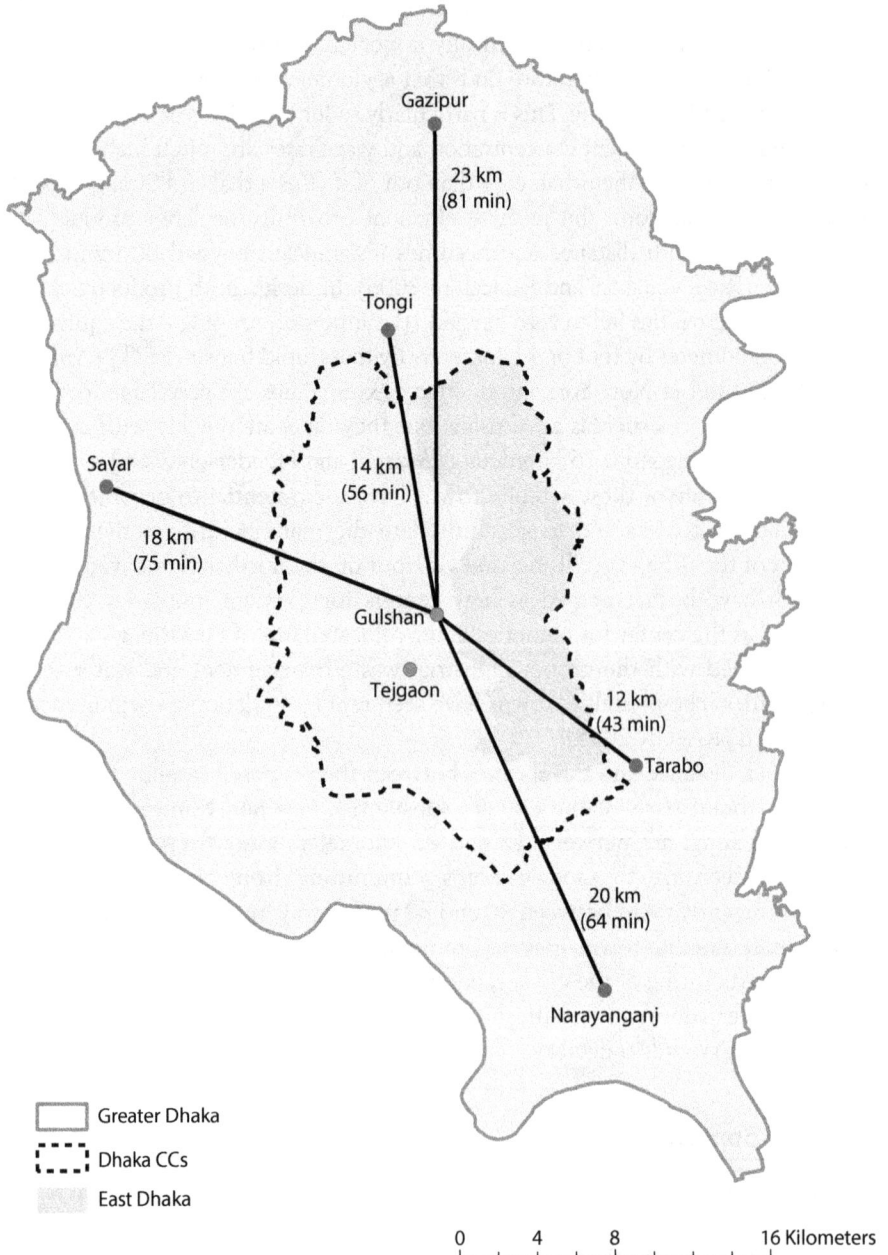

Gazipur

23 km
(81 min)

Tongi

Savar

14 km
(56 min)

18 km
(75 min)

Gulshan

Tejgaon

12 km
(43 min)

Tarabo

20 km
(64 min)

Narayanganj

Greater Dhaka

Dhaka CCs

East Dhaka

0   4   8   16 Kilometers

Sources: Visualization based on Google Maps; Li et al. (2015).
Note: CC = city corporation.

distance between Gulshan and the centers of the 12 unions recently added to the Dhaka CCs is about 6 kilometers. Figures are similar for the distance between the Tejgaon industrial area and East Dhaka.

East Dhaka also sits strategically between West Dhaka and the emerging Sylhet-Chittagong corridor. But transportation networks within East Dhaka barely exist. Until recently, there were only three secondary roads in the east-west direction for the entire area. This situation improved with the completion of the 300 Feet Road, and it would dramatically change if the MRT and road networks proposed by the Revised Strategic Transport Plan (RSTP) for East Dhaka were implemented.

Not surprisingly, the Dhaka Structure Plan 2016–2035 points out that East Dhaka should be converted to urban use to reinforce an eastward spine. And it recognizes that such a conversion is feasible, provided that the appropriate flood prevention measures are in place and geotechnical knowledge is used to guide construction. It also proposes dividing Greater Dhaka into six functional regions with the Dhaka CCs as its core, spanning both West Dhaka and East Dhaka. The eastward expansion of the Dhaka CCs in 2016 shows that the central government endorses this vision for Dhaka's urban development.

Prompted by an ever-growing population and spiraling land prices, Dhaka has quickly begun to expand toward the east. This expansion is occurring despite the recurrent flooding of East Dhaka's low-lying plains. Led mainly by private developers, the eastward expansion reflects the vitality of market forces in Bangladesh. But it has progressed in an organic way, and continuing with this private-led urban development model poses serious risks. Among them are a widening gap between population and transportation infrastructure, a high vulnerability to floods and earthquakes, wetland losses and land value grabbing. It is unlikely, then, that this organic development will be able to put the city on a different growth trajectory.

Building anew in the eastern portion of the city is possible, but based on current trends East Dhaka is likely to increasingly resemble messy West Dhaka over time. And retrofitting East Dhaka later on could be as costly and challenging as retrofitting West Dhaka is today. It is therefore imperative to act now, before East Dhaka is completely encroached on and its layout becomes irreversible in practice. A different urban development paradigm is needed for the eastern part of the city. It requires strategic thinking about the existing policy options and their implementation.

The example of Pudong, Shanghai

In thinking about urban development options for Dhaka, an experience to consider is that of Shanghai, a city in China whose gross domestic product (GDP) per capita already exceeds US$13,500 at 2015 prices, or US$24,000 in purchasing power parity at 2014 prices (Brookings Institution 2015). Such affluence should not obscure the fact that a quarter of a century ago Shanghai was not much richer than Dhaka today. Its takeoff as a global city began in the early 1990s, and it was associated with the development of Pudong, a rural area next to the city center. That area had important similarities with East Dhaka as it is now.

A national-level strategy

Shanghai first rose to prominence in the mid-19th century, and it came to be known as the "Paris of the East" in the early 20th century. It was there that east and west met, creating vibrant networks for capital, technology and ideas to flow. However, after the political events of 1949 Shanghai was largely cut off from the outside world and lost its prestige as a global city. Parts of its city center, such as the historic Bund and the French Concession, maintained their architectural grandeur. But Shanghai's economic activity and urban fabric were restructured in line with the political ideology of the time.

Pudong is located on the east bank of the Huangpu River, only 500 meters from the Bund, an area known for having the highest economic and historic value in Shanghai. In sharp contrast with the long urban development history of Puxi (on the west bank of the river), Pudong was by 1990 still a mix of river port facilities and low-quality housing, with inadequate infrastructure and vast stretches of farmland (photo 4.1). The entire area contributed a meager 8 percent of the city's GDP. Most of its roughly 1,200 businesses were in low-tech, high-polluting industries. The services sector was barely developed, and hardly any banking or insurance companies were located east of the Huangpu River. The only connectivity between the two sides of the river was an old twin-lane tunnel. The popular saying that a Shanghainese "prefers a bed in Puxi to a house in Pudong" illustrates the low standing of the area (Chen 2007; Zhao and Shao 2008).

The idea of developing Pudong was first proposed in the 1980s by local planners as a way to relieve the rising pressure on Puxi. Back then, Puxi's surface size was too limited to accommodate an ever-increasing population and growing economic activity. Its infrastructure was also too obsolete to meet the demands of an emerging modern city. The idea of eastward expansion of the city was embraced by the Shanghai government, which turned it into a strategy for the city to regain its prestige. Indeed, not only had Shanghai lost its status as a global city, it also was less competitive than the southern coastal cities that had engaged earlier in economic reforms.

In 1990 the Pudong idea was finally embraced as a national-level strategy by China's central government. The area initially targeted for reform and development had a surface size of 350 square kilometers and a population of 1.3 million. The intervention area was expanded to 532 square kilometers shortly thereafter, and since 2009 it has covered 1,210 square kilometers.

After a mere two and half decades of development, Pudong has become a vibrant nexus for finance, trade and high-tech industries. By 2011 an area twice the surface size of Manhattan had been constructed there—120 million square meters of floor space by the official tally, including more than 70 skyscrapers. There is less grade A office space empty in Pudong than in Manhattan—9.5 percent

Photo 4.1 Pudong (Shanghai) before and after

a. 1987

b. 2013

Source: © Reuters [Stringer (top); Carlos Barria (bottom)]. Used with the permission of Reuters. Further permission required for reuse.
Note: These photos show the financial district of Pudong in 1987 (top) and on July 31, 2013 (bottom). Both photos were taken at 4:35 p.m., 26 years apart.

versus 10.3 percent. The annual average rent is nearly US$700 per square meter, or more than in midtown Manhattan.

Pudong has attracted many of the world's largest financial and business services firms and emerged as the residential choice for Shanghainese. It has also grown into Shanghai's most populous district, contributing almost 30 percent of the city's GDP. With over 5 million inhabitants, Pudong's population has expanded by 58 percent in just one decade, and the number of internal migrants it hosts by 190 percent. There are now over 20 river crossings and other strategic infrastructures. The area has large green spaces and ecofriendly facilities, as well as efficient public services (Chen 2007; Zhao and Shao 2008). Not surprisingly, these astonishing changes have been called "the propaganda of hope" (Fishman 2005).

From vision to implementation

There are multiple reasons for Pudong's success, and location is one of them. Being next to the Bund, the most affluent part of Shanghai, land was bound to become highly valuable. Skills, technology and management were available nearby, setting it apart from many other districts in China. Tapping into these resources, Pudong transformed itself into an engine powering the economic growth and social development of the city, of the Yangtze River delta and of China as a whole.

However, location is not the full story (box 4.1). Unlike other urban development initiatives, Pudong's rise was a national-level strategy. Its objective was to

---

Box 4.1 The key ingredients of Pudong's success

The development of Pudong was an explicit strategy pursued by Shanghai to revive its economy and regain its prestige as a global city. Due to the lack of housing and infrastructure investment and to the replacement of commercial sites by industries, Shanghai had lost most of its attractiveness. Economically, it had grown much more slowly than the southern provinces, where the open-door policy was first introduced. In the 1980s, Shanghai's local government, researchers and urban professionals began to discuss the idea of developing Pudong. But it was only in 1990, shortly after the Tiananmen Square events, that the central government decided to endorse the proposal and announce it to the world as a way to show its commitment to openness and economic reform.

Pudong was an economic project for a well-defined urban area, which allowed the introduction and testing of a number of preferential policies and regulations. At the time, there was intense debate on economic reforms within the central government. But whatever was decided was likely to face less resistance in it because the area was still relatively poor and underpopulated. This is how Pudong became a testing ground for new institutional arrangements in relation to land ownership and land use rights.

There is no private ownership of land in China. The state owns all urban land, and farming collectives own all rural land. Reforms of the legal framework starting in the 1980s had

box continues next page

Box 4.1 The key ingredients of Pudong's success *(continued)*

effectively separated land use rights from land ownership and made it possible to lease and sell land use rights. The Pudong government regulated the commercialization of existing urban land and the expropriation of collectively owned agricultural land by means of a "land bank" system. Taking advantage of its economic zone status, Pudong was the first area in Shanghai to introduce land lease procedures and to create a local land market.

The Pudong New Area, as it was designated in 1992, was under the purview of three districts and two counties. Rather than deal with the old institutional arrangements and power struggles, the Shanghai local government decided to create a new and more autonomous administrative body. For that purpose, it first set up a transition team, the Pudong Development Office, to examine the existing situation, to coordinate the public institutions involved and to prepare for the new institutional arrangement.

Eventually, an empowered authority, the Pudong New Area Administrative Committee, was established as a unified administrative body. It replaced the old transition team as well as the three districts and the two counties. Personnel were appointed from outside Pudong to minimize power struggles. The new authority was further strengthened by the exclusive status granted to it by the central government, above that of local urban bodies and special economic zones. Despite heading only one district, Pudong officials had the same status as the Shanghai municipal authorities. They were also responsible for a broader set of issues. For example, their trade mandate was more comprehensive than that of the national-level Ministry of Commerce.

Below the Pudong New Area Administrative Committee, development companies and their subsidiaries were set up as implementing agencies for the development in each zone. These development companies handled land transfers, dealt with private investors and communicated with government. They also established subsidiaries to manage different phases of land and infrastructure development. Although there were drawbacks, this two-tiered administrative structure made it easier to handle the process.

Urban planning was given top priority during the development of Pudong, and an integrated and hierarchical approach was followed. The Master Plan for Pudong New Area (1992) articulated the strategy. In accordance with this Master Plan, a series of follow-up plans were prepared for each development zone, specifying functions, zoning criteria and urban design principles. In addition, detailed plans were prepared and put into effect for key areas. The process was characterized by a high degree of openness, including consultations and competition. Planning became a communication tool used to forge a consensus among stakeholders, attract investors and inform the population.

Sources: Based on Chen (2007); Yang (2017); Zhao (2017); Zhao and Shao (2008).

---

revitalize not only Shanghai, but also other peripheral cities. Deng Xiaoping called Pudong "our trump card" to reinvigorate the whole Yangtze River basin. The project received substantial and consistent support from the central government, and it captured the imagination of both the domestic private sector and international players.

Toward Great Dhaka • http://dx.doi.org/10.1596/978-1-4648-1238-5

A new paradigm eastward

Each city has its own history and culture and has gone through its own development process. Each city faces its own unique set of problems as well. Therefore, an approach that proves successful in one city may not be mechanically replicated elsewhere. Different strategies need to be formulated in different places, taking into account their geographical, economic and political circumstances. That said, strategic urban development approaches around the world also have much in common. They are often designed to deal with the same problem: taking advantage of urban land development to improve a city's competitiveness and livability.

From Pudong to East Dhaka

Shanghai's experience has several takeaways for Dhaka, starting with the national dimension of the undertaking. Like Dhaka in Bangladesh, Shanghai was and remains China's largest city, serving as its financial capital and contributing much to its economic dynamism. If apex cities fail, it is difficult for countries to succeed. As such, just as it was vital for Pudong's development to benefit from Deng Xiaoping's strategic push and consistent support, it is critically important for Dhaka's development to receive strategic attention from the highest quarters, framed as part of a national-level growth strategy.

Another takeaway is that nurturing megacities and developing secondary cities are not mutually exclusive choices. Shanghai's development was formulated as a strategy to reinvigorate the entire Yangtze River basin as well as other nearby coastal cities. Dhaka, like Shanghai, is also strategically located in a delta. It lies at the intersection of several emerging transport corridors, and it is the hinge linking Bangladesh's secondary cities. With its still relatively low productivity level, Dhaka has not been able to generate spillovers over a broader area, as megacities like Delhi have done. However, putting Dhaka on a different growth trajectory could change this reality, providing a new impulse for urban development across Bangladesh.

Shanghai's experience is also relevant to Dhaka because of the attention that was paid to the nuts and bolts of urban development. Pudong's transformation was built on large-scale, orderly investments, ranging from backbone infrastructure to commercial projects to residential housing and recreational facilities. These investments vastly changed the local landscape, offering the high-quality urban land sought by firms and households. Dhaka should also focus on critically important investments because it is an infrastructure-hungry city, much like Shanghai a quarter of a century ago.

Last but not least, Shanghai owes its success to its strong focus on policy innovations. In Pudong, priority was given to the high-value-added sectors such as information technology, financial services and logistics. This way, urban development could be combined with structural transformation.

Bangladesh's ambition to become an upper-middle-income country over a relatively short period of time requires sturdy drivers of growth. The ready-made garment sector and other manufacturing industries still dominate its economic landscape. The country needs to diversify its production and climb up the value-added ladder. The difficulties encountered in relocating the traditional heavy-polluting industries, such as the Hazaribagh tanneries, out of Dhaka's urban core illustrate the challenges faced by economic upgrading in West Dhaka. But greenfield development in East Dhaka, building on the Pudong experience, may offer greater space for structural transformation.

Adapting to weaker institutions

The development of East Dhaka faces bigger institutional challenges than Pudong encountered. In Pudong, the urban development strategy was implemented by an empowered local authority with a high degree of autonomy and comprehensive responsibilities. Executive positions were filled by drawing talent from around the country. By contrast, the Dhaka CCs are weak. Responsibilities are fragmented, technical capacity is limited and financial resources are constrained. Multiple national-level agencies work with the Dhaka CCs in key functional areas, but with overlapping mandates and ineffective coordination mechanisms. The consequence is the partial implementation of plans and the weak enforcement of regulations—two traits that have historically contributed to Dhaka's messiness.

In East Dhaka, local governance faces an additional challenge: the recent institutional transition, whereby administrative authority was transferred in 2016 from 12 union councils to the Dhaka CCs. Because of the existing degree of fragmentation, a full institutional integration of East Dhaka with West Dhaka could take quite some time. And it may require adjustments not only in the structure of the Dhaka CCs, but also in other relevant national agencies such as the Dhaka Water and Sewerage Authority (DWASA).

Reforming institutions and creating empowered and capable local authorities are important for Dhaka's revitalization in the longer term. But this will be a protracted process, and in the meantime the risks in East Dhaka are growing as a result of unchecked development by private real estate investors.

Given the institutional constraints, it is worth considering whether a selected set of strategic interventions in East Dhaka could still put Dhaka on a better growth path. Such a set of interventions is likely to be a combination of "hard" and "soft" measures. Infrastructure projects are generally regarded as hard because they require large investments and tend to have irreversible impacts. Building the eastern embankment would be an example of a hard intervention. Policy reforms, on the other hand, are perceived as soft because they typically require smaller amounts of resources, they can be implemented gradually, and they can be adjusted along the way.

However, the institutional arrangements and administrative capacity needed to carry out these interventions could be ranked in reverse order. Conducting policy reforms can be much "harder" than implementing a public investment project (figure 4.1). Economic reforms require analytical clarity, a good grasp of complex political economy issues, and an ability to negotiate without compromising on the essential. Large infrastructure investments are easier to ring-fence, and they can be implemented by a dedicated project implementation unit.

Figure 4.1 Hard infrastructure is easier; soft reforms are harder

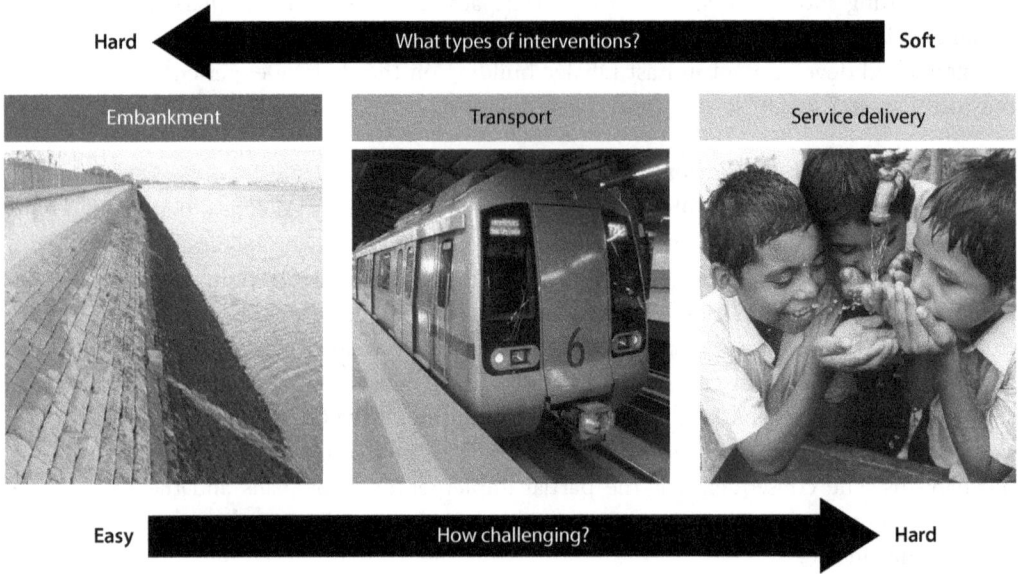

Sources: From left to right: © Peter Church and licensed for reuse under Creative Commons Licence. Wikimedia Commons, https://commons .wikimedia.org/wiki/File:DelhiMetroBlueLineMitsubishiRotem.JPG. Marko Kokic © International Federation of Red Cross and Red Crescent Societies. Used with the permission of International Federation of Red Cross and Red Crescent Societies. Further permission required for reuse.

Mimicking a strategic approach

With less empowered urban authorities and weaker institutional capacity than Shanghai, Dhaka is not well positioned to adopt a comprehensive urban development strategy in the spirit of the Pudong initiative. But the experience of the Hatirjheel project, which successfully transformed an important part of the city over a short period of time, suggests that an alternative approach could be feasible. Such an approach would involve focusing on just a few key interventions—some hard and some soft—that form a package coherent enough to mimic what a strategic approach would aim to accomplish.

To put Dhaka on a different growth path, such interventions would have to be bold in their scale. They would also have to address the three main challenges faced by Dhaka: flooding, congestion and messiness. Fortunately, key interventions meeting these two criteria have been identified in recent master plans and technical studies for Greater Dhaka.

In relation to *flooding*, the analyses conducted by the Institute of Water Modeling (IWM) show that the key intervention is to build the eastern embankment. To address *congestion*, the priority is to build the MRT and road network routes proposed for East Dhaka in the RSTP (DTCA and JICA 2015). Finally, to overcome *messiness* a combination of soft measures can encourage investments in high-value-added activities, upgrade service delivery and protect environmental assets in order to increase both the productivity and the livability of the city as envisaged by the Dhaka Structure Plan 2016–2035 (RAJUK 2015).

The government has an important role to play in relation to each of these three interventions. Flood prevention and mitigation measures, such as the eastern embankment, benefit large numbers of people but require lumpy investments up front. If left to market forces these investments will not be forthcoming because private investors cannot fully appropriate the gains and so have limited interest in these measures. Similarly, road network and mass transit infrastructure generates benefits for society that go beyond the reduction in transportation costs. For example, the value of properties around the network increases. But these are benefits a private investor would not be able to recover, which would result in insufficient infrastructure development. And the same applies to amenities and other services. Wetlands may be valuable to society, but private developers have a clear interest in encroaching on them.

The three interventions can be combined in different ways to generate urban development scenarios toward 2035. At one end, the least ambitious scenario assumes that current economic trends continue unabated. In what follows, this extreme scenario is called *business as usual*, or *scenario A*. Three more ambitious scenarios, inspired by the Pudong example, assume that key urban development interventions are undertaken. Even taken together, these interventions are not as ambitious as Pudong's approach. This more modest stance is intended to reflect the constraints posed by Dhaka's institutional setting.

Scenario A: Business as usual

This, the least ambitious of the scenarios, assumes that Dhaka will continue to be characterized by organic urban development. The city would continue to grow, despite the absence of key interventions. But population size, skills endowment, and productivity growth would remain on the same trajectory as they are now. Ongoing trends would make for a mightier and more affluent city over time, but they may fail to deliver a dramatic transformation. In addition, uneven service delivery, high disaster risk, irreversible environmental loss and land value capture by interest groups would remain unaddressed.

More specifically, in this business as usual environment, private-led real estate activities would be the dominant feature of East Dhaka's development. Because the public sector will not adopt effective measures for flood prevention and mitigation in this area, it is assumed that private investors will continue to fill low-lying areas with sand in order to reduce flood hazards. However, sand filling and construction without proper technical oversight do not result in high-quality urban land.

Progress on transport infrastructure will also be limited in this business as usual scenario. Following on current trends, the public sector is likely to partially implement the transport infrastructure projects proposed by the RSTP. For example, the provision of mass transit will likely see slow progress.

Finally, wetlands will not be appropriately preserved, and access to services will be mainly limited to the private housing projects in line with current developments in East Dhaka. Moreover, no concerted efforts will be made to stimulate high-value-added activities in the area.

Scenario B: Addressing flooding

The more ambitious *scenario B* calls for undertaking the "easiest" of the key interventions, involving hard infrastructure to dramatically reduce the flooding vulnerability of East Dhaka. In practice, this first key intervention involves building the eastern embankment, accompanied by the relevant auxiliary measures.

This intervention was already envisioned in section 8A of the Flood Action Plan. Subsequent studies and plans have confirmed the feasibility and effectiveness of the eastern embankment. In addition to mitigating flooding risks, this intervention reduces the areas subject to soil liquefaction because it makes sand filling unnecessary (BWDB 2017; DWASA 2015; Halcrow Group Limited 2006; World Bank 2016).

The specifics of this key intervention are mainly drawn from the IWM's technical study (BWDB 2017). According to the study, the eastern embankment would be about 26 kilometers long. It would be located on the west bank of the Balu River, all the way from the intersection of the Bangladesh railway with the Tongi Khal to the intersection of Balu River and the Dhaka-Narayanganj-Demra embankment project. Eleven regulators, three navigation locks and five pumping stations also need to be built.

In contrast with previous studies, the IWM study also calls for a reduction in retention ponds and the rehabilitation and protection of more canals. This recalibration, based on a thorough mapping of canals in East Dhaka, would result in greater natural retention and drainage capacity overall. While the rehabilitation and protection of flood retention areas and canals require hard investments, the preservation of wetlands need a strict enforcement of zoning regulations, which is more challenging. Therefore, the embankment intervention includes the rehabilitation of canals and protection of retention areas envisioned by the IWM study, but not the preservation of all wetlands in East Dhaka.

Scenario C: Addressing congestion

Dramatically reducing flooding in East Dhaka would likely attract many more households and firms to the area. In the absence of a substantial improvement in transportation infrastructure, congestion in this part of the city is bound to increase. This is why the even more ambitious *scenario C* envisions combining the construction of the eastern embankment with a key intervention aimed at addressing traffic congestion.

This intervention requires accelerating the investment in transport infrastructure in East Dhaka, with a focus on mass transit. The RSTP also must be tightly implemented, in contrast to the partial implementation in the business as usual scenario. In addition, investments related to East Dhaka, including all mass transit and road network projects, must be accelerated to accommodate the potential influx of households and firms and improve the links between East Dhaka and beyond. Segments of the MRT 1 and MRT 5 (15 kilometers) and the full bus rapid transport 7 line (22 kilometers) would be implemented. The eastern bypass highway (27 kilometers) and the Badda-Golakandial and Progati-Bhulta roads would also have to be built (DTCA and JICA 2015). These transport investments would make East Dhaka more accessible, especially by the poor, and connect it with the emerging Sylhet-Chittagong corridor.

Scenario D: Addressing messiness

One of the main takeaways of the Pudong experience is that the urbanization drive can be used to foster structural transformation. Building on the example of Shanghai, *scenario D* aims to mimic the strategic approach by squarely addressing messiness, in addition to flooding and congestion. This can be done through reforms that foster job creation in high-value-added activities, that boost the availability of amenities and that better protect the environment in East Dhaka. By including a soft intervention, typically more difficult to implement than the construction of hard infrastructure, scenario D is the most ambitious of all.

One of the goals of the soft intervention in scenario D is to reduce the cost of doing business for tradable services in East Dhaka. The tradable services sector includes high-value-added activities such as health care, logistics and finance, which employ large numbers of high-skilled employees. The Dhaka Structure Plan 2016–2035 and other studies have also pointed to the information and communications technology (ICT) sector as a potential driver of growth of the city's economy (Muzzini and Aparicio 2013; RAJUK 2015).

International experience suggests that a broad set of measures can be combined to this effect. The list includes direct support of land acquisition and development, the provision of targeted infrastructure, measures to reduce the regulatory burden and a direct reduction in corporate taxes. For example, in Bangladesh the corporate income tax rate applied to financial services is much higher than for other economic activities. Bringing this higher tax rate in line with the average would therefore translate into a cost reduction for the sector. As another example, the Dhaka Structure Plan 2016–2035 proposes policies such as bonus zoning to encourage private investment by specific sectors in certain locations.

Inspired by the Pudong playbook, in which a new central business district was founded next to the historic Bund district, the government should apply the cost reduction measures to a concentrated zone. An obvious candidate is the area across Pragati Sarani Airport Road, immediately to the east of the Gulshan commercial center and the Tejgaon industrial area. Because of the concentration of tradable services in Gulshan and Tejgaon, such a focused intervention would have the highest potential to attract businesses and form a new ecosystem.

Decent public services and nice amenities are also needed to attract and retain talent. The self-selection of households across locations accounts for from 40 to 50 percent of productivity differences across cities. And residential services and amenities are crucial in explaining where firms and households prefer to concentrate (Ahlfeldt et al. 2015; Combes et al. 2010).

Protecting the environment serves a similar purpose. But in addition to enhancing livability, ecosystems such as wetlands provide services with economic value.

In East Dhaka, wetlands contribute to flood mitigation, biodiversity, water purification and carbon sequestration. Unlike the embankment intervention in scenario B, the preservation of existing wetlands in East Dhaka would be fully implemented in this scenario.

The soft intervention in scenario D, with its emphasis on job creation, service delivery and environmental protection, is consistent with the government's aspirations. The Dhaka Structure Plan 2016–2035 envisages an improvement in the city's livability led by public efforts. Among them are providing more services, protecting the environment, preserving open spaces and recreation areas, and enhancing the urban landscape (RAJUK 2015).

An overview of the scenarios

All three key interventions considered are bold in their scale. But they all require specific institutional arrangements and enhanced administrative capacities. Because building an embankment is predominantly a hard infrastructure intervention, it is arguably the easiest to implement. Road and public transit construction is largely a hard infrastructure intervention as well. But because of the large number of agencies involved in road construction in Dhaka, a certain level of institutional coordination is required. For bus rapid transit (BRT) systems to function effectively, design and enforcement of traffic regulations are critical.

Finally, boosting job creation in high-value-added activities, improving livability and protecting environmental assets involve soft reforms. Therefore, the third key intervention will require the highest degree of coordination and the strongest institutional capacity. But Dhaka has a myriad of overlapping and competing authorities, with no effective coordination mechanisms in place, and plans generated by different agencies are at best partially implemented. These institutional constraints make it appealing to build on the experience of the successful Hatirjheel Lake rehabilitation project, where mandates were clear and strong coordination mechanisms were established.

Because of the implementation challenges posed by the three key interventions, moving from scenario A to scenario D involves a growing level of complexity (table 4.2). Between business as usual and a strategic approach along the lines

Table 4.2 Four development scenarios for Dhaka: from business as usual to a strategic approach

		(A) Business as usual	(B) Embankment	(C) Embankment + transport	(D) Strategic approach
Addressing flooding	One embankment and auxiliary measures				
Addressing congestion	Mass transit and wider roads				
Addressing messiness	More jobs, better amenities and preserved wetlands				

of the Pudong experience, there is a range of options to consider. In choosing their vision for East Dhaka, explicitly or by default, the authorities will be determining the growth trajectory that Greater Dhaka will follow.

References

Ahlfeldt, Gabriel M., Stephen J. Redding, Daniel M. Sturm and Nikolaus Wolf. 2015. "The Economics of Density: Evidence from the Berlin Wall." *Econometrica* 83 (6): 212789.

Ahmed, Shadman Sahir. 2016. "Relocation of Hazaribagh Tanneries." *Independent*, July 5. http://www.theindependentbd.com/printversion/details/50368.

Ali, Sohrab. 2007. "Gulshan Lake: An Ecologically Critical Area." *Daily Star*, October 19. http://www.thedailystar.net/news-detail-7950.

Arzaghi, Mohammad, and J. Vernon Henderson. 2008. "Networking Off Madison Avenue." *Review of Economic Studies* 75 (4): 1011–38.

Baldwin, Richard, Rikard Forslid, Philippe Martin, Gianmarco Ottaviano and Frederic Robert-Nicoud. 2011. *Economic Geography and Public Policy*. Princeton, NJ: Princeton University Press.

Banglanews24. 2015. "Take Action against Gulshan Lake Encroachers in 7-Day." http://www.banglanews24.com/national/article/41800/Take-action-against-Gulshan-Lake-encroachers-in-7-day.

Bhowmik, A. K. 2013. "Industries' Location as Jeopardy for Sustainable Urban Development in Asia: A Review of the Bangladesh Leather Processing Industry Relocation Plan." *Environment and Urbanization Asia* 4 (1): 93.

Blacksmith Institute. 2013. *The World's Worst 2013: The Top Ten Toxic Threats*. New York: Blacksmith Institute.

Brookings Institution. 2015. *Global Metro Monitor 2014*. Washington, DC: Brookings.

BWDB (Bangladesh Water Development Board). 2017. "Technical Study of Flood Control and Drainage Development at Dhaka Circular Road (Dhaka Eastern Bypass) Project, Conducted by Institute of Water Modelling (IWM)." Dhaka.

Chen, Yawei. 2007. *Shanghai Pudong: Urban Development in an Era of Global-Local Interaction*, vol. 14. Amsterdam: IOS Press.

Combes, Pierre-Philippe, Gilles Duranton, Laurent Gobillon and Sébastien Roux. 2010. "Estimating Agglomeration Economies with History, Geology, and Worker Effects." In *Agglomeration Economics*, edited by Edward L. Glaeser, 15–66. Chicago: University of Chicago Press.

Daily Star. 2016. "HC Moved to Protect Gulshan Lakes." http://www.thedailystar.net/city/hc-moved-protect-gulshan-lakes-573553.

Dhaka Tribune. 2017. "35% of Hazaribagh Tanneries Relocated to Savar." http://www.dhakatribune.com/business/commerce/2017/06/11/35-hazaribagh-tanneries-relocated-savar/.

DTCA (Dhaka Transport Coordination Authority) and JICA (Japan International Cooperation Agency). 2015. "Revised Strategic Transport Plan for Dhaka." Prepared by ALMEC Corporation, Oriental Consultants Global and Kathahira and Engineers International. Dhaka.

DWASA (Dhaka Water and Sewerage Authority). 2015. "Storm Water Drainage Master Plan for Dhaka City." Dhaka.

Fatemi, Mohammed Nawrose, and Tahmina Rahman. 2015. "Regeneration of the Hazaribagh Urban Brownfield: An Imperative for Dhaka's Sustainable Urban Development." *Urbani izziv* 26 (2): 132–45.

Fishman, Ted. 2005. *China, Inc.: How the Rise of The Next Superpower Challenges America and the World.* New York: Simon and Schuster.

Fujita, Masahisa, Paul R. Krugman and Anthony J. Venables. 1999. *The Spatial Economy: Cities, Regions and International Trade.* Cambridge, MA: MIT Press.

Halcrow Group Limited. 2006. "Updating/Upgrading the Feasibility Study of Dhaka Integrated Flood Control Embankment cum Eastern Bypass Road Multipurpose Project." London.

Khan, Anisur Rahman. 2016. "No Relocation Despite Taking Compensation: Legal Notice to Errant Tanneries Today; Amu Backtracks on Ultimatum." *Independent*, January 13. http://www.theindependentbd.com/post/30197.

Krugman, P. 1991. "Increasing Returns and Economic Geography." *Journal of Political Economy* 99 (3): 483–99.

Krugman, P., and A. J. Venables. 1995. "Globalization and the Inequality of Nations." *Quarterly Journal of Economics* 110 (4): 857–80.

Li, Yue, Martin Rama, Virgilio Galdo, and Maria Florencia Pinto. 2015. "A Spatial Database for South Asia." World Bank, Washington, DC.

Mahmud, Abu Hayat. 2013. "Gulshan Lake Development Bogged Down." *Dhaka Tribune*, November 23. http://www.dhakatribune.com/bangladesh/development/2013/11/23/gulshan-lake-development-bogged-down/.

Muzzini, Elisa, and Gabriela Aparicio. 2013. *Bangladesh: The Path to Middle-Income Status from an Urban Perspective.* Washington, DC: World Bank.

New Age. 2016. "Dumping Sewage in Gulshan Lake: HC Asks WASA to Report." *New Age*. http://newagebd.net/204063/dumping-sewage-in-gulshan-lake/.

Ovi, Ibrahim Hossain, and Shariful Islam. 2017. "You Will Have to Force Us Out of Here." *Dhaka Tribune*, April 6. http://www.dhakatribune.com/business/commerce/2017/04/06/tannery-owners-will-force-us/.

Rahman, M., and Y. Ara. 2016. "[Re]Structuring Dhaka through Water Urbanism: Visions, Challenges and Prospects." In *Dhaka 2012: An Urban Reader*, edited by M. Rahman, 101–22. Dhaka: University Press.

Rahman, Mohammed Mahbubur, and Sharif Shams Imon. 2017. "Conservation of Historic Waterfront to Improve the Quality of Life in Old Dhaka." *ArchNet-IJAR* 11 (2).

RAJUK (Rajdhani Unnayan Kartripakkha). 2015. "Dhaka Structure Plan 2016–2035." Dhaka.

Rice, Patricia, Anthony J. Venables and Eleonora Patacchini. 2006. "Spatial Determinants of Productivity: Analysis for the Regions of Great Britain." *Regional Science and Urban Economics* 36 (6): 727–52.

Rosenthal, Stuart S., and William C. Strange. 2008. "The Attenuation of Human Capital Spillovers." *Journal of Urban Economics* 64 (2): 373–89.

Roy, P. 2009. "Pollution Gets to Groundwater: Study Finds Hazaribagh Water Most Contaminated." *Daily Star*, April 26.

Ruhani, Rashid. 2017. "Tanneries Move, Waste Doesn't." *Dhaka Tribune*, August 20. http://www.dhakatribune.com/bangladesh/environment/2017/08/20/tanneries-move-waste-doesnt/.

Shaon, Ashif Islam. 2017. "SC Upholds Order to Shut Down Hazaribagh Tanneries." *Dhaka Tribune*, March 12. http://www.dhakatribune.com/bangladesh/court/2017/03 /12/sc-upholds-order-shut-hazaribagh-tanneries/.

UNIDO (United Nations Industrial Development Organization). 2006. "Preparatory Assistance in Relocation of Tanneries from Hazaribagh to Savar." Dhaka.

Venables, A. J. 2017. "Breaking into Tradables: Urban Form and Urban Function in a Developing City." *Journal of Urban Economics* 98: 88–97.

World Bank. 2016. "Unlocking Disaster Resilient: Urbanization of Dhaka East." Unpublished paper, Disaster and Risk Management Team, World Bank, Washington, DC.

Yang, Hongwei. 2017. "The Lessons of Pudong and Its Implications for Other Cities." Interview conducted by World Bank for this report, Shanghai, June 6.

Zhao, Qizheng. 2017. "The Case of Pudong and Its Development in China's Reform and Opening up." Keynote Speech, Towards Great Dhaka: International Conference on Development Options for Dhaka towards 2035, organized by World Bank for this report, Dhaka, July 18.

Zhao, Qizheng, and Yudong Shao. 2008. *Shanghai Pudong Miracle*. Beijing: China Intercontinental Press.

CHAPTER 5

Modeling City Growth

The growth of a city is influenced by locational advantages, but it is also affected by the ways in which economic agents interact across space. Whether productivity increases and livability improves depends on a delicate balance between agglomeration and congestion, two forces whose meanings are intuitively easy to grasp, but whose impacts are difficult to quantify and predict. In the absence of rigorous simulation tools, many discussions of urban development have been anchored in maps and storytelling, conveying the notion that they amount more to art than science. Today, however, a new literature is emerging in urban economics that brings more structure to the discussion of options for urban development.

New research in quantitative spatial economics mimics the behavior of firms—in deciding what to produce and where to do it—and households—in deciding where to live and where to work. Their decisions are reconciled through general equilibrium models, building on an older academic tradition. The main difference with this older tradition is that the new analysis allows study of both locational impacts and sectoral impacts. Indeed, the decisions made by firms and households determine variables such as population density, economic activity, the price of land and the level of wages and incomes for each geographic "cell," or neighborhood.

The new models are not just theoretical; they can be calibrated based on the observed level of variables such as population density and economic activity in each cell. Because of their meaningful connection with real city data, these models can be used to assess the consequences of different urban development options of interest to policy makers (Holmes and Sieg 2015; Redding and Rossi-Hansberg 2017). Until now, this approach has been mainly applied to cities in advanced economies.

Breaking new ground, a comprehensive computable spatial general equilibrium model is used in this report to assess the concrete urban development options for Dhaka (Bird and Venables 2017). The modeling approach is tailored to the city, emphasizing the characteristics of each location in relation to the three critical challenges faced by Dhaka—flooding, congestion and messiness. The approach is also rich enough to differentiate between high- and low-skilled households, between formal and informal housing, and between firms in sectors with different value-added potential.

The model is calibrated on granular data from around the year 2011. Greater Dhaka is divided into 266 cells, each corresponding to an actual union or ward. Detailed data on key variables at the cell level are taken from a spatial database for South Asia compiled by Li et al. (2015). The calibration allows one to infer the value of key variables that cannot be directly measured otherwise, including the productivity and livability scores of each cell.

Once calibrated, the model is used to study the effects of alternative urban development scenarios for East Dhaka. These scenarios range from business as usual to a more strategic approach inspired by the example of Pudong in Shanghai. In between these extremes, construction of the eastern embankment and a substantial upgrade of transport infrastructure are considered as well. Although the scenarios refer primarily to East Dhaka, their impacts are bound to be felt throughout the city. Households and firms may relocate, commuting patterns may change, and the sectoral composition of economic activity may evolve. Therefore, the simulations always assess the consequences of these urban development options for the whole of Greater Dhaka.

The new urban economics

Until recently, the theoretical literature on urban economics was limited to extremely simplified spatial settings. For example, locations within a city were modeled as points on a line, or on a circle. Within these simplified frameworks, some studies were able to offer convincing explanations for the concentration of activities and the growth of cities.

A wave of empirical research was stimulated by this theoretical literature, but overall the analysis has remained sketchy. As a result, it has been difficult to reconcile studies with reality. It has been equally difficult to shed light on the underlying forces at play, let alone simulate alternative scenarios in a meaningful way.

In recent years, however, a new branch of urban economics—quantitative spatial economics—has emerged to study the spatial distribution of activities. Unlike the early theoretical work, its objective is to explicitly incorporate spatial diversity into models. And in contrast to the previous empirical work, its goal is to move beyond partial effects, where some variables are allowed to adjust while others are artificially kept constant. The birth of this literature was facilitated in part by the growing availability of disaggregated spatial data and the rapid progress in computational power.

Studies of quantitative spatial economics draw on both the computable general equilibrium models of international trade and the tradition of economic geography. These studies are rich enough to accommodate concrete spatial features. They do so by including a large number of locations with diverse geographic, productivity, livability and other characteristics. They are also flexible enough to incorporate key spatial interactions such as trade, migration and commuting between locations. These studies are built on solid analytical fundamentals, but they are also tractable enough to match real urban data (box 5.1).

Box 5.1 The available studies are mainly of advanced economies

Research on quantitative spatial economics has advanced substantially in recent years (Redding and Rossi-Hansberg 2017). A noted study used a spatial model to assess the impact of the underground (metro) in Berlin (Ahlfeldt, Sturm and Wolf 2016). Another took a similar approach to quantifying the benefits from a reduction in commuting costs across cities in the United States (Monte, Redding and Rossi-Hansberg 2015).

Applications to developing countries are more limited, in part because of the paucity of spatial data. One notable exception is the assessment of the impact of railroad network expansion in India during the British Raj (Donaldson, forthcoming). Another important exception, and in fact a precursor of the work undertaken for this report, is the analysis of the possible implications of a large transport investment in Kampala, Uganda (Bird and Venables 2017).

Recent studies that build on quantitative spatial economics have shown that multiple urban equilibria may exist. The idea that the fate of a city was not just predetermined, but also depended on the vision and the actions of local authorities, had been a conjecture until recently. Now, however, the multiplicity of urban development outcomes has been revealed in quantitative studies of Berlin, Boston and the urban networks of France and Great Britain (Hornbeck and Keniston 2017; Michaels and Rauch 2016; Redding, Sturm and Wolf 2011).

A critical advantage of quantitative spatial economics, relative to the earlier literature, is its ability to generate predictions of the spatial distribution of economic activity. These predictions take the full equilibrium of the city into account, including the complex spatial interactions between locations through commuting, migration and trade. These interactions and general equilibrium effects were typically not identified in the previous literature. The tighter connection between economic theory and spatial data supports the quantitative evaluation of urban development policy and offers clear insights into the drivers of city growth.

Geography, firms and households

The spatial general equilibrium model of Dhaka developed for this report has three main building blocks. The first one is *geography*. The model allows for unprecedented spatial granularity by dividing the city into a large number of geographical cells. Each cell is characterized by its location, size and shape. The model is also flexible in allowing other factors to affect land supply, such as the flooding risk associated with the cell.

Interactions within this geography are captured by a description of the transport network and a quantification of commuting and transportation costs. For example, workers travel between their place of residence and their place of work, and their commuting costs depend on transportation mode, distance and type of road. Similarly, goods and services need to be delivered from firms to households, as well as between firms. Their transportation costs vary by the type of product carried. Like commuting costs, they also vary with mode of transportation, distance and type of road.

The second building block of the model is a description of economic activity. Production is undertaken by *firms* that choose how much to produce and how much labor, land and other inputs to use in the process. Critically, they also choose where to produce, looking at the costs in each location, accessibility to their customers and suppliers, and possible spillover effects from other firms.

Firms are classified into three sectors: manufacturing, nontradable services and tradable services. Firm size, input mix and location choice vary across these three sectors. The distinction between the two services sectors aims to capture the wide disparities in value added per person that exist between, say, street vending and tertiary education. Retail trade, personal services and informal sector production (nontradable services) are typically spread throughout the city, selling directly to residents and located near their homes and workplaces. Finance, business services and health care (tradable services) cater to customers across the city and outside of it.

The productivity of firms depends not only on the characteristics of their sector, but also on the vibrancy of the locations in which they settle. Positive productivity spillovers from other firms, or agglomeration economies, arise in clusters of economic activity. The strength of agglomeration economies in each spatial cell increases with the number of nearby firms belonging to the sector and decreases with the transportation time between the firms in the cluster (box 5.2).

Box 5.2 Modeling firms and production decisions: the details

In the model, each sector contains a number of firms, and each firm produces its own differentiated product, which it sells across the city. Firms in manufacturing and tradable services may also "export" their products outside the city. The costs of transporting goods and services between places are higher for nontradable services and lower for other sectors. Exports of manufacturing goods and tradable services pass through key access points to the city, at a fixed price.

Firms in each sector use land, labor and intermediate inputs. Food and primary goods are "imported" from outside the city, mainly by firms in nontradable services (retailers who use them as an intermediate input). Each sector is monopolistically competitive, meaning that the number of firms operating in each place is determined by profitability. In equilibrium, the number of firms adjusts until no abnormal profits are earned.

Production technology differs across the sectors. For example, the tradable services sector is the most intensive user of high-skilled labor, whereas the nontradable services sector is the least intensive. Within each sector there may be productivity differences across locations. These differences can stem from aspects of the infrastructure available in the cell. They are also influenced by agglomeration economies because the concentration of firms in a particular sector in a particular location tends to generate positive spillover effects between them (Duranton and Puga 2004). Differences in productivity can also stem from features that are not explicitly described in the model, such as better local governance.

Box 5.3 Modeling households and residential choices: the details

In the model, the total population of the city is constant in the short term, but it varies over time with both demographic growth and migration flows. If real income per capita in the city increases, then population from the surrounding areas is drawn into the city. Migration inflows and income per capita are linked through an elasticity of labor supply.

Each household in the city decides where to live, what type of housing to live in, how much housing to occupy, where to work, and which goods and services to consume. Commuting costs between locations are critically important in making these choices; they are modeled as a loss of real income, with the fraction lost being greater the longer the commuting time. There are also differences in livability across locations. They can be due to factors not explicitly described in the model, such as better residential amenities at the local level.

Two types of housing—modern and traditional—are built by developers, who influence the population density in each type to maximize the profits from their land. For modern housing, density is achieved by building tall structures, at no reduction in quality but at a higher construction cost. The technology of traditional housing is not amenable to building tall. But population density can be increased through "crowding," which reduces both the quality of living and households' willingness to pay for space. Housing construction of both types uses land, labor and intermediate inputs, but construction costs are lower for traditional housing.

The third building block is population and housing. *Households*, and their choices of where to live and where to work, are at the center of this building block. The model distinguishes between high-skilled and low-skilled households to account for the diversity of human capital across the urban population. Regardless of skill, all households derive their income mainly from employment and spend it on accommodation and goods and services produced in the city or imported from outside of it. Households also choose between two types of housing, modern or traditional, with modern housing delivering higher quality of living at a higher price. Households' decisions on where to live and where to work depend on rents, wages and the cost of commuting (box 5.3).

Deriving an urban equilibrium

The three building blocks of the model are connected by the prices, rents and wages that prevail in each locality. Consistent with the idea of a "general equilibrium," these three critically important connectors adjust to balance supply and demand—for goods and services, accommodation and land, and labor—at the level of each cell (figure 5.1). Markets for goods and services determine the prices of products from each sector in each place. Labor markets determine the wages for each skill type, and the land market determines rents for each type of land use. This set of prices, rents and wages reconciles decisions made separately by *firms* and *households*, and it does so across the *geography* of the city.

Land use is at the core of this spatial general equilibrium model. Land can be used for commercial production by firms, for residential housing by households,

Figure 5.1 Households and firms decide where to live, work and operate

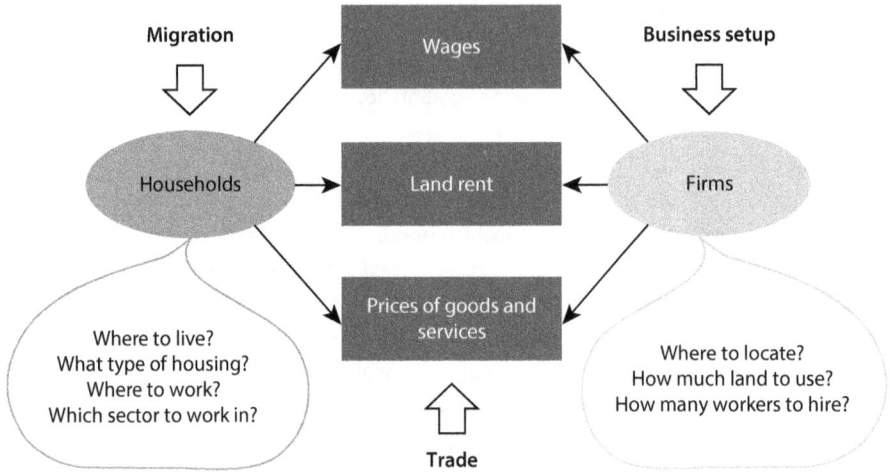

Source: Based on Bird and Venables (2017).

and for other activities such as agriculture. These competing demands are handled by allocating land to the uses that yield the higher rents. The model assumes a constant elasticity of substitution (CES) between land uses; the higher the elasticity the stronger is the intensity of competition between potential tenants.

In equilibrium, the type of land use varies across locations. Cells near the city's edge display a mix of agricultural and urban activities. As urban rents rise, the proportion of cells in urban use increases, enlarging the city's footprint.

To see how this general equilibrium works consider the effects of an increase in land supply in one particular place. For example, better flood control in a cell could make more of its land suitable for construction. Initially, the greater availability of land reduces rents in that place, attracting both households and firms to move in. This internal migration increases the local demand for land, pushing rents back up. The process continues until rents settle at a new level at which the supply and demand for land in each cell of the model are once again equalized.

Despite the bouncing back of rents in the area under consideration, there is now more land per household, and so workers are better off. How much better depends on the types of activities and households that move into the area. For example, if the additional land is occupied by firms that use high-skilled labor intensively, the wages of high-skilled workers will tend to rise more. A new cluster of activity may also form in the area, thereby increasing productivity and yielding additional beneficial effects for both high- and low-skilled households.

Some of these effects may not materialize in the short term. Adjustment costs could slow down the reallocation of firms and households, whereas regulatory frictions could limit the development of land for housing. Failure to consider these costs and frictions would produce rather naïve predictions of the extent of spatial reallocation following the increase in the local supply of land. If urban development suffers from inertia, the response to shocks could even be muted.

But in a city where regulations are weakly enforced and zoning is adjusted to reflect market dynamics rather than to guide it, the reallocation process is bound to happen over time. The new equilibrium can therefore be interpreted as a medium-term outcome.

The model just described is flexible enough to describe any city, but for it to be relevant to Dhaka it must first be localized. The baseline urban equilibrium should reproduce the specific characteristics of the city before it can be used to simulate urban development scenarios. This fitting is carried out in practice through a process called calibration, whereby disaggregated information on key variables at the cell level is used to infer the value of key parameters in the model. Calibration requires assembling reliable data on each of the three building blocks of the model.

Calibrating the geography

A metropolitan area generally consists of a central city and the surrounding areas linked to it through trade, commuting and other interactions. Therefore, the model needs to be calibrated to an area that is large enough to accommodate the interactions between the urban center and its suburbs and, at the same time, compact enough to delineate the city from the rest of the country. Greater Dhaka appears to be the appropriate choice in this respect.

Data on administrative boundaries

There have been various definitions of the exact area covered by Greater Dhaka. The definition used by the Dhaka Metropolitan Development Plan 1995–2015 (DMDP) is retained in what follows. It encompasses an area of 1,528 square kilometers, comprising an urban core as well as several satellite cities, towns and villages (RAJUK 1995). The definition is also suitable from a data perspective because the area has been well diagnosed by all the major urban development plans—the Dhaka Structure Plan 2016–2035, the Strategic Transport Plan 2005–2025 (STP) and the Revised Strategic Transport Plan 2016–2035 (RSTP) (DTCA and JICA 2015; Government of the People's Republic of Bangladesh 2005; RAJUK 2015)—as well as by hydrological and geological studies.

In the calibration, Greater Dhaka is divided into 266 unions or wards. The shape, size and location of these unions and wards are drawn from the administrative boundaries used by the Bangladesh Population and Housing Census 2011 (BBS 2011). Accordingly, 124 unions and wards belong to West Dhaka, whereas East Dhaka comprises only 12 of them. This asymmetry in administrative status reflects the unbalanced development of the city. The census even predates the expansion of the Dhaka city corporations (CCs) that took place in 2016. In 2011 East Dhaka was still governed mainly by union councils.

One of the 12 unions and wards in East Dhaka, union Matuail is crossed by the Dhaka-Narayanganj-Demra drainage project. This line separates East from West in the context of this report. For analytical purposes, union Matuali is therefore treated as part of West Dhaka.

Map 5.1 In the model, Dhaka is treated as 266 locations, with features from 2011 data

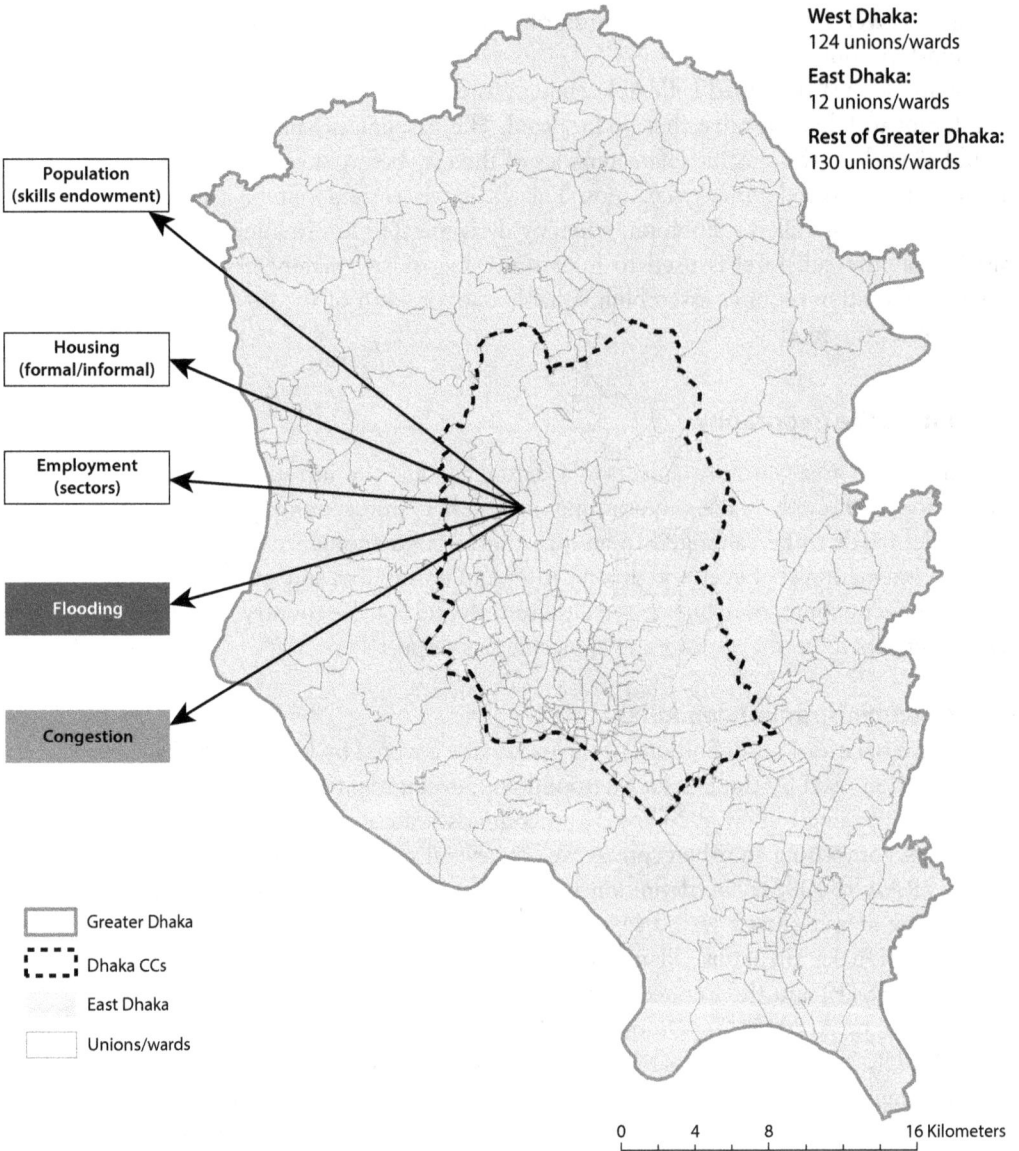

West Dhaka:
124 unions/wards

East Dhaka:
12 unions/wards

Rest of Greater Dhaka:
130 unions/wards

Population
(skills endowment)

Housing
(formal/informal)

Employment
(sectors)

Flooding

Congestion

Greater Dhaka

Dhaka CCs

East Dhaka

Unions/wards

0   4   8   16 Kilometers

Sources: Visualization based on BBS (2011); Bird and Venables (2017); and Li et al. (2015).
Note: CC = city corporation.

Dhaka's 266 unions and wards are described using data for the year 2011, or as close in time to it as possible (map 5.1). Most of the data were curated as part of a broader initiative by the World Bank, "The Spatial Database for South Asia" (Li et al. 2015). This georeferenced data repository integrates in a single platform information from traditional and modern data sources. Traditional sources include censuses, surveys and administrative data; modern sources rely on satellite imagery and crowdsourcing. Along the way, the database addresses the lack of sufficiently reliable and disaggregated information on the geographic boundaries of administrative units.

For the Bangladesh module of the spatial database for South Asia, over 500 indicators from 20 data sources were constructed, with the information presented all the way down to the *mouza* (a nonelective revenue collection unit consisting of one or several villages) and wards of cities. For a large number of indicators, information is also available by tiles of 1 × 1 kilometer. The construction of these indicators builds on close collaboration with the statistical agencies and research institutions in the countries in the region. In Bangladesh's case, the Bangladesh Bureau of Statistics (BBS) and the Institute of Water Modelling (IWM) were important sources of information and expertise.

Data on flooding and congestion

Each ward or union is characterized not only by its shape, size and location, but also by its infrastructure. Embankments, canals, ponds and pumping stations have an impact on the local probability of flooding. Highways, roads and mass transit are critical determinants of the severity of congestion in the area. Infrastructure is treated as part of the geography because neither individual firms nor individual households have the capacity to influence its design and construction.

A high flooding risk amounts to a reduction in the land that can be used in each union or ward. A relevant metric in this respect is the share of land that would be under water during a catastrophic flooding event and therefore not suitable for urban development. The primary data needed to estimate this share are derived from the hydrological model developed by the IWM (Zaman 2014). The model has been validated for over 14 hydrological years and has been used successfully in other studies of flooding hazards in Greater Dhaka (Dasgupta et al. 2015).

The approach used by the IWM consists of three steps. First, a model that reproduces the flows of the major river systems of the Ganges-Brahmaputra Delta is developed. Second, data from this basin-level model are used as an input for region-level modeling that simulates monsoon seasonal flows and water levels in the river networks in the Greater Dhaka area. Finally, the surface runoff flows generated by the previous step allow simulation of the water flows through drainage channels, including canals and ponds, in the Greater Dhaka area. The base year is 2004, when the most recent catastrophic flooding event took place.

This exercise can be used to estimate location-specific flood levels. Water depth during a catastrophic flooding event is computed as the difference between the predicted water level and the actual land level. A location is classified as "under water" if it is estimated to experience a water level more than 0.9 meters in depth during a catastrophic flooding event. The 0.9-meter threshold is set in accordance with the criteria of Bangladesh's Department of Disaster Management (DDM 2016). Based on this approach, the share of surface flooded during a catastrophic event reaches 71 percent in Greater Dhaka and 85 percent in East Dhaka.

Information on transportation infrastructure is critically important to determine the extent of congestion in each ward or union. Commuting times increase as the number of people commuting to or from the ward or union increases, as well as with the amount of goods and services ferried through the area. They decrease with the availability and the quality of infrastructure, both within the ward and across the city as a whole. An example of infrastructure availability is the existence of a road; a measure of its quality is the number of lanes it has. Commuting times are assumed to decrease as the road surface of the cell or the city increases (road surface is the distance covered by roads times the number of lanes of each road). Commuting times also depend on the mode of transportation used. High-skilled households are supposed to be motorized; low-skilled households are not, but they can use mass public transit systems if and when they are built. Goods are also assumed to be shipped around the city by motorized transport.

The transport infrastructure available at the ward or union level can be assessed based on maps in the RSTP for Dhaka (DTCA and JICA 2015) and OpenStreetMaps. The RSTP presents georeferenced information on the existing and planned transport infrastructure in Greater Dhaka. Its maps cover highways, mass transit, major bridges and bus stations; the RSTP maps also include district, primary and secondary roads, but not tertiary roads. For each road, information is provided on the number of lanes and on the status of construction (existing or planned). OpenStreetMaps, a crowd-sourced data repository, incorporates more information on smaller roads. In the calibration, data from OpenStreetMaps are used mainly to fill in the missing data on tertiary roads in the RSTP maps.

Wards and unions also connect via transport infrastructure to places outside Greater Dhaka. The city's imports of food and natural resources and exports of manufacturing products and tradable services pass through 15 access points (map 5.2). These include the international airport and the key nodes of major transport corridors. To the southeast, these corridors connect Dhaka to Chittagong; to the northeast to Sylhet; to the north to the Jamuna Multipurpose Bridge and Mymensingh; to the northwest to Manikganj; and to the southwest to the Padma Multipurpose Bridge (currently under construction), Jessore and Khulna. The share of traffic that goes through each of these access points is influenced by the transport time between the points and the ward or union where exports originate or imports are used.

Calibrating firms and households

The information needed to calibrate these other two key building blocks of the spatial general equilibrium model for Dhaka is taken mainly from traditional data sources such as economic censuses, population censuses and household-level surveys. An input-output matrix is also used to describe the technological relationships linking production sectors.

Assembling data on observable characteristics

Information on the level of activity of each sector of production in each cell of the model is drawn from the Economic Census 2013 (BBS 2013), which covers

Map 5.2 Several corridors connect Dhaka to the rest of the country

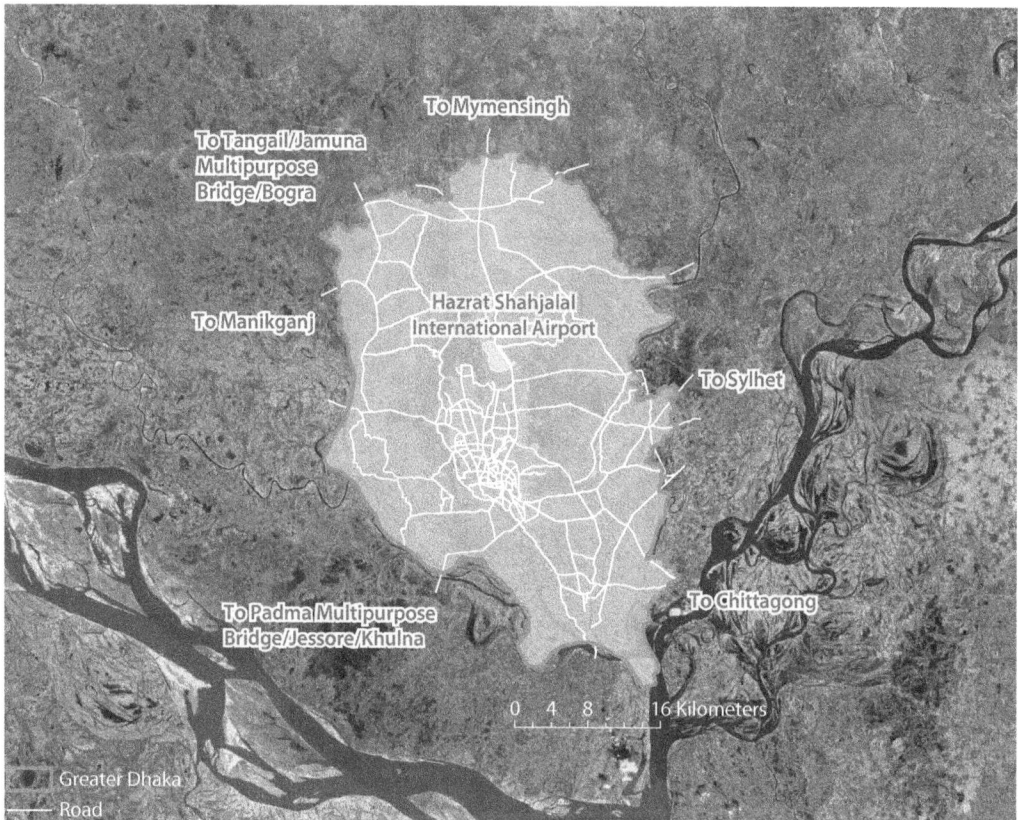

Sources: Visualization based on Bird and Venables (2017); DTCA and JICA (2015); and Li et al. (2015).
Note: Starting from the southeast and going counter-clockwise, the cities noted on the map are Chittagong CC, Sylhet CC, Mymensingh City Corporation (CC), Tangail Municipality and Bogra Municipality, Manikganj Municipality, and Jessore Municipality and Khulna CC.

both formal firms and informal establishments. For each of these economic units, the Economic Census reports an employment level, a four-digit industry code equivalent to International Standard Industrial Classification (ISIC) Revision 4 and a location. Using industry codes, all economic units can be classified into manufacturing, nontradable services and tradable services. Tradable services include finance, professional and business services, information services, hospitals, universities and transportation by air, railway and sea. Calibration also requires assumptions on the specific mathematical form of the relationship between inputs and outputs (box 5.4).

Information on population and housing in each cell is taken from the Bangladesh Population and Housing Census 2011 (BBS 2011). This data source reports the number of households, their educational attainment and their housing type, all by location. According to the census, the total population of the Greater Dhaka area in 2011 was 14.9 million. Roughly 70 percent of this population was of working age, defined as 15 years and older. Households whose heads

---

Box 5.4 Calibrating production and consumption functions

Drawing on the standard economics toolkit, production functions are of the constant elasticity of substitution (CES) type, with elasticity of substitution set at 0.8. This value comes from microeconomic analyses and follows a common practice in the international trade literature. The input shares for each sector are estimated based on the input-output matrices compiled by the Asian Development Bank for Bangladesh (ADB 2007).

Output also depends on a productivity factor that is specific to each sector and cell. This factor is influenced by the characteristics of the cell and by agglomeration economies at the local level. The functional form of the agglomeration economies is drawn from the urban economics literature.

Consumption choices are modeled using a two-layer approach. At the aggregate level, household well-being is linked to the consumption of manufactured goods, tradable services, nontradable services and housing through a Cobb-Douglas function. Consumption of each of the aggregate goods and services is, in turn, decomposed into the different varieties available through a CES function.

The Cobb-Douglas component ensures that the shares of income spent on each aggregate category are constant. These shares are estimated based on Bangladesh's Household Income and Expenditure Survey (BBS 2010). According to this source, households in Greater Dhaka spend 20.5 percent of their income on manufactured products, 10.2 percent on tradable services, 55.2 percent on nontradable services and food and 14 percent on housing. The elasticity of substitution between product varieties in each aggregate category is assumed to be 6.

---

reported that they had completed secondary or tertiary education are considered high-skilled and the rest low-skilled. As a result, 36 percent of the households of Greater Dhaka is characterized as high-skilled.

As for type of housing, *pucka* (good) dwellings are treated as modern housing and the rest as traditional. Living in a *pucka* dwelling is highly correlated with having access to water and sanitation facilities. Based on this criterion, 42 percent of the housing in Greater Dhaka is classified as modern.

The residential housing supply is supported by a construction sector that delivers both modern and traditional housing. For modern housing, the key parameter is the percentage increase in construction costs for every percentage increase in building height. For traditional housing, the key parameter is the percentage decrease in prices for every percentage increase in the crowdedness of the area. Following Henderson, Regan and Venables (2017), these parameters are set at 2 and 4, respectively.

Inferring productivity and livability scores

No direct information is available on two key parameters influencing decisions by firms and households. One of them is the productivity score of each location—a synthetic measure of the attributes of the cell that are not explicitly included in the model, such as the design of infrastructure or the enforcement of regulations at the local level. Other things being equal, firms would prefer to locate in cells with high productivity scores. The other key parameter is the livability score of a location. Characteristics of a cell not explicitly considered—such as the breathability of the air, the level of noise or the quality of amenities—make some locations more pleasant than others. Other things being equal, households would prefer to reside in cells with high livability scores.

Although productivity and livability scores at the cell level are not directly measurable, they can be inferred as part of the calibration process. Conceptually, the model can be used to predict the key variables given the characteristics and the productivity and livability scores. The calibration process works in the opposite direction. The key variables in each cell are observed, as are other characteristics of the cell. The productivity and livability scores of each cell are not observed, but in the calibration process the model is used to infer these scores based on the observed levels of the key variables and characteristics of each cell. Put differently, the calibration process yields the productivity and livability scores that make the solution of the model consistent with the observed distribution of firms and households across locations.

Productivity scores reflect the potential of unions and wards from the point of view of firms. One way to assess how suited a cell is for production is to compute the employment-weighted average of productivity scores across all the firms operating there (map 5.3). On the basis of this metric, the most productive cell in Greater Dhaka is about twice as suitable as the least productive one. As of 2011, the highest productivity scores could be found in West Dhaka.

Livability scores reflect the attractiveness of unions and wards as places of residence. One way to evaluate how attractive a cell is as a place to live is to compute the population-weighted averages of livability scores within the cell (map 5.4). Based on this metric, the most livable cell is about twice as attractive as the least livable one. The highest livability scores can be found around the border between West Dhaka and East Dhaka. They can also be found in the north (Savar Municipality) and in the south (Narayanganj CC).

Constructing the four scenarios

Calibrated around the year 2011, the model is tweaked to simulate four urban development scenarios for East Dhaka. This is accomplished by changing the values of key variables in ways that reflect the impacts the three key interventions considered would have on city dynamics. The four scenarios consist of a continuation of current trends (business as usual) and the adoption of three interventions aimed at addressing the three key challenges faced by Dhaka—flooding, congestion and messiness. These three interventions are introduced sequentially in order to identify the additional impact of each of them.

Map 5.3 The calibration of the model generates productivity scores by location

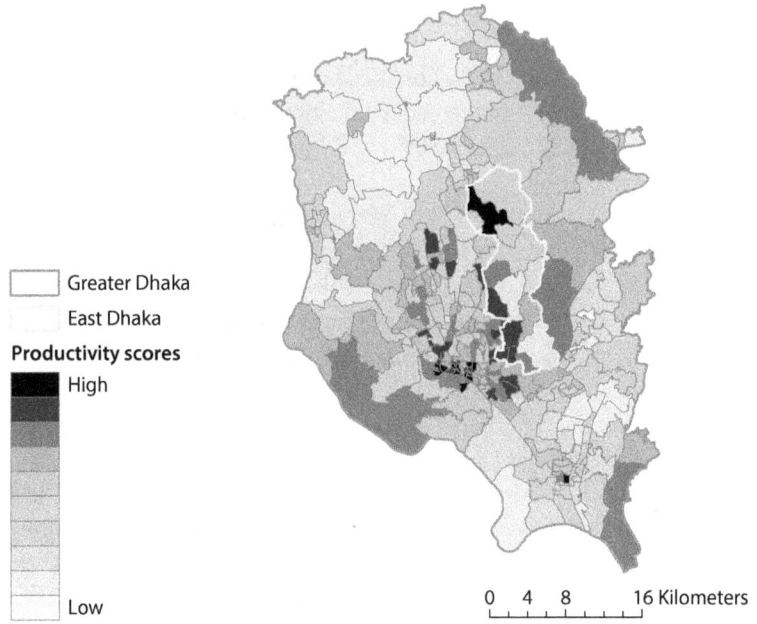

Greater Dhaka

East Dhaka

Productivity scores

High

Low

0   4   8   16 Kilometers

Sources: Visualization based on Bird and Venables (2017) and Li et al. (2015).

Map 5.4 The calibration of the model generates livability scores by location

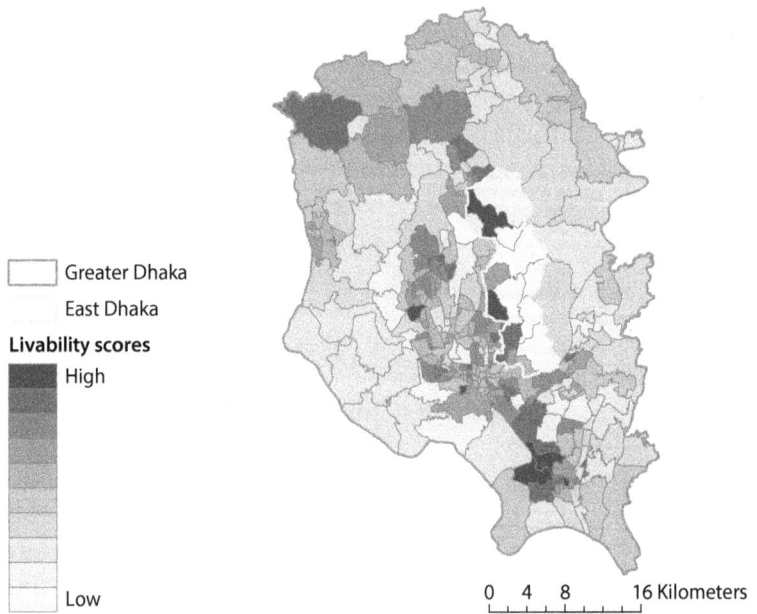

Greater Dhaka

East Dhaka

Livability scores

High

Low

0   4   8   16 Kilometers

Sources: Visualization based on Bird and Venables (2017) and Li et al. (2015).

Assessing Greater Dhaka's urban development in each of the four scenarios involves two broad steps. First, the key interventions are quantified as modifications of the geography of the city, or variations of parameters related to production and consumption, or changes in the distribution of productivity and livability scores across cells, or some combination of these. And second, with new values for some of the parameters and exogenous variables, the model is used to generate a new general equilibrium for the city. This equilibrium is characterized by the values of endogenous variables such as the location of firms and households, the production of goods and services, the type of housing built, and the set of prices, wages and land rent across cells.

Because of adjustment costs and regulatory frictions, it cannot be assumed that the new general equilibrium will be attained immediately. Even with accommodating or weakly enforced regulations, it takes time for households and firms to relocate across Greater Dhaka. Hereafter, it is assumed that the impact of the key interventions considered is fully felt in 2035, almost a quarter of a century after the calibration year.

Scenario A: Business as usual

The *business as usual scenario*, or *scenario A*, assumes that current economic trends continue unabated. This means, in particular, that no key interventions are adopted to address flooding, congestion and messiness. But this scenario still involves changes relative to the current situation, and these changes require adjusting the 2011 calibration of the model.

For example, the average schooling of Greater Dhaka's working-age population is bound to be higher in 2035 than it was in 2011. This will be so even if no key intervention is adopted because younger population cohorts have higher educational attainment and will be reaching working age during this period.

Based on the Dhaka Structure Plan 2016–2035, the population of Greater Dhaka is projected to grow at 3 percent a year, increasing from 14.1 million in 2011 to 24.6 million in 2035 (RAJUK 2015). By then, building on current school enrollment and completion rates, the share of high-skilled households is projected to be 40 percent.

Firms are also bound to become more productive over time, independent of the key interventions. The gross value added of Greater Dhaka is estimated to be US$57.7 billion (at 2015 prices) in 2011. But it is bound to grow as a result of greater population and higher productivity.

Based on historic trends, total factor productivity can be expected to grow by 1 percent a year (BBS 2011; RAJUK 2015). Although productivity gains are lower in agriculture, there is not a clear ranking of the gains across manufacturing, tradable services and nontradable services. Therefore, the 1 percent annual growth rate is applied to all three sectors in the model.

Geography is also bound to change relative to 2011. In the business as usual scenario, the development of East Dhaka is dominated by private-led real estate activities. Because no measures are adopted to address flooding, it is assumed that private investors will continue to fill low-lying areas with sand.

Based on current trends, the sand-filled area of East Dhaka is expected to increase substantially, with the total usable surface of East Dhaka reaching 66 square kilometers by 2035. However, sand filling and construction without proper technical oversight will not generate high-quality urban land.

Transport infrastructure will also likely improve over time, even if messiness is not squarely addressed. In the business as usual scenario, the public sector can be expected to partially implement the transport infrastructure projects proposed by the RSTP, with the pace of implementation remaining on its historical trend. The transportation projects included in the RSTP are divided into four five-year phases. In the business as usual scenario, it is assumed that investments between now and 2035 will be directed mainly at the projects in the first two phases.

Based on experience with the previous transport master plan, the Strategic Transport Plan, it is projected that the road upgrading foreseen in the first two phases of the RSTP is fully implemented, but the implementation is only partial for new construction and the provision of mass transit. As a result, approximately 1,200 kilometers of road lanes are built—a combination of widening existing routes and building entirely new ones—and 42 kilometers of bus rapid transit (BRT) routes and 60 kilometers of mass rapid transit (MRT) routes are established. Because of a lack of focus on East Dhaka in scenario A, it is assumed that no mass transit and only 192 kilometers of road lanes fall in this area.

The expected expansion of the transportation network in the business as usual scenario is modest compared with the growth of vehicle traffic. Population growth means there will be more daily travel journeys. And the growth will be stronger among high-skilled groups, who use motorized transport. With more people relying to a greater extent on vehicles in a context in which the road surface does not increase much, congestion is bound to worsen. In scenario A, there are twice as many vehicles per kilometer of road lane than at present, and travel speed in the city falls by half.

Finally, in the business as usual scenario the public sector will not take additional measures to make East Dhaka more productive or livable. The parts of East Dhaka that are currently developed are expected to maintain their economic potential (productivity score) and their residential attractiveness (livability score). The additional sand-filled surface is assumed to reach the same productivity and livability scores as the existing sand-filled area. But other parts of East Dhaka do not see their economic potential and residential attractiveness improve. And along the way, wetlands become vulnerable to encroachment by the private-led real estate development because they are not protected.

Scenario B: Embankment

The key intervention differentiating *scenario B* from business as usual scenario (A) is construction of the eastern embankment, together with adoption of the auxiliary measures described by the IWM's technical study (BWDB 2017). The eastern embankment, located on the west bank of the Balu River, would span about 26 kilometers, from the intersection of the Bangladesh railway and the Tongi Khal to the intersection of Balu River and the Dhaka-Narayanganj-Dembra embankment project. The auxiliary measures include the construction of 11 regulators, three navigation locks and five pumping stations. Retention ponds and canal rehabilitation and preservation are also part of the intervention.

In terms of the model, the construction of the eastern embankment and its auxiliary measures reduce but do not eliminate the risk of flooding for unions and wards in the eastern part of Dhaka. Location-specific water depth levels in the event of major flooding can be forecast using the same hydrological model as in the calibration process (BWDB 2017; Zaman 2014). As before, water depth is estimated as the difference between the predicted flood level and actual land level. A location is still classified as an area under water if its water level exceeds 0.9 meters in depth during a catastrophic flooding event. Overall, the biggest reduction in flood hazard from this key intervention is projected to be in East Dhaka and in the areas immediately to its north (map 5.5).

This lower flooding risk increases the usable land in East Dhaka by 36 square kilometers, resulting in a total of 102 square kilometers available for urban development by 2035. Also, building the embankment will make the land more productive

Map 5.5 Scenario B, addressing flooding: building one embankment and preserving canals and ponds

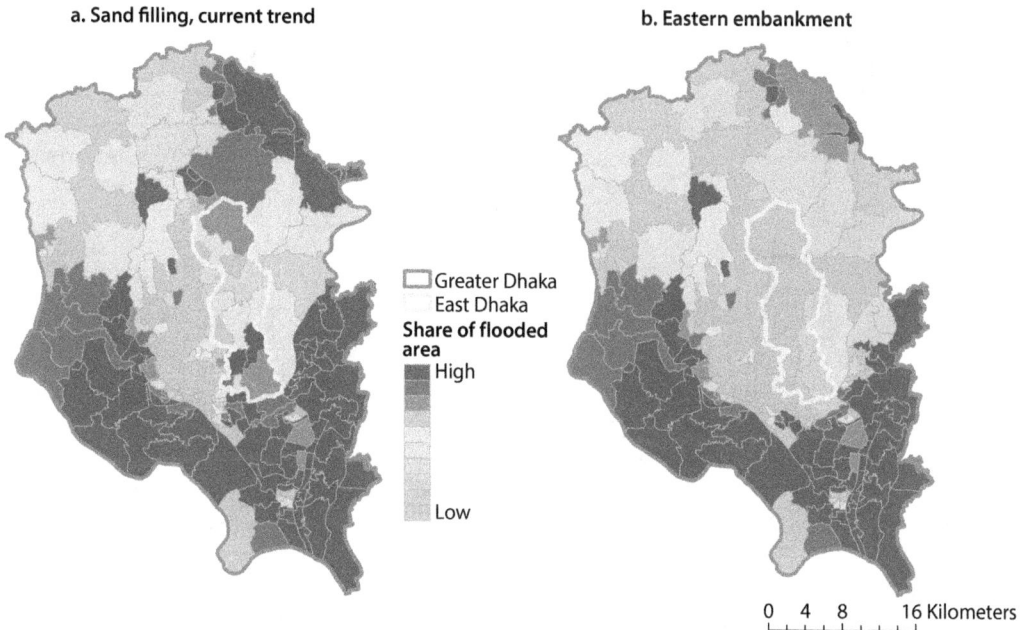

a. Sand filling, current trend

b. Eastern embankment

Greater Dhaka
East Dhaka
Share of flooded area
High
Low

0   4   8   16 Kilometers

Sources: Calculations and visualization based on BWDB (2017); Li et al. (2015); and Zaman (2014).

and more attractive than sand filling. It is therefore assumed that the productivity and livability scores of East Dhaka in 2035 reach the median scores observed in the Dhaka CCs in 2011. More specifically, the productivity score for manufacturing in East Dhaka increases by 8.7 percent, for tradable services by 5.3 percent, and for nontradable services by 2.9 percent. Similarly, the livability score increases by 9.5 percent for modern housing and by 6 percent for traditional housing.

Scenario C: Embankment + transport

The more ambitious *embankment + transport scenario*, or *scenario* C, aims to address traffic congestion in Dhaka, in addition to flooding risk. In practice, it amounts to accelerating transport infrastructure investments in East Dhaka following the RSTP, with a focus on mass transit.

This time, tight implementation of the first two phases of the RSTP is assumed, in contrast with the partial implementation characterizing the business as usual scenario. In addition, investments specified for the last two phases are assumed to accelerate if they are related to East Dhaka (map 5.6). The investments include all mass transit and road network projects located in East Dhaka—such as segments of the MRT 1 and MRT 5, the full BRT 7 line, and the eastern bypass highway. They also include projects connecting East Dhaka to

Map 5.6 Scenario C, addressing congestion: embracing mass transit and building more and wider roads

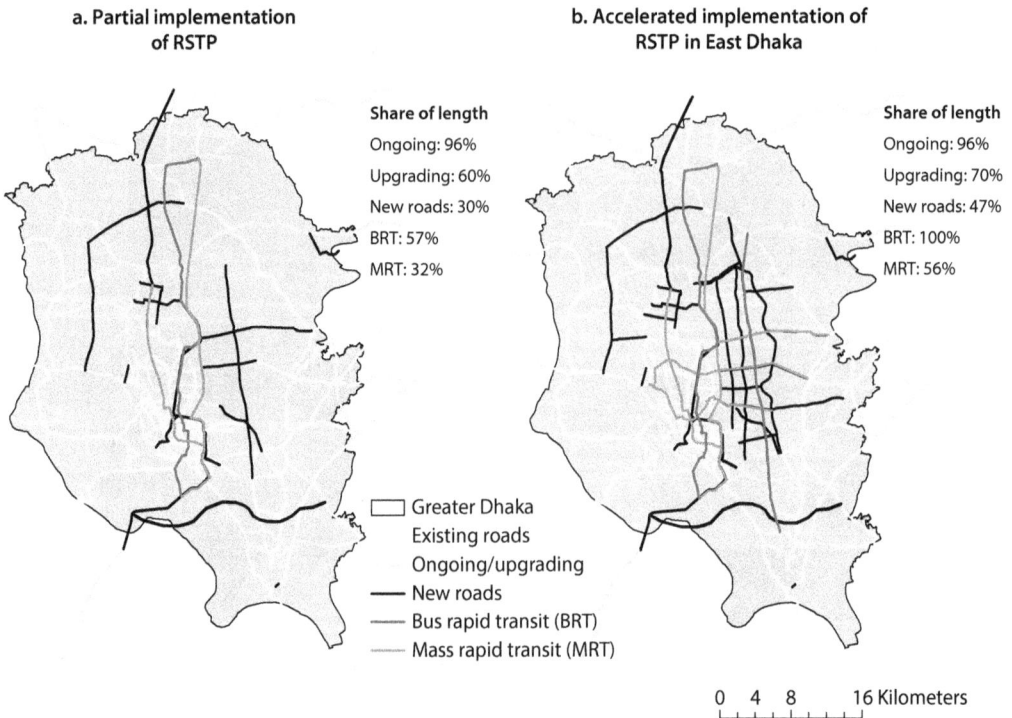

a. Partial implementation of RSTP	b. Accelerated implementation of RSTP in East Dhaka

Share of length (a):
Ongoing: 96%
Upgrading: 60%
New roads: 30%
BRT: 57%
MRT: 32%

Share of length (b):
Ongoing: 96%
Upgrading: 70%
New roads: 47%
BRT: 100%
MRT: 56%

☐ Greater Dhaka
Existing roads
Ongoing/upgrading
— New roads
— Bus rapid transit (BRT)
— Mass rapid transit (MRT)

0   4   8   16 Kilometers

Sources: Calculations and visualization based on DTCA and JICA (2015), and Li et al. (2015).
Note: BRT = bus rapid transit; MRT = mass rapid transit; RSTP = Revised Strategic Transport Plan.

emerging corridors, such as the Badda-Golakandial and Pragati-Bhulta roads in the east-west direction, linking to Sylhet and Chittagong.

By design, the most ambitious investment of this second intervention is in mass transit. In terms of length, the implementation rate in the RSTP for the BRT is projected to increase from 57 percent in the business as usual scenario to 100 percent. The implementation rate for the MRT is supposed to increase from 32 to 56 percent. Overall, this scenario entails the construction of 32 kilometers of additional BRT routes, 50 kilometers of extra MRT lines, and nearly 1,000 kilometers of new road lanes. These investments are in addition to those already considered in the business as usual scenario.

Scenario D: Strategic approach

Finally, the *strategic approach scenario*, or *scenario D*, moves even closer to the example of Pudong in Shanghai. In addition to addressing the flooding and congestion challenges, as in the embankment + transport scenario (C), the strategic approach aims to address the messiness challenge. It does so through soft reforms intended to create more jobs in high-value-added activities, to upgrade urban amenities and service delivery, and to protect the environment. These soft reforms are directed at East Dhaka and, in some cases, at specific cells inside it.

The job creation component of this scenario involves reducing the cost of doing business for the tradable services sector in East Dhaka. From an economic perspective, this is the sector with the highest value added. Supporting its development is consistent with the experience of Shanghai, which converted Pudong into a global financial center. From a spatial perspective, the idea is to foster the emergence of a new economic hub in the area. This may be necessary to boost agglomeration economies at the local level, encouraging a substantial reallocation of economic activity and high-skilled labor across Greater Dhaka. The hub can be interpreted as a new central business district.

In practice, the model is adjusted so that one union in East Dhaka becomes the focus of the intervention. Inspired by the example of Pudong, where a new central business district was established next to the historical Bund district, the union selected sits across the Pragati Sarani Airport Road, immediately to the east of the Gulshan commercial center and the Tejgaon industrial area. The union covers 4.9 square kilometers. Because of the concentration of tradable services in Gulshan and Tejgaon, this union would have the highest potential to tap into existing agglomeration economies, leading to more and better jobs. In view of its lower cost of doing business and its better-serviced land, this union would resemble Pudong more than Gulshan.

For simulation purposes, the union selected sees its productivity score for tradable services become as high as that of the best union in Dhaka. In addition, production costs for the tradable services sector in this particular union decline by a further 20 percent (table 5.1). For example, the current corporate income tax rates in Bangladesh penalize sectors with high value added relative to other sectors. The corporate income tax rate is 25 percent for publicly traded companies and 35 for the rest. But it is as high as 37.5 percent for merchant banks,

Table 5.1 Scenario D, addressing messiness: soft reforms, better services and wetland preservation

	(A) Business as usual	(B) Embankment (C) Embankment + transport	(D) Strategic approach
Jobs	Productivity scores in East Dhaka remain the same as in 2011, except for the new sand-filled areas whose productivity score matches that of existing sand-filled areas.	The productivity scores of all unions in East Dhaka increase to the same level as the median productivity score of the Dhaka CCs.	One union of East Dhaka becomes as productive for tradable services as the "best" union in Dhaka; production costs in that union are reduced by an additional 20 percent.
Amenities	Livability scores in East Dhaka remain as they were in 2011, except for the new sand-filled areas, whose livability scores match those of the existing sand-filled areas.	The livability scores of all unions in East Dhaka increase to the same level as the median livability score of the Dhaka CCs.	The livability scores for modern housing in all unions in East Dhaka increase to the same level as that of the top 20 percent of unions in the Dhaka CCs.
Environment	Wetlands in East Dhaka are partially preserved as part of the embankment intervention.	Wetlands in East Dhaka are partially preserved as part of the embankment intervention.	Wetlands in East Dhaka are fully preserved.

Source: Bird and Venables (2017).
Note: CC = city corporation.

40–42.5 percent for banking, insurance and financial companies, and 40–45 percent for mobile phone operators (NBR 2017). Bringing the tax of these high-value-added sectors down to the average for the economy would be a way to implement the reduction in production costs. In the same spirit, the social security contributions of formal workers could be subsidized in the district selected, and the red tape could be reduced.

The strategic approach also includes an effort to improve the livability of East Dhaka, encouraging the building of modern housing, so that it is more attractive to the high-skilled households who typically work in high-value-added services. Making East Dhaka more livable involves providing basic services, which results in improved urban amenities. In terms of the model, this is accomplished by raising the livability scores for modern housing in East Dhaka to the same level observed in the top quintile of unions across the Dhaka CCs.

Making East Dhaka more livable also involves better protection of the environment. One of the salient features of the area in this respect is the abundance of natural wetlands. In fact, the key intervention in the embankment scenario is expected to reduce the flooding risk more substantially if zoning can be enforced and canals and other natural wetlands can be better preserved. Meanwhile, wetlands are also a source of environmental services and a shield for biodiversity, and their preservation should make East Dhaka a better place.

In the simulation, all existing wetlands in East Dhaka—including rivers, canals and retention ponds—are maintained as they are in 2017 and are not used for urban development (World Bank 2018). Consequently, in the strategic approach the amount of usable land decreases by 12 square kilometers compared with the embankment and the embankment + transport scenarios. Overall, only 90 square kilometers are available for urban development in East Dhaka under the strategic approach.

References

ADB (Asia Development Bank) 2007. "Bangladesh Input-Output Tables, 2006: Model B." Industry Technology Assumption.

Ahlfeldt, G., D. M. Sturm and N. Wolf. 2016. "The Quantitative Evaluation of Urban Transport Infrastructure Improvements." Unpublished paper, London School of Economics.

BBS (Bangladesh Bureau of Statistics). 2010. "Household Income and Expenditure Survey (HIES)—2010." Statistics and Informatics Division, Ministry of Planning, Government of the People's Republic of Bangladesh.

———. 2011. "Bangladesh Population and Housing Census 2011." Statistics Division, Ministry of Planning, Government of the People's Republic of Bangladesh.

———. 2013. "Economic Census 2013." Statistics and Informatics Division, Ministry of Planning, Government of the People's Republic of Bangladesh.

Bird, Julia, and Anthony J. Venables. 2017. "Growing a developing city: A Computable Spatial General Equilibrium Model Applied to Dhaka." Background paper prepared for this report.

BWDB (Bangladesh Water Development Board). 2017. "Technical Study of FCD Development at Dhaka Circular Road (Dhaka Eastern Bypass) Project." Study conducted by Institute of Water Modelling, Dhaka.

Dasgupta, Susmita, Asif Zaman, Subhendu Roy, Mainul Huq, Sarwar Jahan and Ainun Nishat. 2015. *Urban Flooding of Greater Dhaka in a Changing Climate: Building Local Resilience to Disaster Risk*. Directions in Development. Washington, DC: World Bank.

DDM (Department of Disaster Management). 2016. "Hydro-Meterological Hazard, Exposure/Risk Assessment (Flood and Storm Surge)." In *Risk Atlas: Multi-Hazards Risk and Vulnerability Assessment, Modeling and Mapping*, vol. 1. Dhaka: Ministry of Disaster Management and Relief, Government of the People's Republic of Bangladesh.

Donaldson, D. Forthcoming. "Railroads of the Raj: Estimating the Impact of Transportation Infrastructure." *American Economic Review*.

DTCA (Dhaka Transport Coordination Authority) and JICA (Japan International Cooperation Agency). 2015. "Revised Strategic Transport Plan for Dhaka." Prepared by ALMEC Corporation, Oriental Consultants Global and Kathahira and Engineers International, Dhaka.

Duranton, G., and D. Puga. 2004. "Micro-foundations of Urban Agglomeration Economies." In *Handbook of Regional and Urban Economics*, edited by J. V. Henderson and J. F. Thisse, vol. 4, 2063–117. Amsterdam: Elsevier, North-Holland.

Government of the People's Republic of Bangladesh. 2005. "Strategic Transport Plan for Dhaka." Prepared by Louis Berger Group Inc., Bangladesh Consultants Ltd., Dhaka.

Henderson, J. V., T. Regan and A. J. Venables. 2017. "Building the City: Urban Transition and Institutional Frictions." Discussion Paper 11211, Centre for Economic and Policy Research, Washington, DC.

Holmes, T. J., and H. Sieg. 2015. "Structural Estimation in Urban Economics." In *Handbook of Regional and Urban Economics*, vol. 5, edited by Gilles Duranton, Vernon Henderson, and William Strange, 69–114. Amsterdam: Elsevier.

Hornbeck, Richard, and Daniel Keniston. 2017 "Creative Destruction: Barriers to Urban Growth and the Great Boston Fire of 1872." *American Economic Review* 107 (6): 1365–98.

Li, Yue, Martin Rama, Virgilio Galdo and Maria Florencia Pinto. 2015. "A Spatial Database for South Asia." World Bank, Washington, DC.

Michaels, G., and F. Rauch. 2016. "Resetting the Urban Network: 117–2012." *Economic Journal* (September).

Monte, F., S. J. Redding and E. Rossi-Hansberg. 2015. "Commuting, Migration and Local Employment Elasticities." w21706, National Bureau of Economic Research, Cambridge, MA.

NBR (National Board of Revenue, Bangladesh). 2017. "Income Tax at a Glance 2017–2018." http://nbr.gov.bd/uploads/publications/107.pdf.

RAJUK (Rajdhani Unnayan Kartripakkha). 1995. "Dhaka Metropolitan Development Plan 1995–2015." Dhaka.

———. 2015. "Dhaka Structure Plan 2016–2035." Dhaka.

Redding, Stephen J., and Esteban A. Rossi-Hansberg. 2017. "Quantitative Spatial Economics." *Annual Review of Economics* 9 (1). http://www.annualreviews.org/doi/abs/10.1146/annurev-economics-063016-103713?journalCode=economics.

Redding, Stephen J., Daniel M. Sturm and Nikolaus Wolf. 2011. "History and Industry Location: Evidence from German Airports." *Review of Economics and Statistics* 93 (3): 814–31.

World Bank. 2018. "Unlocking Opportunities for Clean and Resilient Growth—Bangladesh Country Environmental Analysis." PowerPoint presentation, Washington, DC.

Zaman, A. M. 2014. "Assessment of Consequences of Climate Change for Urban Flooding: Hydrological Modelling—Final Report." Bangladesh Climate Change Resilience Fund (BCCRF), World Bank, Washington, DC.

CHAPTER 6

Dhaka in 2035

A city's growth can deliver on multiple fronts. By bringing together firms and households, cities amplify the possibilities for prosperity, innovation and competitiveness. By absorbing migrants, offering jobs and stimulating interactions, they hold the promise of mobility and inclusion. Cities also have the potential to reduce the human footprint on the environment by making it possible to lower the unit costs of energy, infrastructure and services (UN DESA 2013; UN-Habitat 2012; World Bank 2015).

In the United States, New York City rose to its status as a world economic center in the late 19th century. With a total economic output of over US$1.5 trillion—the economic size of Canada—and income per capita of over US$70,000 in 2016, the New York metropolitan area continues to be cited as the most prosperous and competitive city by international rankings. New York is also well known for attracting immigrants and thriving from their talents and diversity. Currently, close to 40 percent of New York's residents hail from over 150 nations in virtually every region of the world. The metropolitan area hosts about 20 million people—with the city itself home to 8.5 million (BEA 2015; Brookings Institution 2015; *Economist* 2014; Hymowitz 2016; Mainelli, Yeandle and Knapp 2017; New York State Comptroller 2016; Open Data Network 2017).

In China, Shanghai has thrived since the late 20th century, when the development of Pudong New District took shape. Posting a total economic output of over US$335 billion—nearly US$600 billion in purchasing power parity (PPP) terms in 2014—and income per capita of about US$13,500—comparable to that of Portugal—Shanghai is, according to several major studies, among the top 20 cities globally. The city has invested heavily in connectivity with China's hinterland, and it attracts labor and talent from all over the country: 40 percent of its residents and 50 percent of its most productive labor force are from elsewhere in China. The Shanghai metropolitan area now hosts over 23 million people (Brookings Institution 2015; *Economist* 2014; Lall and Procee, forthcoming; Mainelli, Yeandle and Knapp 2017; Shanghai Pudong New Area Statistical Bureau and Pudong Survey Team of National Statistics Bureau 2016; UN-Habitat 2012).

What will Dhaka's growth deliver in the first half of the 21st century? The answer to this question depends on how the city approaches the development of its eastern part. That decision will be similar to those that shaped the spectacular growth of New York and Shanghai earlier on. In 1881 the commissioners of New York projected the expansion of their city from the southern tip of the island of Manhattan all the way to its north, through a grid of 155 streets. In 1991 Shanghai embarked on the development of Pudong, a mainly rural area to its east, next to the most valuable parts of the city. Dhaka's development path over the next 20 years and beyond will likewise depend on the urban development choices the city makes today.

An important difference with those historic precedents is that tools are now on hand to assess the impact of urban development choices in a quantitative way, with relatively high precision and with rich spatial granularity. The model developed and calibrated for Dhaka can be used to simulate outcomes from several scenarios, all the way from business as usual to a more strategic approach inspired by the Pudong experience. The strategic approach involves building the eastern embankment with the associated measures, establishing a modern transport network (including mass transit), and reducing the cost of doing business, especially for high-value-added sectors. Not only is this approach the most ambitious, but it also reaps the biggest rewards, leading to a much more prosperous and sustainable city than the business as usual scenario.

A more prosperous city

Continuing with business as usual (*scenario A*), the overall size, skill composition and productivity of Greater Dhaka are determined by its recent trajectory. In the projection in the Dhaka Structure Plan 2016–2035 (RAJUK 2015), the city's total population is supposed to reach 24.6 million in 2035, the equivalent of 2.3 percent growth a year from 2011. Over the same period, greater educational attainment among younger cohorts raises the high-skilled share of the population to 40 percent. Productivity also grows across all sectors, at a rate of 1 percent a year.

These increases in total population, in the share of the high-skilled in the population, and in productivity can be fed into the version of the spatial equilibrium model for Greater Dhaka that was calibrated with data from around 2011. Other changes relative to 2011 are private-led sand filling for flood mitigation and some modest improvements in urban transport. The previously calibrated productivity and livability scores of most areas of the city remain the same. And the additional sand-filled surface in East Dhaka is assumed to reach the same productivity and livability scores as the existing sand-filled area. But other parts of East Dhaka do not see their economic potential or residential attractiveness improve.

More ambitious urban development scenarios are constructed incrementally. They entail first building the eastern embankment and associated measures (*scenario B*); then establishing a modern transport network, including mass transit (*scenario C*); and finally reducing the cost of doing business, especially for high-value-added sectors, providing broad-based services, and preserving existing wetlands (*scenario D*). These interventions are location-specific, and they occur in addition to the aggregate trends in the share of high-skilled households and in productivity growth.

The four urban development scenarios considered have diverse impacts on the sectoral structure of economic activity, as well as on the spatial distribution of firms and households across the city. They also have varying impacts on the welfare of residents in ways that are consistent with the number of people the city is supposed to attract.

More and better living space

A key difference among the four scenarios is the amount of land available for firms and households. In the business as usual scenario, the total amount of urban land increases only through private sand filling. In the other scenarios, however, the construction of the eastern embankment and auxiliary measures substantially reduce the probability of flooding in East Dhaka, which amounts to a large increase in the amount of land that can be used for urban development. As the embankment and other key interventions are implemented, the quality of that land improves. Meanwhile, in response to the gradual upgrading in the quantity and quality of land, the total population of the city increases and spreads out differently across West Dhaka, East Dhaka and the rest of Greater Dhaka (figures 6.1 and 6.2).

In the *business as usual scenario (A)*, people continue flocking into highly dense West Dhaka, which intensifies the pressure faced by the existing urban land, infrastructure and services. By 2035, this area is home to about 12.7 million people, or over half of Greater Dhaka's population. And it reaches a density of 64,900 people per square kilometer. East Dhaka, with its lower-quality land subject to flood risks and with its poor access to transport, hosts a little less than 1.6 million people and registers a density of 14,500 people per square kilometer. The share of high-skilled households in the total population is also lower in East Dhaka than in the rest of the city.

In the *embankment scenario (B)*, the more abundant, higher-quality land in East Dhaka creates space for firms to relocate and for households to move in, relieving population pressure in West Dhaka. The additional land available initially reduces rents in the area. In addition, the new land is flood-resilient and thus of higher quality than the private-led sand-filled areas in the business as usual scenario. The consequences of better land quality are simulated through higher productivity and livability scores. Lower rents, together with higher productivity and livability, boost the demand for land in East Dhaka, both by firms seeking greater profitability and by households aspiring to a better quality of life.

East Dhaka can accommodate a larger and more skilled population if developed in a more orderly fashion relative to the current unchecked manner of private sand filling. In the embankment scenario, the population of Greater

Figure 6.1 Key interventions accelerate population growth in East Dhaka, especially for high-skilled households

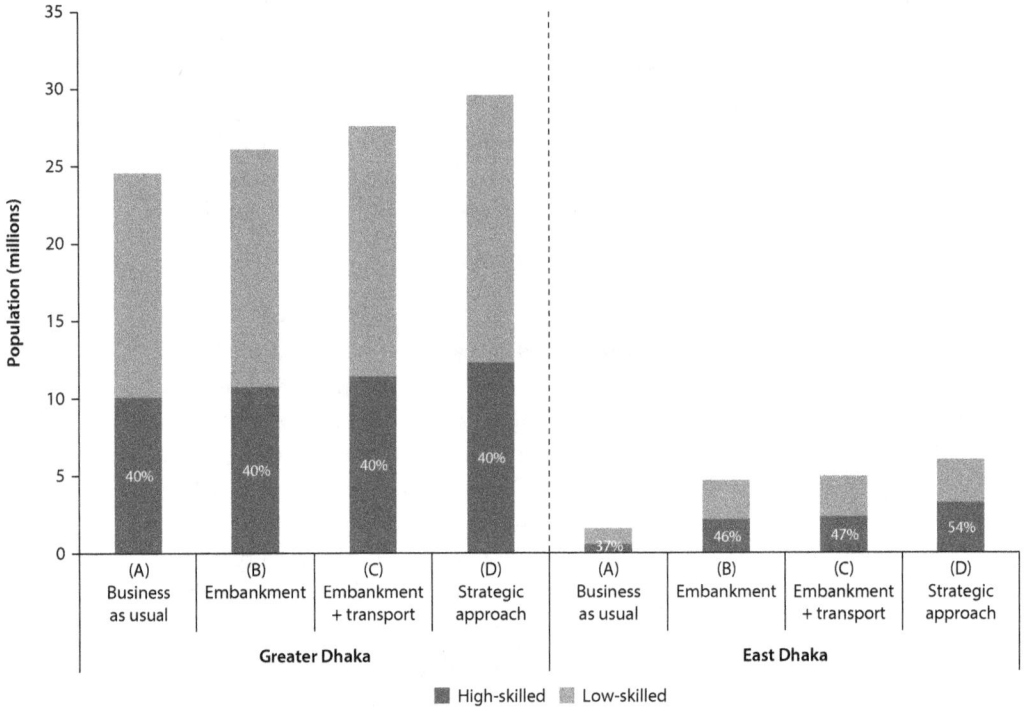

Source: Based on Bird and Venables (2017).
Note: The bars represent the high- and low-skilled population of Greater Dhaka and East Dhaka as determined by simulations of the four scenarios. The numbers are the high-skilled shares of the population.

Figure 6.2 Key interventions lead to a more spatially balanced population density across the city

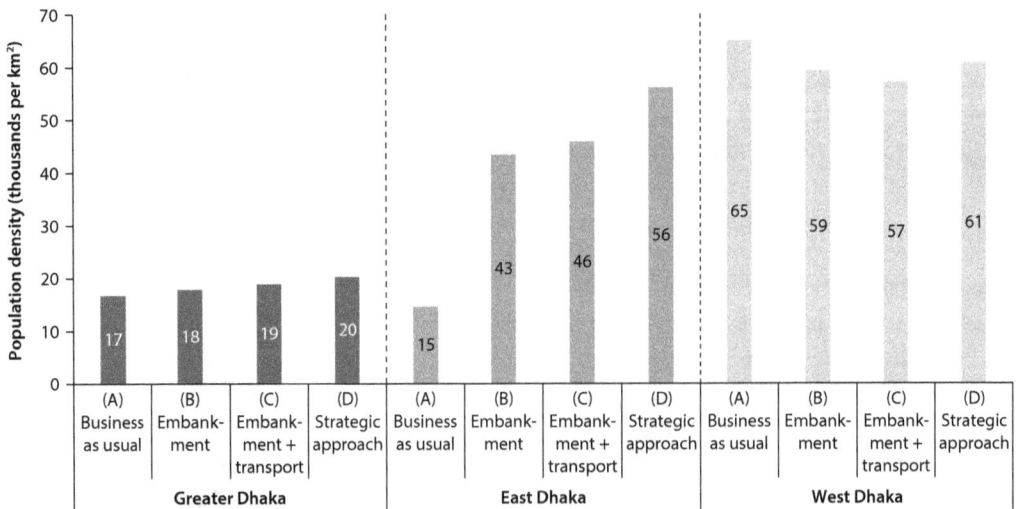

Source: Based on Bird and Venables (2017).
Note: The bars represent the population density of Greater Dhaka, East Dhaka and West Dhaka as determined by simulations of the four scenarios.

Dhaka increases by 1.5 million people, or about 6 percent more than in the business as usual scenario. However, this increase is concentrated in East Dhaka. In fact, despite the growth of the total population of the city, the population density of West Dhaka declines relative to that under the business as usual scenario. The result is a more balanced spatial pattern within the Dhaka city corporations (CCs). This spatial rebalancing is also associated with a greater influx of high-skilled households into East Dhaka, away from West Dhaka and other outlying areas.

In the *embankment + transport scenario (C)*, besides more abundant and better land, connectivity both within East Dhaka and across the city as a whole is significantly improved. Two forces are at work here. First, travel times between many pairs of cells fall, reducing shipping costs for firms and commuting costs for households. Lower transportation costs can strengthen the relocation and migration movements toward East Dhaka as accessing jobs, workers and markets from there becomes easier. But second, jobs, workers and markets become easier to access from other parts of the city. Therefore, improved transportation infrastructure may also attenuate relocation and migration eastward.

Although the net outcome of these two forces is undetermined in principle, the simulation suggests that the first force dominates in practice, so that the population of East Dhaka increases faster in the embankment + transport scenario than in the embankment scenario. The spatial distribution pattern within the Dhaka CCs becomes more homogeneous because the population density of West Dhaka declines slightly and that of East Dhaka increases slightly compared with that under the embankment scenario. Greater spatial homogeneity further reduces congestion pressures in the Dhaka CCs.

Meanwhile, areas to the northeast, east and south of East Dhaka see an increase in population density because they are now better connected to East Dhaka and the rest of the city. The improved connectivity particularly benefits low-skilled residents, who can use the enhanced mass transit system to access jobs in the Dhaka CCs. Better connectivity thus increases the potential of East Dhaka—but also of areas beyond East Dhaka—to support the city's development.

The skills distribution is similar to that in the embankment scenario because the high-skilled population becomes more concentrated in East Dhaka, and less so elsewhere, compared with that in the business as usual scenario. In East Dhaka, the share of the high-skilled population reaches 47 percent—equivalent to 1.7 million more high-skilled people in the area than in the business as usual scenario.

In the *strategic approach scenario (D)*, the cost reduction in the tradable services sector in the selected union, together with improved urban amenities, generate a new dynamic in the city. Initially, the lower cost of doing business prompts tradable services firms to relocate to the union, to benefit from the incentives. This concentrated cluster of activity stimulates growth in the wider area of East Dhaka, boosting the city's wealth and household incomes.

Higher household incomes draw additional migration into the new area, and improvements in livability scores further encourage relocation into East Dhaka.

Productive and residential externalities reinforce one other in this scenario, leading to a significantly larger population in Greater Dhaka—and a much higher concentration in East Dhaka—than in the other scenarios. This is so despite the fact that the existing wetlands are preserved, effectively reducing the usable land in East Dhaka by more than 10 square kilometers relative to what is available in the embankment and embankment + transport scenarios.

The spatial distribution of the population within the Dhaka CCs becomes almost balanced because population density in East Dhaka undergoes a remarkable increase and its gap with West Dhaka narrows significantly. Population density in East Dhaka reaches 56,100 people per square kilometer, which is only slightly below the 60,700 people per square kilometer in West Dhaka. This spatial rebalancing reduces pressures on the historical core of the city.

Greater Dhaka can absorb 5 million more people in the strategic approach scenario than in the business as usual scenario, and 2 million more people than in the embankment + transport scenario. East Dhaka becomes home to over 6 million people, quadrupling the population size expected in the business as usual scenario and accommodating 1.1 million more people than in the embankment + transport scenario. With East Dhaka becoming a hub for the tradable services sector and with its livability improving, high-skilled households are attracted to the area in larger numbers. In the strategic approach scenario, 54 percent of East Dhaka's population is high-skilled, which is equivalent to 2.7 million more than under the business as usual scenario.

Productive new jobs

East Dhaka can emerge as a new growth pole and support millions of new jobs if the government embarks on an urban development path more ambitious than business as usual. As key interventions are implemented, job opportunities increase in East Dhaka faster than its population grows, resulting in notable gains in employment density (figures 6.3 and 6.4). And yet this economic buoyancy does not come at the expense of other areas: in West Dhaka employment density remains at a similar level across all four scenarios. But with East Dhaka booming, Greater Dhaka as a whole becomes more productive, and the total number of jobs increases substantially.

In the *business as usual scenario (A)*, the assumptions made about population growth, skills composition and productivity gains imply that Greater Dhaka supports 8.7 million jobs by 2035. Much of the job creation relative to 2011 is at the fringes of the city, where previously undeveloped land becomes available, and in West Dhaka, which densifies further. In this scenario, West Dhaka hosts 55 percent of the total number of jobs in Greater Dhaka, with an employment density of 24,300 jobs per square kilometer. There is some job creation on sand-filled land in East Dhaka, but total employment in the area amounts to just 0.44 million jobs (or a mere 5 percent of the Greater Dhaka total). East Dhaka's employment density reaches only 4,200 jobs per square kilometer.

Toward Great Dhaka • http://dx.doi.org/10.1596/978-1-4648-1238-5

Figure 6.3 As key interventions are implemented, many more jobs emerge overall but fewer in manufacturing

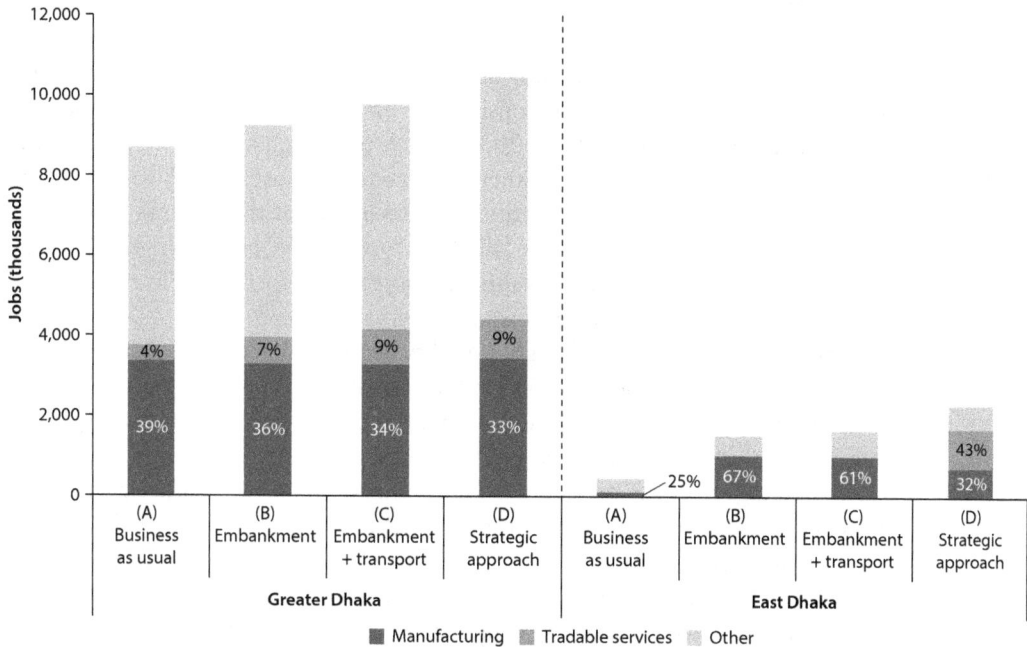

Source: Based on Bird and Venables (2017).
Note: The bars represent employment in the manufacturing, tradable services and other sectors resulting from simulations of the four scenarios. The numbers are the employment shares of the manufacturing and tradable services sectors.

Figure 6.4 Higher employment density in East Dhaka comes at no expense to West Dhaka as key interventions are implemented

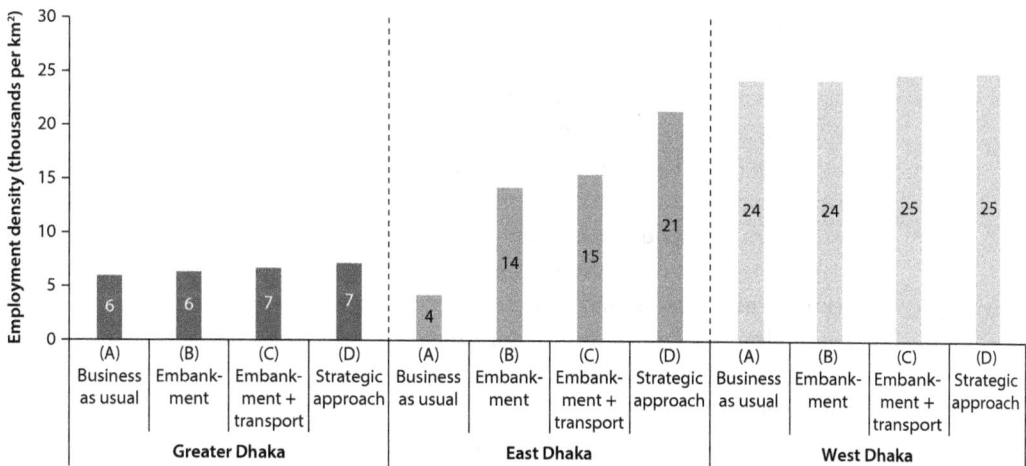

Source: Based on Bird and Venables (2017).
Note: The bars represent the employment density of Greater Dhaka, East Dhaka and West Dhaka as determined by simulations of the four scenarios.

In this scenario, most of the increase in employment in Greater Dhaka is associated with the manufacturing sector, in line with the city's current comparative advantage. By 2035, 40 percent of all jobs are in manufacturing. The projection is based on a relatively conservative assumption on the growth rate of total factor productivity in the manufacturing sector, in line with the trend of the last two decades. The projection is also consistent with the growth patterns foreseen in the Dhaka Structure Plan 2016–2035, which predicts a sustained expansion of the ready-made garment and leather processing industries (RAJUK 2015). The growth in manufacturing employment occurs in part at the expense of employment in tradable services, which falls from 9 to 5 percent of Greater Dhaka's total, or a loss of 26,000 jobs. As the city increasingly specializes in manufacturing, it becomes a net importer of tradable services.

The more abundant and higher-quality land available in the *embankment scenario (B)* stimulates job creation in East Dhaka. Some of the new jobs are the result of businesses relocating from within the city or from outside, while others can be attributed to start-ups. Employment growth is reinforced by greater labor pooling, stronger production linkages, and enhanced market access. The process results in a remarkable employment concentration in East Dhaka and an overall employment increase in Greater Dhaka when compared with the business as usual scenario. The number of jobs in Greater Dhaka exceeds 9.2 million in this scenario, or 6 percent more than in the business as usual scenario. By 2035, there are 1.5 million jobs in East Dhaka, or 2.5 times more than under the business as usual scenario. This amounts to 8 percent annual growth from 2011. The area now accounts for 17 percent of total jobs, and employment density grows to 14,200 workers per square kilometer from 4,200 in the business as usual scenario.

Most of the employment growth in East Dhaka is in manufacturing, which increases almost ninefold relative to the business as usual scenario, rising from 0.11 million to 1 million. This emerging concentration of the manufacturing sector in East Dhaka is at the expense of other parts of the city, especially West Dhaka. However, the net job loss across all sectors in West Dhaka is small because the contraction in manufacturing reduces the demand for land and allows other sectors to expand.

In the *embankment + transport scenario (C)*, improved connectivity results in a broad-based cost reduction across the city. Although the new transport infrastructure investments are concentrated in and around East Dhaka, they reduce the shipping costs of all sectors and the commuting costs of a large number of workers. This broad-based cost reduction stimulates production and job creation in almost all parts of Greater Dhaka. Meanwhile, this force works alongside the greater availability and better quality of land in East Dhaka. The combination of the two forces leads to the creation of more jobs in Greater Dhaka, a slightly higher concentration of jobs in East Dhaka, and lower job losses elsewhere relative to the embankment scenario. Greater Dhaka now hosts 9.8 million jobs, of which 1.6 million (17 percent) are in East Dhaka. In comparison with the embankment scenario, employment density increases further in most parts of Greater Dhaka. In East Dhaka, it reaches 15,500 jobs per square kilometer.

Manufacturing employment becomes relatively less important than in the embankment scenario, but it increases noticeably to the northwest of the Dhaka CCs, around the Savar municipality. Presently an industrial hub, this area is better positioned to take advantage of the increased access to labor and markets made possible by improved connectivity. However, manufacturing remains the dominant sector of employment in East Dhaka.

In the *strategic approach scenario (D)*, the substantial and spatially concentrated cost reduction for tradable services generates a momentous boost for the sector in East Dhaka, but also in the city as a whole. Firms specializing in tradable services respond to the interventions by relocating from everywhere in the city to the targeted union and by setting up new facilities there. A new cluster gradually emerges in this small area, increasing the productivity of businesses located in and around it. But the productivity of tradable services firms decreases elsewhere because the agglomeration benefits decline sharply with distance. This spatial gap in productivity, in turn, encourages more relocation and stimulates the creation of more start-ups. Eventually, this new cluster replaces the existing tradable services center in West Dhaka and depletes the sector elsewhere. The sector dominates economic activities in East Dhaka and emerges as the new driver of growth for Greater Dhaka.

Energized by this strong stimulus, Greater Dhaka hosts 10.5 million jobs in this scenario, 7 percent more than in the embankment + transport scenario, or 20 percent more than in the business as usual scenario. Employment is more concentrated in East Dhaka, which now accounts for 2.3 million jobs, or 22 percent of the city total. This represents a 38 percent increase from the embankment + transport scenario—over five times the total employment in the business as usual scenario—despite all existing wetlands being protected from urban development. Employment density in East Dhaka undergoes a particularly large boost, reaching 21,400 jobs per square kilometer, but West Dhaka also sees a significant increase in employment density.

An important feature of this scenario is the growth in the number of tradable services jobs in the city as a whole. Employment in this sector increases to nearly 1 million, or 9 percent of Greater Dhaka's total employment, compared with 0.39 million (or 4 percent) in the business as usual scenario. Most of these jobs are in the new cluster in East Dhaka, with the remainder in the surrounding areas. In absolute numbers, manufacturing employment in Greater Dhaka increases, remaining important in outlying areas of East Dhaka. Its share of total employment decreases, however.

An engine of economic growth

Bangladesh is bound to grow faster if the government proactively develops East Dhaka, because Greater Dhaka becomes a much more prosperous city by 2035 under the strategic approach than under the business as usual scenario. This is so

Figure 6.5 Dhaka becomes an even stronger economic powerhouse for Bangladesh if key interventions eastward are implemented

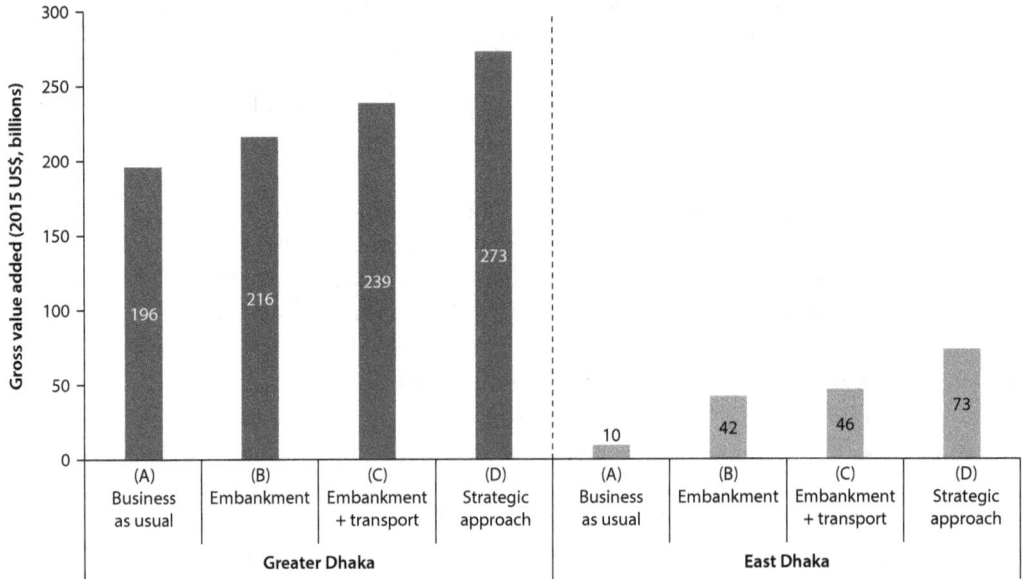

Source: Based on Bird and Venables (2017).
Note: The bars represent the total economic output or gross value added of Greater Dhaka and East Dhaka as determined by simulations of the four scenarios.

in terms of both overall output and income per capita. Given the weight of the city in the country, faster economic growth in Greater Dhaka should result in stronger growth performance at the national level. Gains are also substantial if the authorities choose to implement only the interventions in the embankment scenario, or those in the embankment + transport scenario. But the gains are not as large as in the strategic approach (figure 6.5).

Greater economic output

In the *business as usual scenario (A)*, productivity growth rates are assumed to be in line with historical trends and to be the same across all sectors of the economy. Together with a larger and more skilled population, these productivity gains translate into stronger growth in output. The total output of Greater Dhaka increases by 5.3 percent a year. By 2035 it reaches US$196 billion (at 2015 prices). However, East Dhaka only contributes US$9.5 billion, or 5 percent of the city's total output.

In the *embankment scenario (B)*, the more abundant land of greater quality in East Dhaka translates into greater labor productivity, which, in turn, attracts a larger inflow of firms and migrants to the area. This leads to higher employment density and subsequently to larger agglomeration benefits, providing a further impulse to income growth. The total economic output of Greater Dhaka reaches US$216 billion, or nearly 10 percent more than in the business as usual scenario.

As the most dynamic part of the city, East Dhaka sees its economy grow by 6.4 percent a year. By 2035 the area generates US$42 billion in output, or nearly one-fifth of the city's total. This represents an astounding 343 percent increase from the business as usual scenario.

In the *embankment + transport scenario (C)*, better connectivity within and around East Dhaka leads to a broad-based reduction in costs and thus to higher incomes. Higher living standards attract even more firms and migrants to the city and support an even higher employment density, which is conducive to greater agglomeration economies. The economic dynamism of Greater Dhaka is further strengthened as a result. The output of the city reaches US$239 billion, or US$43 billion more than under the business as usual scenario. East Dhaka generates US$46 billion in output, which represents an almost fivefold increase over the business as usual scenario.

In the *strategic approach scenario (D)*, the place-based, sector-specific cost reduction creates a pivotal stimulus of total production. A tradable services cluster emerges close to the existing business centers, which not only ensures greater dynamism in East Dhaka, but also leverages agglomeration benefits more broadly. Much as in the embankment and embankment + transport scenarios, higher productivity makes the city more attractive to firms and migrants, thereby achieving even higher employment density and productivity. Greater Dhaka becomes an economy of over US$273 billion by 2035, or more than US$77 billion bigger than in the business as usual scenario. East Dhaka emerges as the new center of gravity of the city, generating nearly US$73 billion in output by itself, or nearly 27 percent of the city's total output. This represents a sevenfold increase over the business as usual scenario.

Higher income levels

Moving from business as usual to the more ambitious urban development scenarios delivers not only higher aggregate output for the city, but also higher incomes for its residents. In each of the three more ambitious scenarios, both total output and total population are higher than in the business as usual scenario. But total output grows faster than the total population, resulting in improved living standards and pulling Greater Dhaka closer to the global cities with which it aspires to compete (figure 6.6).

In the business as usual scenario, the income per capita of Greater Dhaka reaches US$7,976 (at 2015 prices) by 2035, or almost double that in 2011. In the embankment and embankment + transport scenarios, income per capita is 4 and 8 percent higher, respectively, than in the business as usual scenario. In the strategic approach scenario, income per capita is further boosted to US$9,225, a 16 percent increase over the business as usual scenario.

These comparisons reveal that Dhaka can move up the ranking of global cities more rapidly if it embraces an ambitious urban development vision. The income per capita figures compiled by the Brookings Institution's Global Metromonitor for nearly 300 metropolitan areas around the time of the calibration of the spatial equilibrium model for Greater Dhaka provide a useful benchmark.

Figure 6.6 With key interventions, Dhaka can catch up with global cities in income per capita

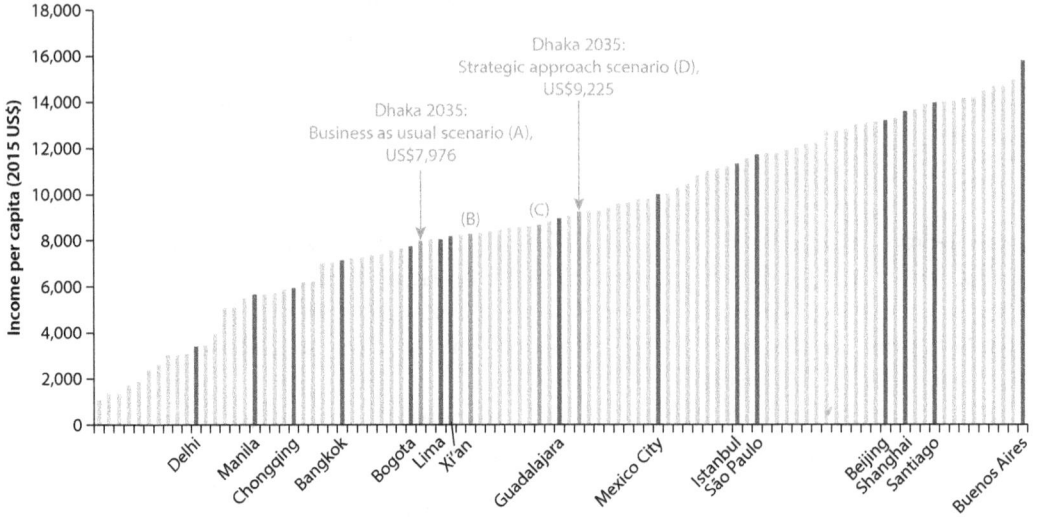

Sources: Based on Bird and Venables (2017) and Global Metromonitor 2014 (Brookings Institution 2015).
Note: The orange bars represent the income per capita of Greater Dhaka in 2035 from simulations of the four scenarios. The blue and green represent the income per capita of international metropolitan areas in 2014, as reported by the Brookings Institution's Global Metromonitor 2014.

If the government could deliver a strategic approach for the city rather than continue on a business as usual trajectory, Greater Dhaka would become more prosperous than cities such as Lima (Peru), Xi'an (China), and Guadalajara (Mexico) are nowadays. It would also be able to significantly close its gap with Shanghai, an emerging global city thanks to its strategic approach to the development of Pudong.

Tighter links with the Sylhet-Chittagong corridor

Dhaka's economy is intrinsically linked with those of Bangladesh's secondary cities and the rest of the country. The spatial general equilibrium model for Dhaka primarily allows studying dynamics within the city. A different modeling exercise would be needed to fully understand the impacts of Greater Dhaka's development across the urban hierarchy of Bangladesh. And yet the current model does offer some hints on those broader impacts through its results on Greater Dhaka's trade with the outside economy.

In the simulations, Greater Dhaka's trade with the rest of the country is assumed to be split across 15 access points to the city. These include the international airport and the key nodes on the road transport corridors. But the relative importance of these 15 access points varies across scenarios, with 9 of them accounting for the lion's share of total trade (map 6.1). Two main forces shape the distribution of trade with the outside economy: the distribution of total output across locations within Dhaka and the distribution of transport costs between these locations and the access points. The size and composition of the economy

Map 6.1 Greater Dhaka spreads prosperity through the emerging Sylhet-Chittagong corridor

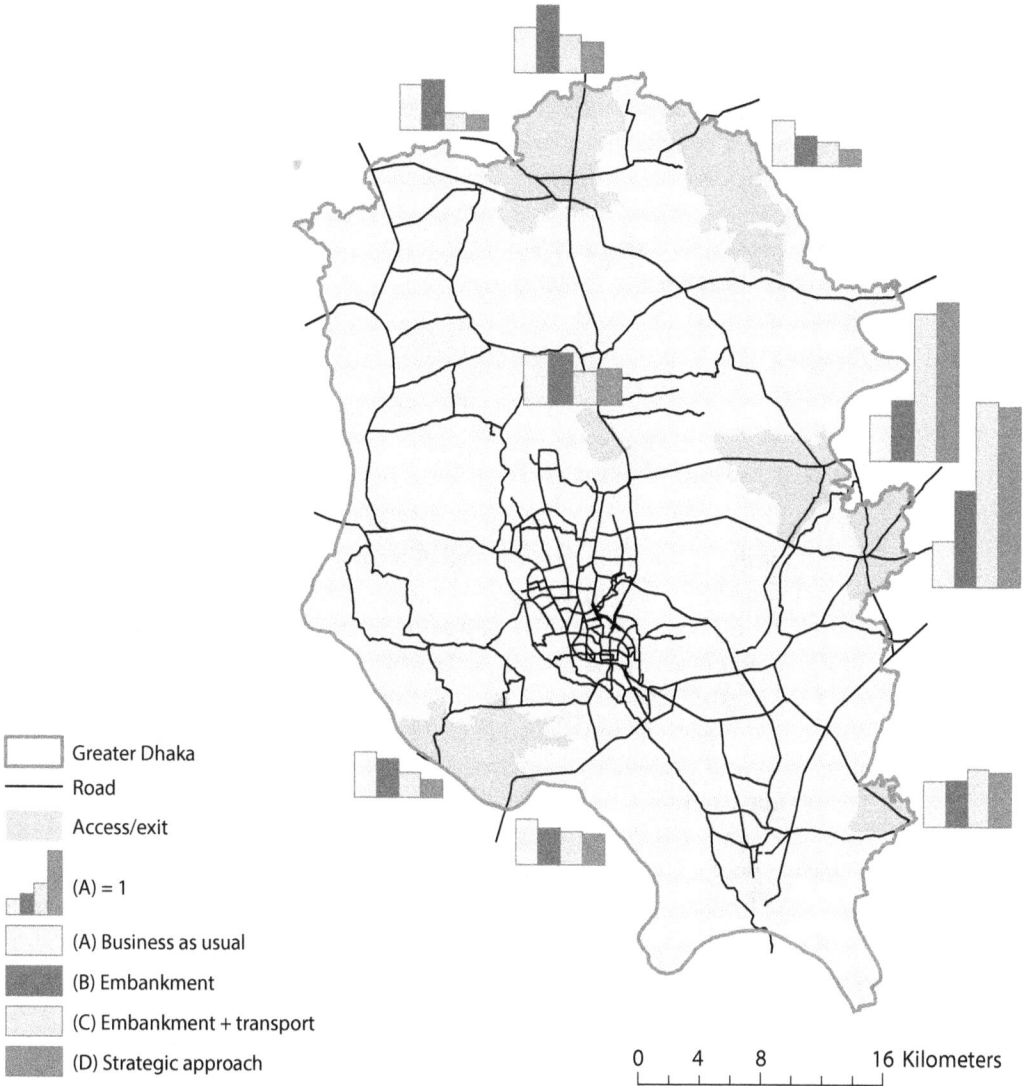

Greater Dhaka
Road
Access/exit
(A) = 1
(A) Business as usual
(B) Embankment
(C) Embankment + transport
(D) Strategic approach

0   4   8   16 Kilometers

Source: Visualization based on Bird and Venables (2017).
Note: The bars represent normalized trade shares across the 9 access points to the city from simulations of the four scenarios. Normalized trade shares divide trade shares in each scenario by trade shares in the business as usual scenario for each access point.

outside Dhaka along these different access routes is not taken into account explicitly in the model.

In the *embankment scenario (B)*, total output in East Dhaka grows much faster than in the rest of the city. This faster growth leads to more trade with the rest of the country through the two access points on the eastern edge of Greater Dhaka. One of these points is on the continuation of the 300-Feet Road, and the other is along the Pragati Sarani–Bhulta Road proposed by the Revised Strategic Transport Plan (DTCA and JICA 2015). Both roads run in an east-west direction and link to Chittagong and Sylhet. In the embankment scenario, the share of the city's total trade going through these two eastern access points rises to 17 percent, from 11 percent in the business as usual scenario.

In the *embankment + transport scenario (C)* and the *strategic approach scenario (D)*, improved road connectivity within and around East Dhaka makes these two eastern access points more advantageous relative to the other 13 access points to the city. The economy of East Dhaka continues to grow faster than that of the rest of Greater Dhaka, and it is natural for its trade to pass through the two closest access points on the eastern fringe. In addition, for businesses located in other parts of the city it becomes less costly to transport their goods across East Dhaka and trade through these two access points. These combined forces increase even more the total trade share of the two eastern access points, to about 37 percent of the total.

The distribution of gains

An ambitious vision for the development of East Dhaka results in greater economic output for the city and substantially higher incomes for its residents, but the gains are not distributed uniformly. Some locations prosper more than others, some households do better than others, and some investors benefit disproportionately. Rapid economic growth is often associated with greater inequality, and one relevant question in this respect is whether high-skilled households are bound to prosper more than the low-skilled ones. Higher population density and a greater number of jobs per square kilometer also make land more valuable. The ownership of property, from small informal housing to large sand-filled areas, is unevenly distributed and so is the capital gain associated with land appreciation.

Higher productivity levels in all sectors, together with a larger supply of land and agglomeration economies, deliver significant increases in real incomes for both high- and low-skilled households (figure 6.7). The average real income of high-skilled households increases by 5, 10 and 18 percent over business as usual in the embankment, embankment + transport and strategic approach scenarios, respectively. Gains are larger for high-skilled households than for the low-skilled ones because manufacturing and tradable services expand more than nontradable services, enhancing the demand for high-skilled labor. The real incomes of low-skilled households are 5, 9 and 16 percent higher in scenarios B, C and D, respectively, than in the business as usual scenario. Therefore, inequality by skill does not increase much.

Gains from higher land value are distributed less evenly. Although the direct impact of increasing the supply of land is a drop in rents, the full effect—once economic adjustments are factored in—is a large increase in the total land rent generated in the city. But trends are different across neighborhoods. Land prices increase sharply in East Dhaka in line with the much higher productivity and livability scores, compared with those under the business as usual scenario. By contrast, lower population pressure eases land prices in West Dhaka.

The composition of the stock of housing also evolves in the process. In the business as usual scenario, 54 percent of housing in East Dhaka is modern, and

Figure 6.7 Key interventions in East Dhaka boost average household incomes

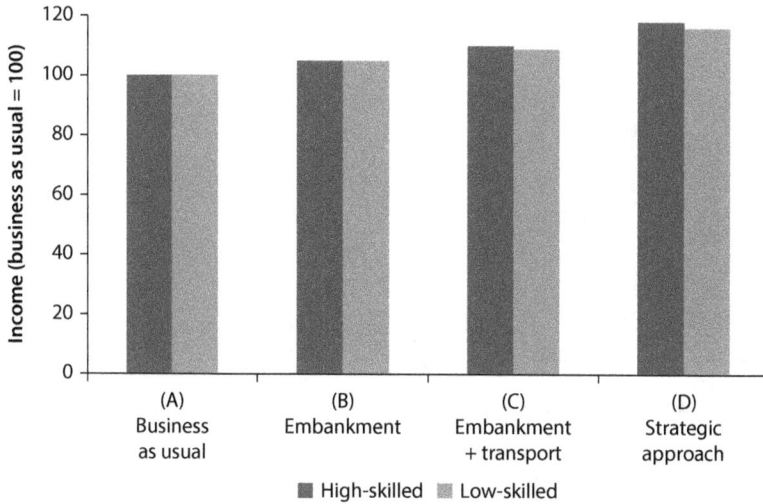

Source: Visualization based on Bird and Venables (2017).
Note: The bars represent the income levels of high- and low-skilled households in Greater Dhaka from simulations of the four scenarios. The values are normalized so that the income levels are 100 in the business as usual scenario for both high- and low-skilled households.

the remaining is constructed using traditional technology, leading to crowded, poor-quality dwellings. The interventions in the embankment and embankment + transport scenarios encourage households and firms to move to East Dhaka because the flood risks are reduced and the transport links are improved. But a larger population by itself does little to encourage the construction of modern housing. In the embankment + transport scenario, its share of the total housing stock barely rises to just 56 percent. On the other hand, in the strategic approach scenario the livability scores for modern housing increase to match the scores of the top 20 percent of cells in West Dhaka. This increase captures the effect of better laid-out infrastructure, as well as more attractive amenities. As a result, the share of modern housing rises to 72 percent of the building stock in East Dhaka.

Total rents in East Dhaka increase from US$1.8 billion in the business as usual scenario to US$8.7 billion in the embankment scenario—a nearly fivefold rise (figure 6.8). However, this increase is in part at the expense of the rest of the city. For example, total rents in West Dhaka fall by US$1.2 billion over those in the business as usual scenario. Combining the gains and losses, the city as a whole generates an additional US$3.3 billion in land rents, or a 9 percent increase over those in the business as usual scenario.

With the additional transport infrastructure in scenario C, land rents in Greater Dhaka are even higher, increasing by US$6.9 billion over those in the business as usual scenario. Just US$0.7 billion of this increase is generated in East Dhaka. The remainder is largely from areas that are now better connected to East Dhaka and the central part of West Dhaka.

Figure 6.8 Key interventions increase total rents considerably in East Dhaka, but much less elsewhere in the city

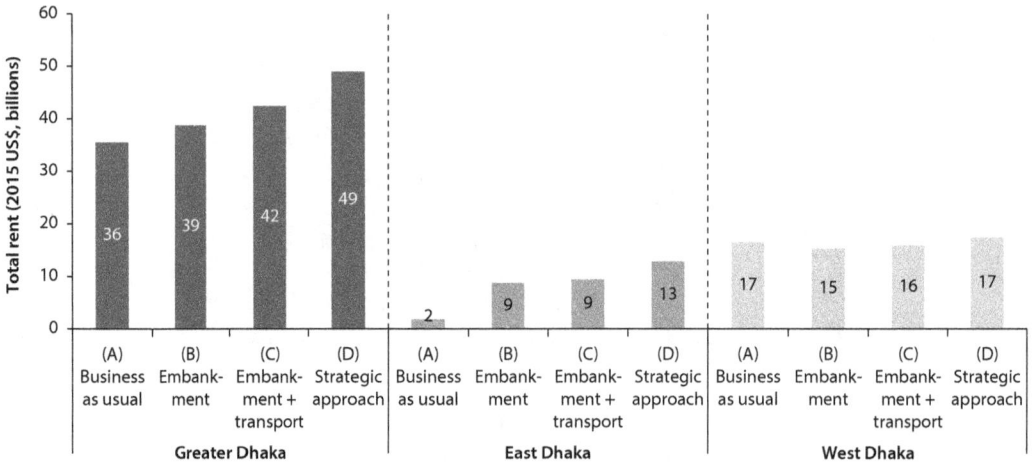

Source: Visualization based on Bird and Venables (2017).
Note: The bars represent the total land rents in Greater Dhaka, East Dhaka and West Dhaka from simulations of the four scenarios.

The strongest increase in total rents, however, takes place in the strategic approach scenario. Citywide rents are US$13.3 billion higher, which represents a 38 percent jump over the business as usual scenario. The biggest gains are again in East Dhaka, the site of the new tradable services hub, home to millions of people and the source of plentiful jobs. In the strategic approach scenario, total rents in East Dhaka are US$11.1 billion higher than in the business as usual scenario. However, the rest of the city also benefits from the increase in productivity in East Dhaka, with total rents elsewhere in Greater Dhaka rising by over 6 percent relative to the business as usual scenario.

Higher rents translate into higher land prices, and the gains accrue to those who own the land, both in East Dhaka and throughout the city. But the gains are a direct result of key interventions by the government, including the construction of the embankment, the upgrading of transport infrastructure, and the adoption of soft policies to make East Dhaka a better place.

Depending on how landowners are taxed, these key interventions can have significant distributional effects. If taxation on land is low or nonexistent, landowners make very substantial gains. The gains can be very substantial for the private developers who currently own large patches of East Dhaka (figure 6.9). Investors who buy land there at the currently low prices can also make sizable capital gains. However, increases in land value can also be captured by the government through taxation and other financial instruments such as impact fees. In this case, the proceeds can be redistributed to the population at large through further investments in urban development, through the delivery of social services, and through measures to preserve the environment and enhance resilience.

Figure 6.9 Key interventions make high-quality urban land become increasingly pricey, especially in East Dhaka

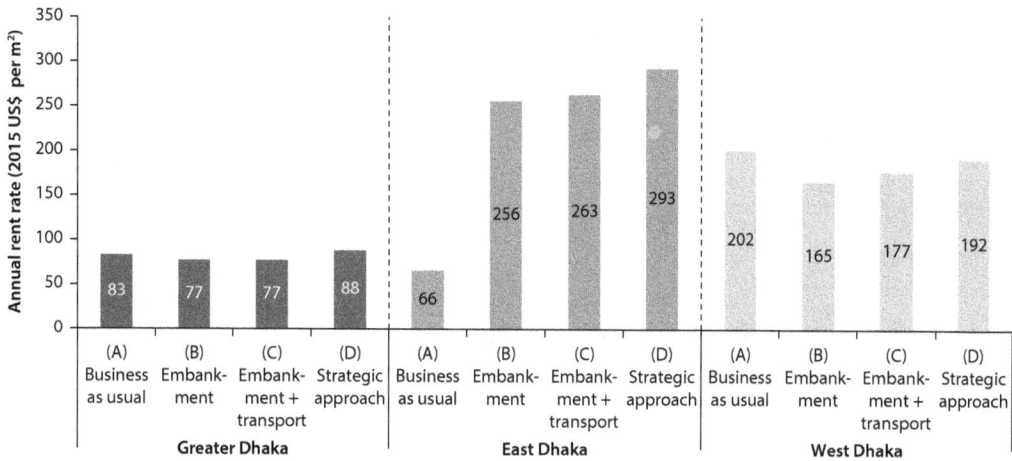

Source: Visualization based on Bird and Venables (2017).
Note: The bars represent the land rent rates in Greater Dhaka, East Dhaka and West Dhaka from simulations of the four scenarios.

References

BEA (Bureau of Economic Analysis). 2015. "Economic Growth Widespread Across Metropolitan Areas in 2014." News release, U.S. Department of Commerce, Washington, DC. https://bea.gov/newsreleases/regional/gdp_metro/2015/pdf/gdp_metro0915.pdf.

Bird, Julia, and Anthony J. Venables. 2017. "Growing a Developing City: A Computable Spatial General Equilibrium Model Applied to Dhaka." Background paper prepared for this report.

Brookings Institution. 2015. "Global Metromonitor 2014." Metropolitan Policy at Brookings, Washington, DC.

DTCA (Dhaka Transport Coordination Authority) and JICA (Japan International Cooperation Agency). 2015. "Revised Strategic Transport Plan for Dhaka." Prepared by ALMEC Corporation, Oriental Consultants Global, and Kathahira and Engineers International, Dhaka.

Economist. 2014. "Ending Apartheid—The Rural-Urban Divide." April 19. https://www.economist.com/news/special-report/21600798-chinas-reforms-work-its-citizens-have-be-made-more-equal-ending-apartheid.

Hymowitz, Kay. 2016. "New York Values: How Immigrants Made the City." New York Times, November 1. https://www.nytimes.com/2016/11/06/books/review/city-of-dreams-history-of-immigrant-new-york-tyler-anbinder.html.

Lall, Somik, and Paul Procee. Forthcoming. "Shanghai 2050: From Made in Shanghai to Create in Shanghai." World Bank, Washington, DC.

Mainelli, Michael, Mark Yeandle and Alexander Knapp. 2017. "The Global Financial Centers Index." Z/Yen Group Limited, London. http://www.zyen.com/component/content/article.html?id=240.

New York State Comptroller. 2016. *A Portrait of Immigrants in New York.* Albany, NY: Office of the New York State Comptroller.

Open Data Network. 2017. "Demographics: New York Metro Area." https://www.open datanetwork.com/entity/310M200US35620/New_York_Metro_Area_NY_NJ_PA /demographics.population.count?ref=suggest-entity&year=2016.

RAJUK (Rajdhani Unnayan Kartripakkha). 2015. "Dhaka Structure Plan 2016–2035." Dhaka.

Shanghai Pudong New Area Statistical Bureau and Pudong Survey Team of National Statistics Bureau. 2016. *Shanghai Pudong New Area Statistical Yearbook 2016.* Beijing: China Statistics Press.

UN DESA (United Nations Department of Economic and Social Affairs). 2013. "Towards Sustainable Cities." In *World Economic and Social Survey 2013: Sustainable Development Challenges.* New York: United Nations.

UN-Habitat (United Nations Human Settlements Programme). 2012. *State of World's Cities 2012/2013: Prosperity of Cities.* London: UN-Habitat.

World Bank. 2015. *What Makes a Sustainable City? A Sampling of Global Case Studies Highlighting Innovative Approaches to Sustainability in Urban Areas.* Washington, DC: World Bank.

CHAPTER 7

Implementing the Vision

A coherent set of urban interventions in East Dhaka could result in a fundamental transformation of Greater Dhaka, and in the process it could boost Bangladesh's economic growth. But implementing this vision is as important as defining it. Implementation requires not only technical capacity among urban authorities, but also rigorous upstream analysis to inform urban development choices. Before the vision can become a reality, the government must assess economic returns and evaluate fiscal implications. It has to mobilize finance for the required investments and design the complementary "soft" policies. And it should identify the possible risks and design measures to mitigate them.

A significant challenge is that the economic benefits are bound to materialize many years after the investment costs are incurred. The key interventions to seize the opportunities provided by East Dhaka need to be carried out relatively soon, before spontaneous development makes the area as messy as the rest of the city is today. But it takes time for households to migrate and choose where to live and work and settle. And it takes time for firms to adjust their location and sector of activity and to invest and hire personnel. As a result, two decades could well elapse before the benefits of the urban development choices made today can be fully reaped.

In light of this extended time horizon, investment costs and additional output need to be compared in present value terms to determine which scenario—the embankment, the embankment + transport, or the strategic approach—yields the highest economic returns. Intertemporal trade-offs also need to be considered when assessing the fiscal implications of developing East Dhaka. And because of the time lag between investment costs and increased output, the mobilization of various forms of finance becomes critically important to implementation of the vision.

Important decisions also have to be made about soft policies. Cities are characterized by inertia: once a production cluster has emerged, individual firms have little interest in moving somewhere else. By being in the cluster, firms make each other more productive, and so the first one to move to another, emptier location would be at a disadvantage. This is true even if that other location is better and could support a more productive cluster. East Dhaka is potentially that other location, but strong incentives may be needed before a new business center can emerge there. Economic analysis can help determine the threshold for policies to trigger the shift to a superior equilibrium.

A transformation of this sort is not without risks. The successful development of East Dhaka means that many more people will be living off the Madhupur Tract in areas more exposed to strong ground shaking in the event of an earthquake. Success will also lead to a bigger and richer city, and this implies there will be many more commutes, and a larger fraction of them will be motorized. The goal of reducing congestion by adding a vast expanse of high-quality urban land to the city could thus be undermined, with traffic speeds declining and air pollution increasing. Last but not least, land prices in East Dhaka will surge. With weak land titling systems in place, there could be strong incentives for land grabbing. Thus before the vision can be implemented, it is necessary to assess how serious these risks are and discuss which measures could be put in place to mitigate them.

Returns and financing

The three urban development scenarios proposed for East Dhaka to depart from business as usual entail both up-front costs and long-term benefits. The first key intervention in these scenarios is to build the eastern embankment with the appropriate retention, drainage and waste treatment systems. The second key intervention is to establish a modern transport network, including mass transit. And the third key intervention involves reducing the cost of doing business—especially for high-value-added sectors—and providing comprehensive public services. Compared to the business as usual scenario (A), undertaking the first key intervention leads to the embankment scenario (B), adding the second one to the embankment + transport scenario (C), and adding the third one to the strategic approach scenario (D). These scenarios can be assessed along a range of dimensions, including their economic returns, their fiscal implications, and the potential financing choices.

Costs and benefits

From an economic point of view, a key question is whether the overall benefits are greater than the investment costs. The question is particularly relevant because of the magnitude of the expenditures to be incurred. Reducing the cost of doing business in the new area may not be expensive because it mainly requires an institutional effort to ensure leadership and coordinate across agencies. But the cost of the infrastructure investments associated with the other key interventions and the cost of providing comprehensive public services are substantial.

The Bangladesh Water Development Board (BWDB) has estimated the cost of building the eastern embankment. Including construction, maintenance, land acquisition and resettlement expenses, the bill would amount to US$1.9 billion to US$2.0 billion. The range stems from the variation in the composition of the auxiliary facilities, such as the number of pumping stations (BWDB 2017). The higher investment cost figure of US$2 billion is used in what follows.

Building the critically important transport infrastructure for East Dhaka is more expensive. The Revised Strategic Transport Plan (RSTP) presents detailed cost estimates for all of its infrastructure projects (DTCA and JICA 2015). Based on these estimates, the cost of building a road is about US$3.5 million per lane-kilometer, whereas the cost of building 1 kilometer of bus rapid transit (BRT) is close to US$9 million and that of building 1 kilometer of mass rapid transit (MRT) is roughly US$120 million. As a result, the construction and maintenance costs for the plan as a whole amount to US$35.6 billion, excluding land acquisition and resettlement expenses.

The key intervention proposed for East Dhaka is a subset of the overall RSTP package. The RSTP provides cost estimates on a project-by-project basis, and for each project the cost can be prorated according to project length. Following this logic, the cost of the transport infrastructure that is critically important for East Dhaka amounts to US$8.0 billion, with mass transit alone accounting for US$6.1 billion. These investments are in addition to the transport investments envisioned in the business as usual scenario, which should cost around US$14 billion.

Estimating how expensive the third intervention would be is more challenging. Reducing the cost of doing business is mainly a regulatory undertaking, but providing comprehensive public services does require substantial spending. International benchmarks from cities with high-quality service delivery offer some guidance in this respect. In Singapore, the infrastructure expenditure was on average 6.4 percent of total output over 2007–10—at the time the city was experiencing robust economic growth (5.9 percent a year during the 2000s). In Hong Kong SAR, China, spending on infrastructure was on average 2.6 percent of total economic output over 2007–10—and the city grew at a rate of 4.4 percent a year during the 2000s. Infrastructure expenditures were higher in Pudong, reaching between 6 and 12 percent of total output during 2005–09—a period when the area thrived (Ingram, Liu and Brandt 2013; Shanghai Pudong New Area Statistical Bureau and Pudong Survey Team of National Statistics Bureau 2016).

Based on these benchmarks, a reasonable infrastructure investment target for East Dhaka would be 6 percent of the area's annual economic output. In the strategic approach scenario where such a comprehensive investment is proposed, the simulations suggest that East Dhaka's economy grows at 14.8 percent a year. Combining the investment target and the growth rate, the infrastructure investment needs of East Dhaka between 2016 and 2030 are a grand total of about US$15 billion. Because building the eastern embankment and developing East Dhaka's transport infrastructure are expected to cost US$2 billion and US$8 billion respectively, the cost of upgrading service delivery can be estimated at US$5 billion (= 15–2–8).

The private sector will also incur investment costs as households build housing and firms erect factories and commercial facilities. These costs are undertaken because they lead to better living conditions for households and to higher profits for firms. Counting private investment expenditures as part of the cost of the various scenarios would be misleading because these expenditures are induced by the key interventions rather than being part of them.

Although the investment costs associated with the three interventions are large, the resulting economic benefits are enormous. Compared with the business as usual scenario, the economic output of Dhaka increases between US$20 billion (at 2015 prices) and US$77 billion a year from 2035 onward, depending on the scenario. Part of this gain is at the expense of the agricultural sector elsewhere, because more people will migrate from rural areas to Dhaka. The expected reduction in agricultural output amounts to US$4–$24 billion a year from 2035 onward. Consequently, the economic benefits for Bangladesh as a whole are US$16–$53 billion. Put differently, a single year of future output gains more than covers the entire cost of the infrastructure investments associated with the three key interventions (figure 7.1).

Figure 7.1 The investments needed in East Dhaka are affordable, and their economic returns are very high

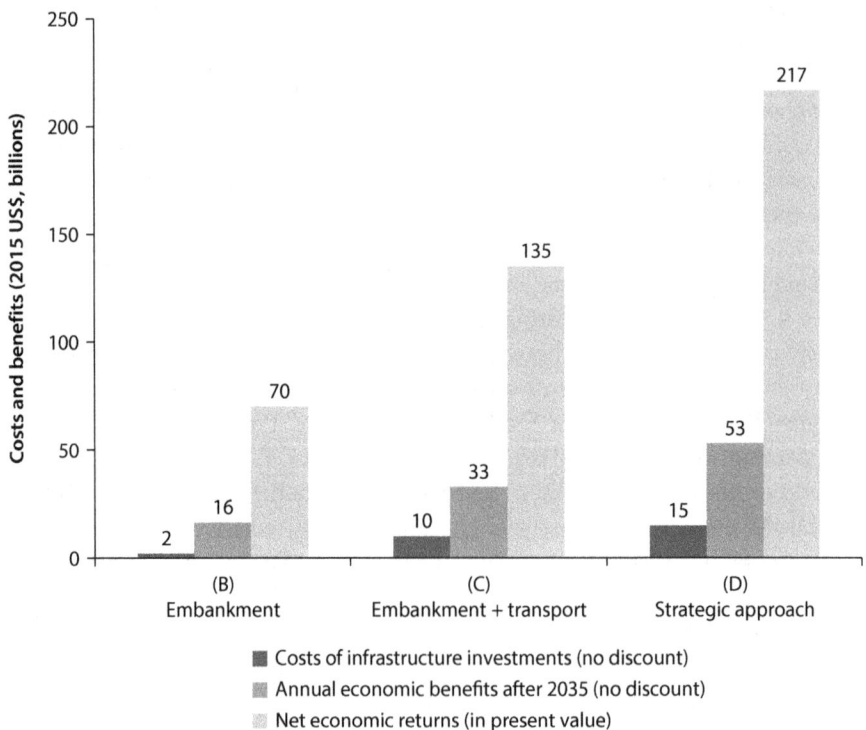

Costs and benefits (2015 US$, billions)

	(B) Embankment	(C) Embankment + transport	(D) Strategic approach
Costs of infrastructure investments (no discount)	2	10	15
Annual economic benefits after 2035 (no discount)	16	33	53
Net economic returns (in present value)	70	135	217

■ Costs of infrastructure investments (no discount)
▨ Annual economic benefits after 2035 (no discount)
▨ Net economic returns (in present value)

Sources: Calculations based on Bird and Venables (2017); BWDB (2017); DTCA and JICA (2015); Shanghai Pudong New Area Statistical Bureau and Pudong Survey Team of National Statistics Bureau (2016).
Note: The bars represent (1) the estimated costs of the infrastructure investments as proposed by the three scenarios; (2) the annual economic gains after 2035 when the impact of the investments and policy reforms is assumed to materialize and the economy of Greater Dhaka is assumed to reach its equilibrium; and (3) the net economic returns from the investments. The net economic returns are computed as the present value of the economic gains net of investment costs, assuming a 10 percent discount rate. No discount rate is applied for the other two bars.

Admittedly, the investment costs would have to be incurred early on, whereas the economic benefits would only accrue gradually, and mostly after 2035. But even under very conservative discounting assumptions, the present value of net benefits remains large because infrastructure investment costs are a one-time expenditure, whereas the benefits accrue indefinitely. The present value of the flow of benefits is much larger than the investment cost.

A somewhat extreme calculation can help make this point. Suppose for simplicity's sake that the additional spending starts in 2016, and that it takes five years to build the eastern embankment, 10 years to put the transportation infrastructure for East Dhaka in place, and 15 years to upgrade its service delivery. Suppose also that the benefits from these interventions fully materialize only after 2035 and that the growth rate of the city's output between 2016 and 2035 is constant under each scenario.

Assessing the economic returns requires expressing the associated streams of costs and benefits in present values. Assume that the discount rate is 10 percent, meaning that 100 units of output in 2017 (measured in real terms after removing inflation) are valued as the equivalent of 90 units of output in 2016. With this discount rate, 100 units of additional real cost in 2021 are valued as 62 units of cost in 2016, and 100 units of real output in 2035 are valued as 24 units of output in 2016. Similar conversions of costs and benefits can be computed for the other years.

Adding the resulting flows of discounted economic benefits and subtracting the flow of discounted investment costs yields the net present value of the different scenarios, measured in 2016 terms. This net present value ranges from US$70 billion under the embankment scenario to US$217 billion under the strategic approach. The present value of the net benefits is thus very substantial, on the same order of magnitude as the current gross domestic product (GDP) of Bangladesh. And 10 percent is a very high discount rate; under more plausible assumptions, the net economic returns would be even higher.

Fiscal implications

An important question is whether the government of Bangladesh would have the means to carry out the key interventions associated with the proposed urban development scenarios. It could well be that society as a whole gains from the development of East Dhaka, but the government lacks the resources to undertake the necessary investments. Which is why, in addition to conducting a cost-benefit analysis for society as a whole, it is necessary to assess the fiscal implications of the proposed approach.

The government would need to incur large investment costs, but it would also gain from the development of East Dhaka because the economic benefits would translate into a large revenue stream for the public sector. The implications for both national and local tax revenue have to be considered in this respect.

The main sources of national tax revenue in Bangladesh are the value-added tax (VAT) and supplemental duties, personal and corporate income taxes, and the tariffs and other duties applied to imported products. The ratio of tax revenue to GDP has remained relatively stable over the years, hovering at around 8.5 percent of GDP despite rapid economic growth. In comparison with other countries, Bangladesh has, then, limited fiscal space for development spending, and so the government has been keen to expand tax revenues. For 2017, the official target was 10.7 percent of GDP (IMF 2017). Although meeting such targets may take time, it is reasonable to assume that at least 11 percent of the additional output generated by the development of East Dhaka will translate into additional tax revenue, bringing an extra US$1.8 billion to US$5.8 billion a year to state coffers after 2035, depending on the scenario. However, this is a conservative estimate because the ratio of tax revenue to GDP tends to increase as countries develop.

Cities around the world also raise revenue from various forms of property tax. In Bangladesh, the main tax instrument at the local level is the holding tax, which is set at 12 percent of the rental value of properties in the Dhaka city corporations (CCs). Very little revenue is raised from this instrument at present because of inaccurate valuations, low coverage and poor collection. In fiscal 2014/15, the two Dhaka CCs earned about US$50 million in holding tax. The situation is similar in the other local urban governments in Greater Dhaka such as in the Gazipur CC and Narayanganj CC (Huda and Hasan 2009; *Independent* 2017; Rahman 2017b; World Bank 2016, 2017a). However, the holding tax could become a more relevant source of revenue if the recorded rental values of properties were increased to their actual levels. It is hoped that this will have been done by 2035.

Both land and housing rental values in Greater Dhaka increase substantially as a result of the three key interventions proposed. In the embankment scenario, annual housing rents in Greater Dhaka increase by US$4.1 billion over those in the business as usual scenario. The expected gains in the embankment + transport and strategic approach scenarios are even greater, reaching US$9.0 billion and US$17.9 billion, respectively. If a 12 percent holding tax is applied to these gains, the revenue of the Dhaka CCs and other local urban governments in Greater Dhaka increases by US$0.5 billion to US$2.1 billion a year after 2035, depending on the scenario (figure 7.2).

To assess the fiscal implications of the three interventions proposed, one could consider a present value approach along the lines of the cost-benefit analysis discussed earlier. Again, the same time profile is assumed for both the investment costs and the increases in output and rental value of property, where 2016 is assumed to be the initial year, and the tax revenue gains will increase gradually, fully materialize after 2035 and continue indefinitely afterward. With a 10 percent discount rate, there is a net fiscal gain of US$8.4 billion in present value in the embankment scenario. The gain increases to US$12.6 billion in the embankment + transport scenario and to US$24.2 billion in the strategic approach scenario. The proposed interventions would thus solidify the fiscal position of the government rather than weaken it.

Figure 7.2 High economic gains from the proposed interventions will translate into larger fiscal revenue

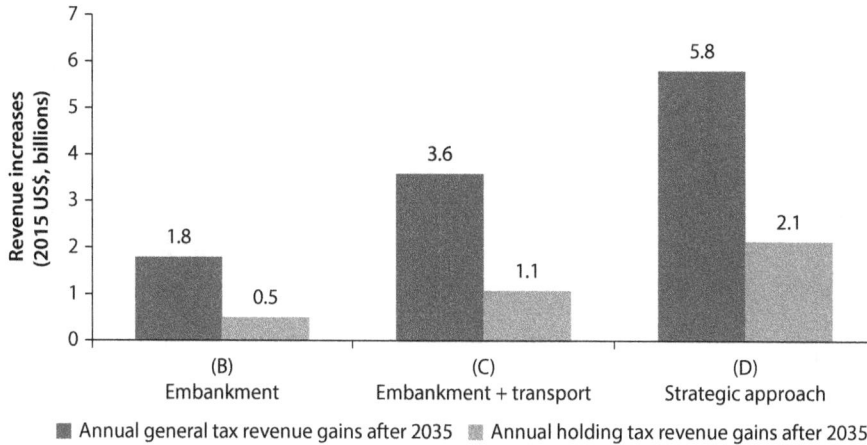

Sources: Calculations based on Bird and Venables (2017); IMF (2017); Rahman (2017a); World Bank (2017a).
Note: The bars represent the estimated annual revenue gains from the general tax and the holding tax under the three proposed scenarios after 2035, when the impact of the investments and policy reforms in East Dhaka is assumed to materialize and the economy of Greater Dhaka is assumed to reach its equilibrium.

Financing the investments

The proposed interventions have important financial implications. The economic benefits associated with them would be much higher than their costs, and the flow of tax revenue they would generate would be sufficient for the government to afford the necessary investments. But there is a mismatch in the timing of expenditures and income. The infrastructure investments would need to be undertaken relatively soon, whereas higher incomes and tax revenues would not fully materialize until much later.

Consider the strategic approach. As noted earlier, the investment expenditures associated with the three key interventions amount to US$15 billion, with the eastern embankment built in five years, the new transport infrastructure for East Dhaka in place in 10 years, and investments related to improved service delivery spread out uniformly over 15 years. With these assumptions, to implement the strategic approach the government of Bangladesh would need to spend an additional US$1.5 billion a year over the next five years, over US$1.1 billion a year over the following five, and US$0.3 billion a year afterwards until 2030. Because additional income and tax revenue would materialize only much later, mostly after 2035, the government would have to rely on long-term financing to cover this additional spending.

The kind of long-term development financing provided by development partners and international financial institutions is ideally suited for this purpose. Key counterparts in this respect might include the Asian Development Bank, Asian Infrastructure Investment Bank, European Investment Bank, Islamic Development

Bank, Japan International Cooperation Agency and World Bank. The combined lending to Bangladesh of these development partners and international financial institutions amounted to US\$3.6 billion in 2016, and it is expected to increase in the coming years (ADB 2016; AIIB 2016; EIB 2016; JICA 2017; World Bank 2017c). This is more than twice the additional volume of annual government spending the strategic approach would require.

Private resources could also be leveraged. Because the proposed interventions result in a fiscal gain over a longer time horizon, borrowing for the development of East Dhaka should improve debt sustainability, not undermine it. This opens the door to the issuance of long-term bonds in international markets.

Finally, experience from other countries suggests that land-based financing could be tapped as well to help cover the upfront costs. In each of the three scenarios considered, land rents see steep increases in East Dhaka. This means that the benefits from public investments in urban infrastructure not only are capitalized into land values, but also fall into a relatively well-defined "benefit zone." Such localization of the gains is ideal for land-based finance.

The capture of land value by the government also makes for a more equitable distribution of the benefit of urban development across the population. Those who own property in East Dhaka, and especially in and around the areas in which transport investments would take place, are bound to make large capital gains. The gains would be substantial even if these property owners did not invest their own resources. And they would be made possible by infrastructure investments undertaken with money from taxpayers around the country. Capturing part of those windfall gains and reducing the burden on taxpayers are only fair.

As early as 1879, Henry George, one of the leading thinkers of the Progressive Era in the United States, argued that the increments in land value due to public investment belong to the public and are thus naturally subject to value capture by the fiscal authority (George 1987 [1884]). Since then, many land-based financing instruments have been developed to fit different institutional settings and country contexts.

During the 19th century, when advanced economies experienced rapid urbanization, cities in these countries were innovative in using land value capture to meet their development needs. New York City financed its first city hall by selling "water lots" that required private purchasers to fill in their sites. When rebuilding Paris, Baron Haussmann financed the grand avenues and utility lines along them by acquiring land around the planned avenues and using it as collateral for borrowing. To this day, this approach remains central to municipal finance in advanced economies (Alterman 2012; Gielen, Salas and Cuadrado 2017; Harvey 2003; Ingram and Hong 2012; Peterson 2009).

In developing countries, Pudong was in the vanguard of using land-based financing instruments. It raised most of the resources for its ambitious infrastructure blueprint by leasing public land and borrowing against land collateral. But Pudong is not alone. Delhi, Kolkata and a handful of other large Indian cities paid for their modern urban airports by contributing public land to joint development ventures or public-private partnerships (Lall and Procee 2016; Peterson 2009; Pethe 2013; Wong 2013).

An in-depth analysis would be needed to design land-based financing instruments that suit East Dhaka's circumstances. Such an in-depth analysis is beyond the scope of this report, but examples from other countries and the lessons of experience can shed light on East Dhaka's options.

Meanwhile, regardless of the option retained, better land asset management is a prerequisite for moving in this direction. A large portion of East Dhaka falls in the category of *khas* land, meaning water bodies and low-lying floodplains that do not support permanent human settlements. *Khas* land is owned by the government and held under the Ministry of Land. But the pressure to develop this land for urban uses will be tremendous in the near future. It is thus critically important for the government to build a comprehensive inventory of its land assets in East Dhaka, including *khas* land and public lands owned by different agencies. This inventory would help the government to think strategically about the most appropriate uses, including preservation. Indeed, only after these public assets have been inventoried can active land asset management take place. In practice, active land asset management would involve exchanging some of these assets or their developments through market mechanisms and using the proceeds from the transactions to finance public infrastructure expenditures.

The payoffs to being strategic

Net economic returns are highest under the strategic approach scenario, but reducing the cost of business and upgrading service delivery in the new area will be challenging because it requires consistent political support and concerted institutional efforts to implement bold reforms. If the reforms are not bold enough, those larger benefits for society may not materialize.

The threshold of change

Urban economic theory suggests that multiple equilibria may exist in the presence of increasing returns to scale in production. In plain language, the concentration of firms in one location makes all firms in that location more productive. There could well be a better location, in the sense that total production would be higher if all firms migrated there. But there is a first-mover dilemma: no one wants to take the initiative to locate a firm in an empty place, preferring to wait until others are there. As a result, the better location may never take off.

One key policy implication of multiple equilibria is that policies may need to reach some minimum threshold to be effective. Because more than one stable equilibrium exists, inertia prevents a city from shifting from one equilibrium to the other. In this situation, bold changes in policies, or bold reforms, are required to convince private agents to overcome the inertia. Once the threshold of change is reached, policy effects tend to reinforce themselves and keep the city moving toward the new equilibrium (Baldwin et al. 2011; Fujita, Krugman and Venables 1999; Krugman 1991; Krugman and Venables 1995; Venables 2017).

In the strategic approach, a 20 percent reduction in business costs is applied to the tradable services sector in one union of East Dhaka. In a way, this intervention amounts to selecting one relatively small area as a potential new business district. The tradable services sector is chosen for this intervention because it generates more value added, is more intensive in skills, and is less polluting than other sectors. The reduction in the local cost of doing business leads to the formation of a tradable services cluster in the chosen union, replacing tradable services in the rest of Greater Dhaka. The sector receives a significant boost on productivity as a result of this more favorable clustering. The flip side is that manufacturing industries are crowded out of East Dhaka, and out of Greater Dhaka more generally.

The choice of a 20 percent reduction in the cost of doing business is not arbitrary. Because of inertia, ensuring that a new area in East Dhaka has the same underlying productivity score as the "best" area in central Dhaka is not enough to trigger the formation of a new large productive cluster—thus the need for an additional incentive. But even if tradable services expand in East Dhaka as business costs continue to fall, the new cluster does not form until the incentive becomes sufficiently large (figure 7.3).

When the government does not reduce the cost of doing business in the selected union, making it only as attractive as the most business-friendly area in the Dhaka CCs, only 135,100 jobs in tradable services are created in East Dhaka. This is just a small fraction of employment in the sector citywide. When the government introduces a cost reduction of 2.5 percent, the number of jobs in tradable services in East Dhaka more than doubles, to 295,000, or about a third

Figure 7.3 Soft reforms need to reach a threshold to make a real difference

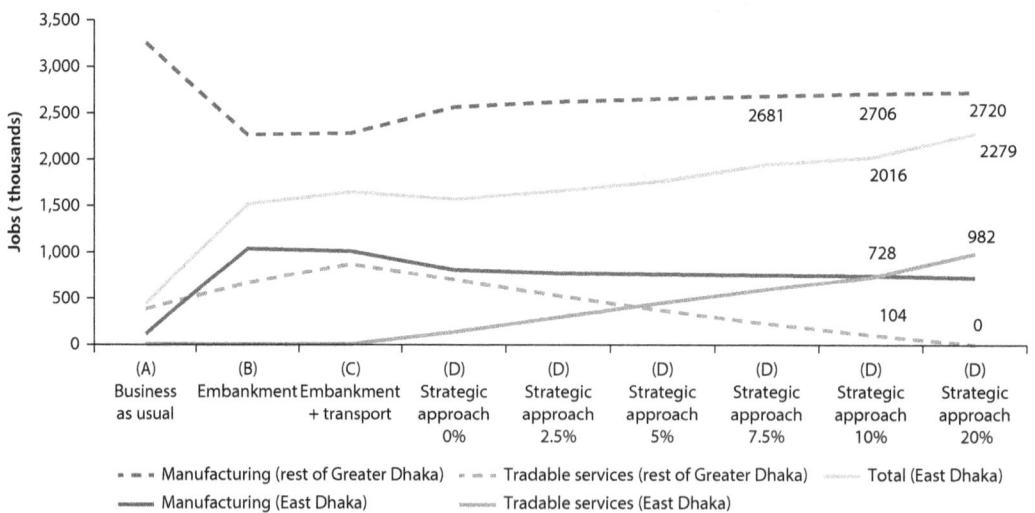

Source: Calculations based on Bird and Venables (2017).
Note: The lines represent the employment of different sectors in East Dhaka and in the rest of Greater Dhaka in different scenarios. In the strategic approach scenario, the cost reduction for the tradable services sector in the selected East Dhaka union ranges from 0 to 20 percent.

of total employment in tradable services. But the share expands as the cost of doing business in the selected union is further reduced. With a 20 percent reduction in cost, all tradable services firms relocate to East Dhaka.

The encouragement of tradable services also has implications for employment in manufacturing. The construction of the eastern embankment increases the supply of land in East Dhaka and attracts firms in manufacturing, which is the most land-intensive sector. However, as transport investments proceed and incentives for firms in the tradable services sector are introduced, the population and level of economic activity in East Dhaka increase. A higher demand for land boosts rents and reduces the initial advantage manufacturing firms enjoyed by locating to this area. As long as the reduction in the cost of doing business for the tradable services sector is less than 10 percent, manufacturing remains the main employer in East Dhaka. But when the reduction exceeds 10 percent, tradable services overtake manufacturing and become the largest source of employment.

At the citywide level, the total number of manufacturing jobs increases as the cost of doing business for tradable services is reduced in the selected union, but only until the reduction reaches 10 percent. At that point, the tradable services cluster in East Dhaka becomes large enough to generate sizable productivity spillovers, pushing the city to respecialize in this sector.

The size of agglomeration economies in the tradable services sector also affects the impact of soft reforms. The stronger the agglomeration economies, the greater is the productivity advantage of being close to the old center and the harder it is to persuade firms to locate elsewhere. But stronger agglomeration economies also imply that the benefits from the new East Dhaka cluster, if it ever emerges, are greater, too.

Agglomeration economies are captured by the return to greater effective employment at the local level. Effective employment is the weighted aggregate employment of tradable services in the union and in its vicinity, where the weights decline with travel times between union pairs. The return to effective employment is the percentage increase in the productivity of tradable services in a union when effective employment in the union doubles. Three cases are considered to illustrate the role of agglomeration economies: (1) no returns to effective employment, (2) a 1 percent return and (3) a 3 percent return (figure 7.4).

If agglomeration economies are substantial, then more jobs are created in the selected union. The reason is that relocating firms and new firms form a new large cluster and benefit from the substantial return to effective employment. Although some of the jobs in the selected union are relocated from the current center, many are new.

These simulation exercises suggest that a city's growth prospects depend on the competitiveness of the activities that dominate its economy. The introduction of significant incentives for tradable services firms in East Dhaka, together with improvements in amenities, leads to US$77 billion in gains in output, or US$53 billion if the associated decline in agricultural output is taken into account. But small incentives do not have nearly as large an impact because of

Figure 7.4 The stronger the agglomeration effects, the greater is the impact of soft reforms

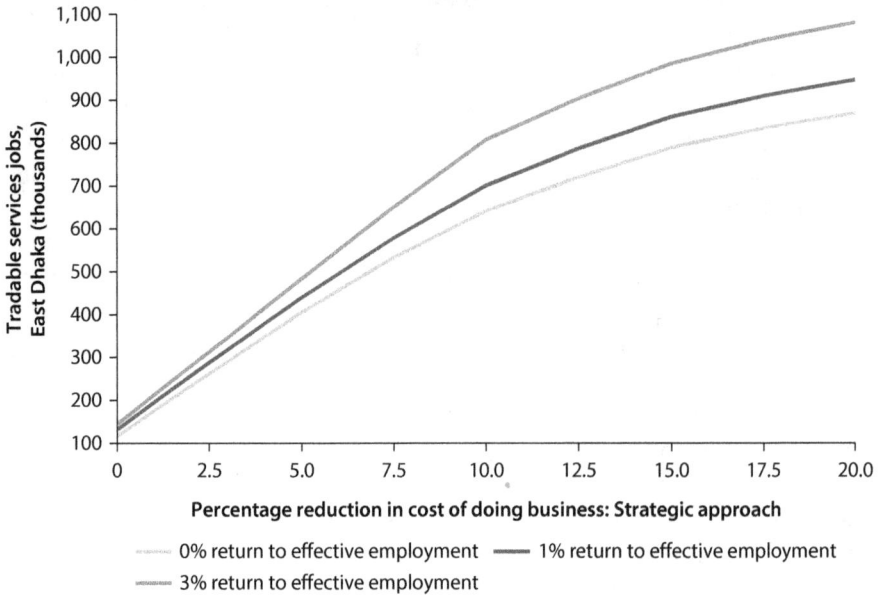

Source: Calculations based on Bird and Venables (2017).
Note: The lines represent employment in the tradable services sector in East Dhaka under three different levels of return to effective employment. All three lines are for the strategic approach scenario, with the cost reduction for the tradable services sector in the selected East Dhaka union ranging from 0 to 20 percent.

the threshold effect faced by this type of soft policy. The stronger the agglomeration economies in production, the higher is the threshold and the greater is the need for bold reforms.

Implementing the bold reforms

Bold policy reforms often face strong resistance. In the case of the proposed intervention, resistance could come from the vested interests who benefit from the dominance of manufacturing industries in the Dhaka CCs. The resistance could also come from well-meaning groups who see low-skilled employment in manufacturing as an avenue for poverty reduction. Or it could originate in analysts who have legitimate reservations about what could be perceived as a spatial version of industrial policy.

Whatever the source of the resistance, strategic support from the central government would be critically important for bold reforms to see the light of day. Pudong's transformation from stretches of farmland to a hub of finance, trade and high-tech industries could not have taken place without the impetus provided by Deng Xiaoping, the "chief architect of China's economic reforms." Deng viewed Pudong's development as part of a national growth strategy, with potentially vast spillovers to secondary cities. Shanghai received consistent political support from the Chinese government to sustain Pudong's development momentum (Chen 2007; Zhao and Shao 2008).

In addition to political support from the top, strong institutions may be needed for bold reforms to be implemented. At times, a purpose-built governance structure could be required. In Shanghai's case, the Pudong New Area Administrative Committee was set up to replace the old institutions fragmented across three districts and two counties. This committee was largely free from the power struggles and constraints entangling Puxi, the more prosperous part of Shanghai at the time. In fact, Pudong officials had the same status as the Shanghai municipal authorities, despite the fact that they were heading only a district of the Shanghai municipality. Pudong officials were also responsible for a broader set of issues than usual (Chen 2007; Zhao and Shao 2008).

The special governance structure allowed the implementers of Deng's vision to be entrepreneurial and take calculated risks in policy reforms. Against this backdrop, Pudong became the true testing ground for policies and regulations related to capital, labor, land, trade and foreign investment.

At present, Dhaka has a myriad of overlapping and competing authorities. No effective coordination mechanisms are in place, and plans generated by different agencies are, at best, partially implemented. If a full-blown reform of local urban bodies is out of reach, then a purpose-built governance structure could be set up for East Dhaka. There are reasons for optimism that a new governance structure of this sort could work. In a few cases in which the mandates have been clear and strong coordination mechanisms have been established, exceptional implementation capacity has emerged. The successful Hatirjheel Lake rehabilitation project is a relevant example in this respect.

Risks and mitigation

Urban development in East Dhaka offers the prospect of very large economic gains, but it also entails substantial risks. Greatly expanding the population that lives off the Madhupur Tract will lead to a greater vulnerability to earthquakes. Rapid urban growth could also undermine the chances of reducing traffic congestion and could increase pollution. And on the social side, there will be an unfair appropriation of the gains from rapid urban development if property rights to the potentially valuable land in East Dhaka are not well defined and protected.

Earthquakes: Enforcing construction codes

The rapid development of East Dhaka triggered by the proposed urban development scenarios reduces some disaster risks and increases others. Flood risks are lessened if the eastern embankment is built and canals and retention ponds are maintained. But earthquake risks become more substantial.

Greater Dhaka is exposed to high levels of seismic activity because most of the Madhupur fault line is located within 60 kilometers of the city. East Dhaka is particularly vulnerable because its generally softer soil potentially amplifies ground shaking in an earthquake. In addition, private real estate development projects have reclaimed vast amounts of land through hydraulic fill. Sand filling, in combination with a high groundwater table, makes the soil more susceptible to liquefaction and thus to the collapse of buildings. The sites of some private real estate projects have already been flagged as suffering from a high liquefaction risk (Ahamed 2005; Hore 2013; Hossain 2009; Islam et al. 2010; World Bank and EMI 2014).

In principle, the development of East Dhaka has conflicting implications for the city's vulnerability to earthquakes. On the one hand, the construction of the eastern embankment would make additional sand filling unnecessary, and this would reduce the overall area susceptible to soil liquefaction compared with that in the business as usual scenario. On the other hand, more people would live in areas off the Madhupur Tract, where ground shaking is potentially more severe.

In practice, the second effect dominates by a vast margin, so that vulnerability to earthquakes would rise. For example, in the strategic approach scenario the population of East Dhaka is nearly four times larger than in that in the business as usual scenario. Consequently, the population residing off the Madhupur Tract and exposed to earthquake risks increases from fewer than 0.6 million to 2.3 million. Similarly, the population living on land parcels reclaimed through sand filling, which are exposed to high liquefaction risks, increases almost three-fold (figure 7.5).

This increased vulnerability to earthquakes cannot be ignored when thinking about options for the development of East Dhaka. Hard interventions, including building the eastern embankment and developing the transport infrastructure of the area, need to be complemented by soft interventions for this risk to be contained.

Figure 7.5 Vulnerability to earthquakes increases in more ambitious urban development scenarios

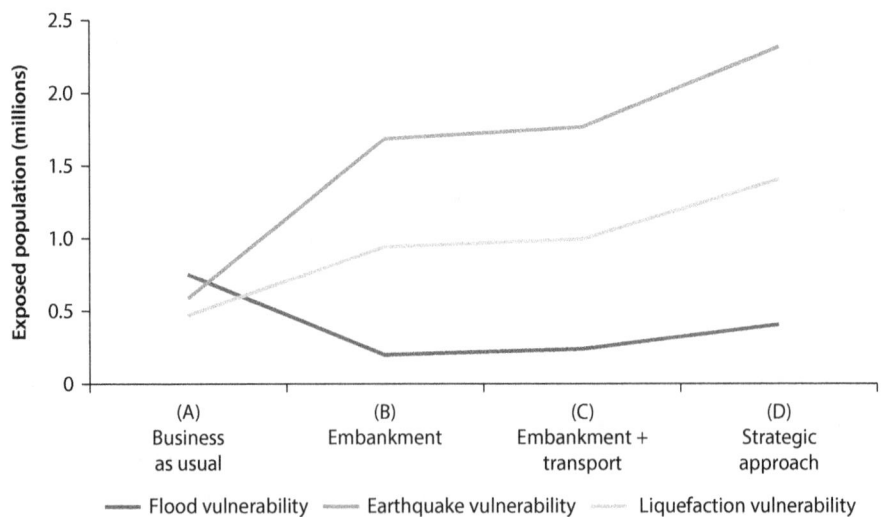

Sources: Calculations based on Bird and Venables (2017); GISAT (2017); GSB and BGR (2014); private developers' websites.
Note: The lines represent the population in East Dhaka who would be vulnerable to disaster risks in the four urban development scenarios considered.

Building standards have proven effective at limiting the risks posed by earthquakes. In advanced economies, risk reduction and hazard adaptation have relied in large part on construction codes. Over the past decade, high-income countries experienced 47 percent of disasters globally, but thanks to more advanced building standards, they accounted for only 7 percent of disaster fatalities. For example, in the United States the state of California passed the Field Act in 1933, which required special earthquake designs for public schools. Since then, no school building in the state has collapsed (World Bank 2015).

Bangladesh has enacted a series of laws and regulations for building safety. The most prominent ones in Dhaka's case are the Building Construction Act of 1952, Bangladesh National Building Code of 1993 (which was made a legally binding document in 2006 and has been periodically updated since then), Building Construction Rules of 1996, Dhaka Metropolitan Building Rules of 2008, Local Government Act of 2009 and Real Estate Development and Management Act of 2010 (HBRI 2015; LGED 2013; Shafi 2010).

Although some of these laws and regulations are outdated and should be improved, the most serious challenge is the lack of enforcement. The reality is that construction in Bangladesh does not follow even basic standards. Tragically, buildings continue to collapse, even in the absence of earthquakes. The Rana Plaza disaster, one of the deadliest accidental structural failures in modern history, is the most recent and extreme example. The death toll from this tragedy exceeded 1,100, and about 2,500 people were injured (BBC 2013; HBRI 2015; LGED 2013; Shafi 2010).

If the urban development initiatives proposed here are embraced, it would be imperative for the authorities to strictly enforce the existing building codes in East Dhaka. Apart from the potentially large benefits from compliance, it is also much more cost-effective to make new construction disaster-resistant than to retrofit existing buildings. New construction, built to the appropriate design, could be made disaster-resistant for a small percentage of the investment cost—on the order of 5 to 10 percent. By contrast, the retrofitting of existing vulnerable structures may require major expenditures, in the range of 10 to 50 percent of value of the buildings (World Bank 2015).

The need for soft interventions aimed at containing earthquake vulnerability further stresses the payoffs to being strategic. Hard interventions alone will certainly bring more prosperity to Greater Dhaka, but they will also increase the risks faced by many of its inhabitants.

Congestion and pollution: Developing mass transit

By substantially increasing the amount of high-quality urban land available, the development of East Dhaka should relieve some of the population pressure on the city, thereby reducing the current levels of traffic congestion. However, Dhaka's population is bound to increase substantially. It will also become considerably wealthier, which will lead to a larger number of commutes and a greater reliance on motorized transport. Already, about 42 percent of trips on a normal working day are made in motorized vehicles, and the number of private cars is estimated to have grown between 5 and 10 percent a year over the last five years. The number of motorcycles has grown by over 10 percent annually (DTCA and JICA 2015; World Bank 2017b). These trends are bound to continue.

Income growth accelerates when moving from the business as usual scenario to the more ambitious urban development scenarios. As a result, the reliance on motorized transport becomes even higher. The greater dependence on motorized transport, in combination with a substantially larger population, would put enormous pressure on Dhaka's already burdened road network. Which is why the risk of greater congestion remains, even with successful infrastructure investments to form a modern transport network in East Dhaka.

The number of trips made in motorized vehicles on a normal working day almost doubles in the business as usual scenario between 2011 and 2035. In the embankment scenario, the number of motorized trips increases by another 7 percent over the business as usual scenario. The increase would become 13 percent in the embankment + transport scenario and 22 percent in the strategic approach scenario.

Although mass transit systems are much better established in the embankment + transport and the strategic approach scenarios, they would mostly be utilized by those who would otherwise walk. A majority of the people who nowadays walk are projected to take mass transit to complement their commutes in these two scenarios, while less than half of them will do so in the business as usual scenario. By contrast, an almost negligible proportion of those with a private car will utilize mass transit as part of their commutes. Therefore, the coverage of mass transit system in the embankment + transport and strategic approach scenarios is not sufficiently comprehensive to change the transport habits of those with motorized vehicles.

The greater reliance on motorized transport is also likely to worsen air pollution. At present, Dhaka suffers from some of the poorest air quality among Asian cities. In 2016 the air quality reading in Dhaka revealed about 90 micrograms of fine particulate matter ($PM_{2.5}$) per cubic meter, or nine times higher than the safe level. About 19 percent of the concentration of fine particulate matter was due to motor vehicles and 18 percent to road dust (WHO 2016; World Bank 2018). If no other measures are taken and the reliance on motorized trips grows as predicted by the simulations, the $PM_{2.5}$ concentration would increase to a level that is simply too dangerous for human life.

Establishing a comprehensive public transport system is the most viable solution to mitigate the risk of congestion and to contain air pollution. According to international comparisons, Dhaka is at the lower end of the spectrum in terms of mass transit density, and the transportation investments envisioned in the RSTP would not be sufficient to substantially improve its position (figure 7.6). In the embankment + transport and the strategic approach scenarios, 32 kilometers of additional BRT routes and 50 kilometers of additional MRT lines are introduced. However, even with these improvements, Dhaka reaches only from 3.7 to 4 kilometers of MRT per million people. This is less than a quarter of what Shanghai has achieved and less than half of what Delhi has constructed.

Figure 7.6 In Dhaka, mass rapid transit will remain underdeveloped compared with that in other major cities today

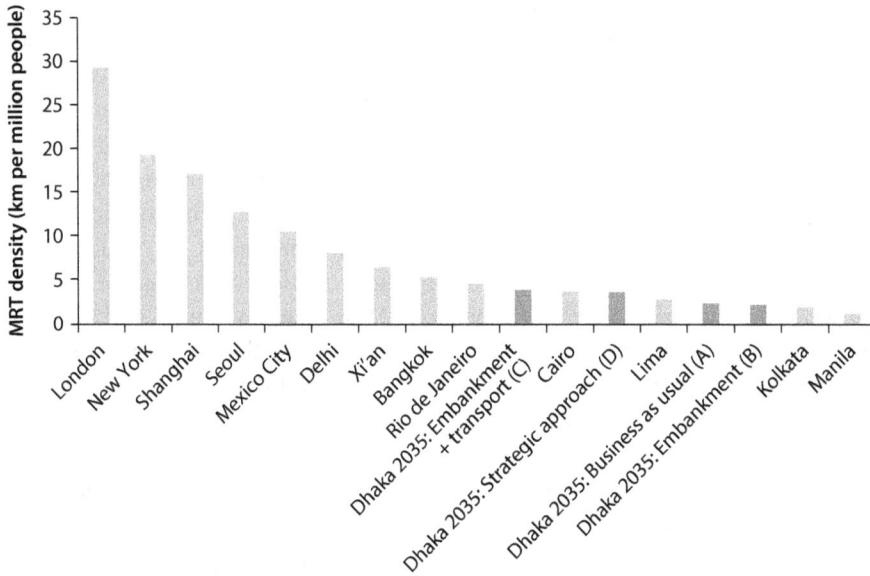

Sources: Calculations based on Bird and Venables (2017); UN (2015); metro operators' corporate websites.
Note: The green bars represent the MRT density for different metropolitan areas around 2015. The orange bars represent the MRT density in Greater Dhaka around 2035 in the four urban development scenarios.

Consistent with the RSTP, the two most ambitious scenarios for the development of East Dhaka envision construction of BRT line 7 and the road corridor alongside it. In these two scenarios, this new transport infrastructure becomes the backbone of north-south traffic in East Dhaka. But the potential demand is higher than what this backbone transit infrastructure can accommodate. Addressing congestion risk would require upgrading the BRT line into an MRT line and converting the four-lane road next to it into a six-lane road (ALMEC Corporation 2017).

Surplus grabbing: Improving land administration

A final risk, and not the least worrying, has to do with the unfair distribution of the gains from rapid urban development in Dhaka. The main concern is not related to growing inequality in labor earnings. Although a shift in the specialization of the city from manufacturing to tradable services can be expected, the ratio of skilled to unskilled wages may not change much. The real risk is related to the distribution of capital gains. In the more ambitious scenarios, the population density of East Dhaka will increase considerably, leading to a surge in land prices. Much of the land in East Dhaka remains agricultural, and many current residents are relatively poor farmers. Whether they are able to benefit from higher land prices, or find that the surplus is being appropriated by private developers, is unclear.

Comprehensive data on land records are not available, but an in-depth study of a single *mouza* illustrates the concern. The *mouza* Purba Durgapur, introduced

earlier in this report, provides a clear illustration of the risks. This *mouza* is arguably representative of the areas in East Dhaka that have not yet been touched by
private developers. Located in the south of East Dhaka, it sits between the Balu
River and the Dhaka-Narayanganj-Demra project in a medium low-lying, flood-
prone area. The union consists largely of agricultural land and small-scale rural
settlements. It used to be part of union Demra and is now under the purview of
the Dhaka South CC.

According to the *mouza*'s official records on paper at the local office, there
were 84 property titles in 2017, 76 of which were private. This number of private titles exceeds the number of households in the *mouza* in 2001, but by
2011, 92 households were already living there, and so their number would
be substantially higher in 2017 (figure 7.7). More than one household may live
on a property, and some households may have more than one property, but
overall a correspondence between the number of land titles and the number of
households can be expected.

The case of the *mouza* Purba Durgapur suggests that many East Dhaka households may be living on untitled properties. And in the absence of rapid development of land titling, the gap could become alarmingly large. The number
of households living in this *mouza* would remain roughly unchanged in
the business as usual scenario. But the number would increase to more than
600 households in the more ambitious scenarios. It is not clear from whom these
hundreds of new households would buy or rent their property.

Meanwhile, the average land value in East Dhaka surges. Land rent increases
from US$9 per square meter per year in 2011 to US$86–$143 in 2035, depend-
ing on the scenario. The consolidated land rent gain across the entire area is

Figure 7.7 There may be many fewer property titles than households in East Dhaka in the more ambitious urban development scenarios

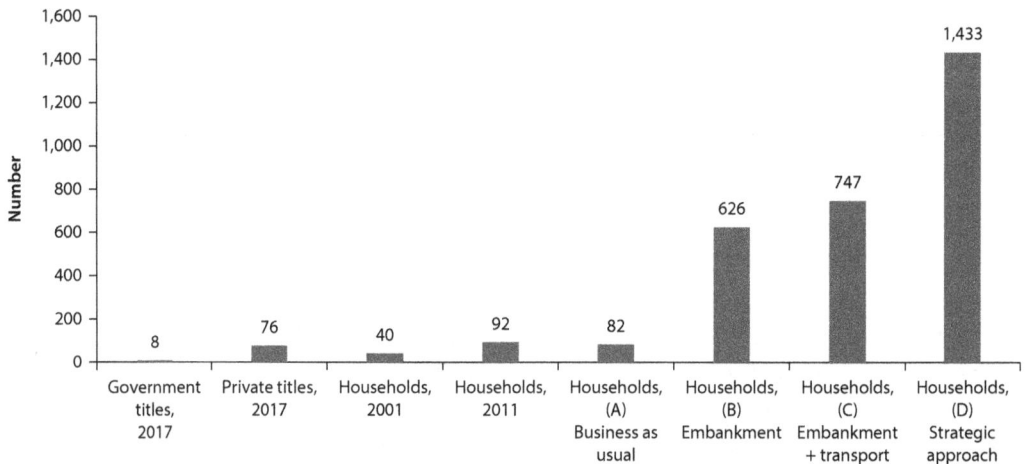

Sources: Calculations based on BBS (2001, 2011); Bird and Venables (2017); *Khatian* book (records of rights) of the *mouza* Purba Durgapur.
Note: The bars represent the number of official land title records for the *mouza* Purba Durgapur in 2017, the number of households in the same *mouza* in 2001 and 2011, and the estimated number of households in the four urban development scenarios considered.

somewhere between US$6.9 billion in the embankment scenario and US$11.1 billion in the strategic approach. It is reasonable to expect that land prices increase proportionately to land rent. Appropriating even a small part of this surplus would make for huge gains, a prospect that could encourage dubious practices by private developers in a context of weak governance.

The current land administration system seems ill-equipped to address this challenge. Land titling information is scattered across different agencies, and coordination among them is limited. Land transactions have to be recorded with the subregistry office under the Ministry of Law and Parliamentary Affairs, and a mechanism exists in principle to update land titles with the Deputy Commissioner Office under the Ministry of Public Administration. But the process is cumbersome and slow. Consequently, land titling information is likely to be outdated. All titles are paper-based, in the form of *Khatian* books. In East Dhaka alone, there are over 1,000 of them, and each contains nearly 200 titles. Land administrative offices are currently digitizing the roughly 200,000 existing paper records. But they are doing so starting with the historical records that date back to 1899. It may be a long time before the digitization process moves to more recent land records (Office of the Deputy Commissioner Dhaka 2017).

A modern land administration system, including accurate and accessible land titles records, is essential to ensure a fair distribution of land value gains and to mitigate the risk of surplus grabbing. A well-functioning land administration system is also needed to return land to its lawful owners when needed and to transparently reclaim land for legitimate public uses. This challenge should be urgently addressed before any serious infrastructure investments and policy reforms are implemented in East Dhaka.

Since the mid-1990s, there have been multiple attempts to improve land administration in Dhaka. These efforts have often involved support from international donors. But, unfortunately, not much headway has been made. The limited progress accomplished so far suggests the need for a special and particular effort for East Dhaka, which may be more feasible than overhauling the land administration system of the entire city.

References

ADB (Asian Development Bank). 2016. "Asian Development Bank and Bangladesh: Fact Sheet, 2016." Mandaluyong, Philippines.

AIIB (Asian Infrastructure Investment Bank). 2016. "Project Summary Information." Beijing. https://www.aiib.org/en/projects/approved/2016/bangladesh-distribution -system.html.

Ahamed, Selim. 2005. "Soil Characteristics and Liquefaction Potential of Selected Reclaimed Areas of Dhaka City." M.Sc.Engg. thesis, Department of Civil Engineering, Bangladesh University of Engineering and Technology, Dhaka.

ALMEC Corporation. 2017. "Impact of Urban Growth Scenario on Urban Transport in Dhaka." Background paper prepared for this report.

Alterman, Rachelle. 2012. "Land Use Regulations and Property Values: The 'Windfalls Capture' Idea Revisited." In *Oxford Handbook of Urban Economics and Planning*, edited by Nancy Brooks, Kieran Donaghy and Gerrit-Jan Knaap. New York: Oxford University Press.

Baldwin, Richard, Rikard Forslid, Philippe Martin, Gianmarco Ottaviano and Frederic Robert-Nicoud. 2011. *Economic Geography and Public Policy*. Princeton, NJ: Princeton University Press.

BBS (Bangladesh Bureau of Statistics). 2001. "Population and Housing Census 2001." Statistics and Informatics Division, Ministry of Planning, Government of the People's Republic of Bangladesh.

———. 2011. "Population and Housing Census 2011." Statistics and Informatics Division, Ministry of Planning, Government of the People's Republic of Bangladesh.

Bird, Julia, and Anthony J. Venables. 2017. "Growing a Developing City: A Computable Spatial General Equilibrium Model Applied to Dhaka." Background paper prepared for this report.

BBC (British Broadcasting Corporation). 2013. "Bangladesh Factory Collapse Toll Passes 1,000." May 10. http://www.bbc.com/news/world-asia-22476774.

BWDB (Bangladesh Water Development Board). 2017. "Technical Study of Flood Control and Drainage Development at Dhaka Circular Road (Dhaka Eastern Bypass) Project, Conducted by Institute of Water Modelling (IWM)." Dhaka.

Chen, Yawei. 2007. *Shanghai Pudong: Urban Development in an Era of Global-Local Interaction*. Vol. 14. Amsterdam: IOS Press.

DTCA (Dhaka Transport Coordination Authority) and JICA (Japan International Cooperation Agency). 2015. "Revised Strategic Transport Plan for Dhaka." Prepared by ALMEC Corporation, Oriental Consultants Global and Kathahira and Engineers International, Dhaka.

EIB (European Investment Bank). 2016. *EIB 2016 Financial Report*. Luxembourg: EIB.

Fujita, Masahisa, Paul R. Krugman and Anthony J. Venables. 1999. *The Spatial Economy: Cities, Regions and International Trade*. Cambridge, MA: MIT Press.

George, Henry. 1987 (repr. 1884). *The Land Question*. New York: Robert Schalkenbach Foundation.

Gielen, D. Muñoz, I. Maguregui Salas and J. Burón Cuadrado. 2017. "International Comparison of the Changing Dynamics of Governance Approaches to Land Development and Their Results for Public Value Capture." *Cities* 71: 123–34.

GISAT. 2017. "Urban Land Use Update and Mapping for Greater Dhaka Region." Background paper prepared for this report. Prague, Czech Republic.

GSB (Geological Survey of Bangladesh) and BGR (Bundesanstalt für Geowissenschaften und Rohstoffe). 2014. "Infrastructure Suitability for Shallow Foundation of Dhaka Metropolitan City." Dhaka. Printed map issued by GSB, Dhaka.

Harvey, David. 2003. *Paris, Capital of Modernity*. Paris: Routledge.

HBRI (Housing and Building Research Institute). 2015. "Bangladesh National Building Code: Final Draft." Dhaka.

Hore, Ripon. 2013. "Liquefaction Potential of Selected Reclaimed Areas of Dhaka City Based on Cone Penetration Test." M.Sc.Engg. thesis. Department of Civil Engineering, Bangladesh University of Engineering and Technology, Dhaka.

Hossain, T. 2009. "Estimation of Earthquake Induced Liquefaction Potential of Selected Reclaimed Areas of Dhaka City Based on Shear Wave Velocity." M.Sc.Engg. thesis, Department of Civil Engineering, Bangladesh University of Engineering and Technology, Dhaka.

Huda, M. S., and M. R. Hasan. 2009. "Problems and Prospects of Municipal Holding Taxation System: A Study on Bhairab Pourashava." *Journal of Bangladesh Institute of Planners* 2: 126–35.

IMF (International Monetary Fund). 2017. "Bangladesh 2017 Article IV Consultation—Press Release; Staff Report." IMF Country Report 17/147, IMF, Washington, DC.

Independent. 2017. "Dhaka Property Owners Protest New Holding Tax." October 22. http://www.theindependentbd.com/post/120058.

Ingram, Gregory K., and Yu-hung Hong, eds. 2012. *Value Capture and Land Policies.* Cambridge, MA: Lincoln Institute of Land Policy.

Ingram, Gregory K., Zhi Liu and Karin Brandt. 2013. "Metropolitan Infrastructure and Capital Finance." *Metropolitan Finance in Developing Countries* 339–66.

Islam, Mohammad Shariful, Md Tanvir Hossain, Syed Fakhrul Ameen, Eqramul Hoque and Selim Ahamed. 2010. "Earthquake Induced Liquefaction Vulnerability of Reclaimed Areas of Dhaka." *Journal of Civil Engineering* 38 (1): 65–80.

JICA (Japan International Cooperation Agency). 2017. *Annual Report 2017.* Tokyo: JICA.

Krugman, Paul, 1991. "Increasing Returns and Economic Geography." *Journal of Political Economy 99* (3): 483–99.

Krugman, Paul, and Anthony J. Venables. 1995. "Globalization and the Inequality of Nations." *Quarterly Journal of Economics* 110 (4): 857–80.

Lall, Somik, and Paul Procee. 2016. *Shanghai 2050: From Made in Shanghai to Create in Shanghai.* Washington, DC: World Bank.

LGED (Local Government and Engineering Department). 2013. *Safe Buildings and Planned Development—A Need of the Time.* English version of *Nagar Sangbad: A Quarterly UMU Publication of LGED* 9 (32): April–June.

Office of the Deputy Commissioner Dhaka. 2017. "The Status of the Record of Rights in Dhaka CCs." Interview conducted by World Bank for this report, Dhaka, July.

Peterson, George. 2009. *Unlocking Land Values to Finance Urban Infrastructure.* Washington, DC: World Bank.

Pethe, Abhay. 2013. "Metropolitan Public Finances: The Case of Mumbai." In *Financing Metropolitan Governments in Developing Countries*, edited by Roy W. Bahl, Johannes F. Linn, and Deborah L. Wetzel. Cambridge, MA: Lincoln Institute of Land Policy.

Rahman, Hossain. 2017a. "Transforming Dhaka East: A Political Economy Perspective on Opportunities and Challenges." Background paper prepared for this report.

Rahman, Shamsur. 2017b. "Holding Tax Varies from City to City." *Daily Prothom Alo.* October 13. http://en.prothomalo.com/bangladesh/news/162925/Residents-face-disparity-in-holding-tax-rates.

Shafi, Salma A. 2010. "Keynote Paper on National Building Code and Its Implementation." Round Table Discussion on Implementation of National Building Code, National Press Club, Dhaka.

Shanghai Pudong New Area Statistical Bureau and Pudong Survey Team of National Statistics Bureau. 2016. *Shanghai Pudong New Area Statistical Yearbook 2016.* Shanghai.

UN (United Nations). 2015. "World Urbanization Prospects: The 2014 Revision." Department of Economic and Social Affairs, Population Division, United Nations, New York.

Venables, Anthony J. 2017. "Breaking into Tradables: Urban Form and Urban Function in a Developing City." *Journal of Urban Economics* 98: 88–97.

WHO (World Health Organization). 2016. *WHO Global Urban Ambient Air Pollution Database.* Geneva: WHO.

Wong, Christine. 2013. "Paying for Urbanization in China: Challenges of Municipal Finance in the Twenty-First Century." In *Financing Metropolitan Governments in Developing Countries,* edited by Roy W. Bahl, Johannes F. Linn, and Deborah L. Wetzel. Cambridge, MA: Lincoln Institute of Land Policy.

World Bank. 2015. *Building Regulation for Resilience: Managing Risks for Safer Cities.* Washington, DC: World Bank.

———. 2016. "Land and Legal Diagnostic: Proposed Embankment on Balu-River/Eastern Bypass Project." Unpublished paper, Disaster and Risk Management Team, World Bank, Washington, DC.

———. 2017a. "Dhaka Megacity: Development Issues, Plans and Prospects with Particular Reference to East Dhaka." Background paper prepared for this report. Washington, DC.

———. 2017b. "Urban Transport in Dhaka: Review of Plans and Institutional Set-up." Background paper prepared for this report. Washington, DC.

———. 2017c. "The World Bank in Bangladesh: Overview." Washington, DC. http://www .worldbank.org/en/country/bangladesh/overview#2.

———. 2018. "Bangladesh Country Environmental Analysis." Washington, DC.

World Bank and EMI (Earthquakes and Megacities Initiative). 2014. "The Dhaka Profile and Earthquake Risk Atlas." Manila, Philippines.

Zhao, Qizheng, and Yudong Shao. 2008. *Shanghai Pudong Miracle.* Beijing: China Intercontinental Press.

www.ingramcontent.com/pod-product-compliance
Lightning Source LLC
Chambersburg PA
CBHW081435270326
41932CB00019B/3215